The Power Of CALL

The Power Of CALL

Edited by
Martha C. Pennington

ATHELSTAN

© 1996 Athelstan

ISBN: 0-940753-04-9 (cloth)
ISBN: 0-940753-03-0 (paper)

Athelstan
2476 Bolsover, Suite 464
Houston, TX 77005
USA

www.athel.com
info@athel.com

Martha C. Pennington
Powdrill Professor of English Language Acquisition
Spires Research Centre
2 Adelaide St.
University of Luton
Luton LU1 5 DU UK
e-mail martha.pennington@luton.ac.uk
fax 44 1582 743701

To the Reader:

This book provides a comprehensive overview of the field of computer-assisted language learning (CALL) written by specialists in specific areas of electronic media. It is designed to be an accessible treatment of CALL for educators as well as the general public. It would also make a suitable textbook for a course on CALL.

The book includes nine chapters, each written by an authority in the area of the chapter content. The material is divided into three sections. *Part 1. Background* includes an introductory chapter discussing the power of CALL, a chapter on software design and evaluation, and one on the research base for CALL. In *Part 2. Technology*, the technologies of networking, hypermedia, and concordancing are described in the context of how these are applied in CALL. *Part 3. Language Skills Areas* addresses applications of CALL in reading, writing, and speaking instruction in a second language.

Beyond being a systematic and comprehensive overview of the field of computer-assisted language learning, the book aims to present some new ideas which the contributors hope might fire the imagination of teachers, course developers, and software designers to project the next generation of applications of the computer in the language curriculum. If we succeed in lighting the way down some new paths of instruction for practitioners in language education or in sparking some new developments in language learning software, then we will all feel that the two-year process of bringing this collection to completion will have been well worth the effort.

> \- Martha C. Pennington
> Hong Kong
> January 1996

CONTENTS

PART 1. BACKGROUND

1. The Power of the Computer in Language Education 1
   Martha C. Pennington
2. Elements of CALL Methodology: Development, Evaluation, and Implementation 15
   Philip L. Hubbard
3. Second Language Classroom Research Traditions: How Does CALL Fit? 33
   Carol Chapelle, Joan Jamieson, and Yuhsoon Park

PART 2. TECHNOLOGY

4. Computer Networks: Webs of Communication for Language Teaching 55
   Robert Hoffman
5. Hypermedia and CALL 79
   David Ashworth
6. Concordancing in Language Learning 97
   John Flowerdew

PART 3. LANGUAGE SKILL AREAS

7. A Principled Consideration of Computers and Reading in a Second Language 115
   Tom Cobb and Vance Stevens
8. Exploring the Virtual World: Computers in the Second Language Writing Classroom 137
   Marianne Phinney
9. Computer-Assisted Development of Spoken Language Skills 153
   Martha C. Pennington and John H. Esling

   References 191

   Name Index 217

   Subject Index 223

1. The Power of the Computer in Language Education

Martha C. Pennington

1.1. INTRODUCTION

As the introductory chapter in a book that seeks to bring the reader up to date about computer-assisted language learning, this preliminary discussion aims to develop some historical and thematic background to frame the discussion of the remaining chapters, while at the same time introducing the content of the individual chapters of the book.

The power of CALL in language learning and language teaching is to introduce new types of input, from both a quantitative and a qualitative perspective. The added quantity of input leads to a richer language learning environment, while the unique quality of CALL input means different possibilities for accessing and developing information. CALL makes for better quality of input as well in being more focused and more individualized than many other learning media. Thus, CALL modes of teaching and learning can increase the variety or diversity of learning opportunities and the quality of the learning experience in making input of more varied kinds learnable and accessible to each individual learner. Qualitatively different learning modes in CALL may increase the effectiveness of instruction for some individuals or populations of learners. In short, CALL promotes a better learning/teaching process.

A presentation on computer may be inherently more salient, less threatening, and more easily available than some other presentational modes and so add an extra dimension to the accessibility of information (Pennington, 1986). Accessibility can be thought of as both physical access to information—bringing information to the user's fingertips—as well as psychological and cognitive access. Information is **psychologically accessible** to the extent that it is harmonious with or neutral in relation to the user's current or long-term psychological condition. Psychologically inaccessible information, in contrast, is negative in relation to the user's mental state or ego in a particular context or in general and thus produces or enhances such mental states as may be counterproductive to learning (e.g., anxiety or frustration). The **cognitive accessibility** of information is the degree to which it is congruent with the user's mental schemata or knowledge structures and so tends to activate these structures (Kruglanski, 1989) and to be learned in relation to them.

In addition, by means of CALL, language learners are led to produce more language (Phinney, this volume), i.e., more comprehensible input for each other and potentially of better quality as well, i.e., more comprehensible output (Swain, 1985). Moreover, as a consequence of the amount and variety of types of input made accessible by the machine, students often increase their risk-taking behavior and experimentation with learning and with language (Pennington, in press, a). This in turn can result in development of new modes of communication such as Hoffman (this volume) notes, where electronic networks offer a real audience for English among Chinese students who would not ordinarily speak the second language with each other.

With more opportunities and different opportunities to negotiate input in a computer environment come not only a greater quantity of language, particularly, the second language, but also more focused, explicit, and specific uses of language (Pennington and Esling, this volume). When married to a network, the computer also allows or encourages different voices and personas of students (Hoffman, this volume) and teachers (Phinney, this volume) to emerge. The greater variety of voices and roles may eventually lead to better—clearer, more logical, more fluent, and more productive—voices and roles.

The computer can scaffold learning by invoking contexts as structures of a learning activity or as virtual worlds within which the computer user navigates language and the communication process more generally. In the "decontextualized" environment of the computer, the learner may be led to invoke context more explicitly and in a more explicit linguistic form, i.e., by explicit grammatical means, than in some other environments. Thus, the simple "de-grammatical" (or ungrammatical), "high-context" (Hall, 1976) form of language that will suffice in fully contextualized communication seems to occur less in a computer environment. The more explicit invocation of context within the "decontextualized" computer environment may cause students to work in a more concentrated manner, more intently, and for longer periods of time. In addition, work around computers provides for both private, cognitive-focused work and more public, interpersonal aspects of communication. In these ways, CALL extends the human learning zone—what Vygotsky, in his book, *Thinking and Speech* (originally published in Russian in 1934) called the "zone of proximal development" (translated version in Rieber and Carton, 1987, p. 211).

In the view of Lea (1992):

> [T]he relatively cueless environment of CMC [computer-mediated communication], coupled with additional features of the technology and the environmental contexts in which CMC typically occurs, promote social psychological conditions (e.g., de-individuation and

heightened self-awareness) that enhance sensitivity to the social context in which CMC takes place. (p. 2)

Spears and Lea (1992) cite research suggesting a "stylistic spontaneity in CMC that ... is promoted because of the relatively cueless environment" (p. 36). They further note that communicators in a computer environment, where social cues are reduced, tend to be relatively uninhibited and to take more risks in their communication than they would in a face-to-face environment (Spears and Lea, 1992, p. 37). In short, computer-mediated communication offers relatively easy accessibility to information and relatively risk-free social accessibility as well.

Use of CALL may reconfigure the boundaries between the personal and the social, the cognitive and the linguistic—in short, between the user's inner and outer worlds. The computer seems to promote the externalization of the thinking process (Pennington, in press, a), as learners reconstitute their thoughts in the processes and outputs of the medium, e.g., in word-processing or logic games. It also seems to encourage the externalization of the reasoning process, as Mohan (1992) has discussed in relation to his observations of student groups working together around one computer. The computer also makes it possible to externalize the structure of thought and of reasoning by linguistic means, when language is used to invoke the context and steps in the reasoning process, making it more transparent and explicit. As a device which simulates and at the same time partners the user's processes of thinking, reasoning, and communicating, the computer also has the potential to change these processes.

In what follows, I trace these attributes and potentials of the electronic medium from the early applications of computers in education through language learning theory and into the present-day field of CALL. The chapter ends with a discussion of how the power of CALL helps to realize learning potentials as actualities.

1.2. THE EVOLVING PRESENCE OF COMPUTERS IN EDUCATION

As detailed in Pennington and Singer (forthcoming), in the history of their development, computers became increasingly available to humans as a result of:

- Decreasing size and expense;
- Vastly increasing quantity and variety of software;
- Changes in software design to make use of the medium more attractive and less imposing to the average user; and
- Changing attitudes about computers as a result of advertising and "word-of-mouth" from an increasing number of users.

The increasing socialization of the human population to computers and the evolution of education via computers can be summarized as a series of phases, as shown in Figure 1.1.

Phase 1. Calculating for the Elite
Phase 2. Education for the Elite
Phase 3. Educational Access for All
Phase 4. Capitalization of Computers
Phase 5. Educators Take Possession of Computers
Phase 6. Universal Computer Literacy
Phase 7. Networking the World

Figure 1.1. Phases in Evolution of Computers in Education

In Phase 1, computers were used by an elite group of mathematicians and scientists for purposes of calculation. In Phase 2, the circle of users was widened somewhat as computers became accessible in education to professors and their students at a few major, prestigious universities. Access to computers was still denied to all but the most clever minds, and to all of those outside scientific, mathematical, or technical fields. This was an era in which the computer was transformed from a fearsome image to an esoteric aura associated with "eggheads" and "nerds".

Phase 3 brought the computer within reach of the masses, in the beginning of the period of educational access for all. Access for the masses was first provided by programmed instruction and later by Apple software aimed at the public schools, extending Phase 3 into Phase 4, the capitalization of computers. In Phase 4, the first big efforts were undertaken to market computers to the masses, and access to computers became virtually universal for the middle class. In less than ten years, this highly successful marketing effort resulted in the mass conversion of educators to computer use. As educators took possession of computers in Phase 5, the machines became even more firmly entrenched in the society, as the schools hooked kids into them. This phase made possible the phase of universal computer literacy, Phase 6, which is currently taking over and setting up the conditions for Phase 7, in which there will be virtually universal access—via hypermedia, networking, and the "information superhighway"—not only to information but also to people, their minds as well as their other communications and creative resources and products.

At this point in time, computers are viewed as a way of extending the range of availability of data, calculations, and other functions that have added new symbolic representations of ideas and systems to human society. A major step forward occurred when it was realized that computers can do more than calculate or present sequential text. They can extend our range of thoughts and representations by simulation of complex processes and systems. Once it is seen that computers can do more than calculate and present information, people begin to realize the computer's vast potential for creating new learning environments, by combining the different computer applications already known and bringing to the fingertips of all users the data that was once reserved for only a few privileged insiders.

1.3. EXPANDING THE LEARNING ZONE IN LANGUAGE EDUCATION

The use of computers in language instruction would appear to be based on the coalescence of three "megatrends" in education of the 1950's and 1960's:

> (1) The availability of computers to educational institutions, particularly at first to those involved in government-sponsored research and development;

> (2) The development out of behaviorist psychology of the educational approach of Programmed Learning—an instructional approach which is well-suited to the computer capabilities of presenting and manipulating information sequentially and individually;

> (3) Audiolingualism—a theoretical and methodological approach to language learning, also with behaviorist roots, that was based on habit formation and so amenable to implementation by programmed learning on computer.

The early applications of computers to language learning followed the same basic approach as self-teaching courses in mathematics or psychology, building up a knowledge base by presenting small bits of information in sequence, allowing the learner to work at his/her own pace, and then reinforcing that knowledge by frequent testing. Often these PI courses supplemented regular classroom instruction, though in some cases, students could take the computer self-teaching section of a course instead of a section with a teacher, working alone except for occasional consultation with the instructor or a tutor and major examinations.

The technological developments made possible in the era of the 1980's were coupled with emerging new theoretical and methodological thrusts in language teaching which moved computer-assisted teaching away from PI approaches and games, and towards other orientations such as simulations and problem-solving software. Moreover, in the Apple give-away phase, along with traditional CAI like grammar exercises or vocabulary games for English learners (native or non-native), word processing was made available to young writers. During this period, computers were allied to voice synthesis and analysis, audio and video media, and telecommunications, thus opening up a very big range of possibilities for software development and curriculum in the teaching of English and language learning more generally.

Since in every era, the use of media has been tied to the view of education that was current at that time, in order to see how these expanded computer media are being and might be used in the current era, it will be valuable to consider current thinking about the nature of language learning. By considering the nature of language learning in its various aspects, we can get some idea of the types of computer capabilities that will be understandable and that will be considered useful in the present era.

1.3.1. A Current Perspective on Language Learning and Teaching

Drawing on the discussion in Pennington (in press, b), language learning is a process of "creative construction" in which the learner builds a cognitive representation of the second language based partially on knowledge of the mother tongue and partially on knowledge of universal principles of language and of learning, such as generalization, simplification, and analogy. Creative construction of a language is a long and effortful process in which the learner needs to be motivated to sustain effort and actively engaged to carry out the problem-solving, hypothesis-formation, and hypothesis-testing which this construction process entails.

Learning based on these unconscious and natural processes can be refined by knowledge learned consciously, in the classroom or through self-study, as the learner deliberately applies learning strategies to control the content, the rate, and the conditions of learning. By means of a combination of creative construction and language practice through which performance is adjusted, the learner gradually builds up knowledge and skills for ready comprehension and fluent production of the language.

For successful construction of the system (the grammar) of the second language, the learner must be in a favorable psychological state and willing to experiment and take risks, learning by making errors and receiving feedback on performance to improve knowledge, skills, and subsequent performance. In the creative construction process, the assistance and input of others is needed to support, to facilitate, to supplement, and to scaffold the learner's developing knowledge of the second language. The role of the teacher or expert in this process is to act as both a resource provider and a mentor, with students as apprentices who gradually advance themselves in the "zone of proximal development", to gain an increasing measure of skill and independence over time.

Language learning is a process of interacting not only with input but also with people through various senses and modalities: face-to-face or eye-to-eye (as in ordinary conversation), ear-to-ear (as over the telephone), and mind-to-mind (as in reading and writing). It is thus a process of learning to communicate with others, both immediately and over time and space, usually in terms of new cultural and social milieus requiring new rules of speaking. At the same time, the purpose of language learning may vary substantially from one learner to the next, with some seeking full integration into a new culture or society and others pursuing more limited instrumental goals related to their academic studies or occupation. In all cases, however, learning a new language means learning new forms of expression in new contexts of communication.

Based on the discussion above, the ideal teacher or teaching system will be one which:

- Helps learners develop and elaborate their increasingly specified cognitive representation for the second language;
- Allows learners to experiment and take risks in a psychologically favorable and motivating environment;
- Offers input to both conscious and unconscious learning processes;
- Offers learners opportunities to practice and to receive feedback on performance;
- Allows learners to learn according to their own purposes and goals;
- Puts learners in touch with other learners;
- Promotes cultural and social learning;
- Promotes interactivity in learning and communication;
- Exposes the learner to appropriate contexts for learning;
- Expands the learner's "zone of proximal development";
- Builds to learner independence.

In all these ways, the computer stands, along with the teacher, as a uniquely effective medium.

1.3.2. Computers in the Context of Current Views of Language Learning

Computers may partner the learner in developing language skills and help to elaborate their cognitive system for the second language in many different ways. Thus, computers can model—retrospectively, prospectively, or simultaneously—the cognitive and physical processes required for linguistic perception and production, as in the visual modeling of speech characteristics (Pennington and Esling, this volume), thought processing programs (Phinney, 1989), many reading comprehension or story schema programs (Cobb and Stevens, this volume), and the on-line modeling by the computer of problem-solving or thought processes which a user might undergo to complete a task on screen (Dickson, 1985). To the extent that this modeling represents the real process which a learner must undergo in skilled performance and makes it transparent enough or simple enough for a learner to imitate the computer's performance, the machine aids the learner in developing a cognitive representation of the task and skilled, routinized performance.

Computers assist in the construction and elaboration of the second language grammar by structuring the learner's input and output in certain ways, e.g., by limiting and focusing the language and the tasks which will be performed. They also offer an especially favorable environment, or environments, for language learning. The control of the computer environment makes it conducive to language learning, as does the nature of individual applications. For example, networking promotes language learning by putting learners in touch with other learners and with a multitude of other resources (Hoffman, this volume). Word processing, with or without enhancements such as speech (Pennington and Esling, this volume) or multimedia (Phinney, this volume) is an environment which creates a "natural partnership" (Pennington, in press, a) between the capabilities of the machine and the needs of the non-native writer, thereby helping the learner to develop a natural and effective writing process.

In addition, the computer environment is a highly motivating one to many learners and a private workspace where they can take risks and experiment in ways that might be psychologically threatening in a classroom or real-life communication situation. When writing over a network, for example, the anonymity and ease of communication seem to encourage a spontaneous and playful form of "speak-writing" that results in more creative and natural language than in some other environments (Esling, 1991c; Hoffman, 1994, this volume; Pennington, in press, a). Computer training systems for pronunciation (Pennington and Esling, this volume) seem to be one of the few environments where learners' consciousness of their own spoken language errors does not interfere with their learning. The computer environment, especially when married to hypermedia (Ashworth, this volume), is a rich one which allows the user to enter new worlds and traverse new territory. Using hypermedia, the learner is able, for example, to:

- Create a path through hyperspace that leads to increasingly deep and diversified coverage of a topic, using a variety of me dia to organize different "passes" through the material; or
- Virtually experience walking down the street in a foreign land and conversing with its inhabitants.

In addition, the computer offers many opportunities for exploration of language, such as through concordancing (Flowerdew, this volume), including now video concordancing (Price and Imbier, 1993), and text manipulation software of various sorts (Cobb and Stevens, this volume).

In being highly salient and not only physically accessible but also psychologically and cognitively accessible to the learner (Pennington, 1991d), the presentation on computer is an especially memorable form of input that can assist both conscious and unconscious intake and uptake of information. In addition to deductive presentation of rules and models in a highly salient form (Doughty, 1992), by use of such utilities as hypermedia and concordancing, the computer can vary the types of input and the amount of context presented to enable the user to learn inductively and at a pace that matches a natural acquisition order or is just ahead of the learner's current level of knowledge or stage of acquisition—the "i+1" level in Krashen's (1982) terms.

With the computer, language learners gain many different kinds of opportunities to practice and to receive feedback on performance, including practice and feedback levels and types which are tailored to the learner's current level (Hubbard, this volume; Stevens, 1989, 1992). In this capability, the electronic medium serves as a self-teaching system which adjusts the level of the task to fit the student's ability level. The amount and the difficulty of the input offered to the learner is then just what the learner can use, thereby avoiding the discouragement and frustration of "information overload". In addition, the computer can function as a non-threatening intermediary to pass on a person's feedback without the threat of face-to-face confrontation or embarrassment. Alternatively, the computer can itself analyze the user's performance and give the feedback, as a sort of neutral observer. In addition, the computer is nowadays providing new types of feedback and more variety of types which can more and more be selectively accessed as desired by individual users (Hubbard, this volume).

The natural feedback of e-mail messages sent between students and teacher, or among the students themselves, is also of a relatively simple, psychologically and cognitively accessible, engaging, and non-threatening form of input on performance. As noted by Hoffman (this volume), through such feedback, the language learner gains a real communicative response which indirectly promotes language acquisition as a by-product of completing another task that is the focus of the learner's conscious attention.

To the extent that the type of computer access involves choice and programs give over control to the user, to that extent does the computer allow learners to learn according to their own purposes and goals. More and more, computer applications are becoming self-contained, multimedia management and presentation systems suitable for self-access in the computer lab, the office, or the home. In addition, with hypermedia, the user can decide to a large degree the level and content of access within the system. Such systems offer the maximum in the way of learner control and creativity in interrelating different communications media such as text, graphics, and sound, thus encouraging learning by juxtaposing different symbol systems (Dickson, 1985; Salomon, 1979) to create different modes of interpreting and understanding information.

The computer in its role of networking users with each other puts them in touch with other learners and communicators. Through networking and hypermedia, the user can in fact gain access to users around the globe as well as to all the different forms of information which those users have created and which are available in databases and in the creative products of visual and sound media. On the rapidly expanding communications superhighway, learners gain access not only to other people, but also to their ideas. Even without the benefit of networking, the computer seems to bring people together and to encourage communication (Abraham and Liou, 1991; Chapelle, Jamieson, and Park, this volume; Phinney, this volume), e.g., as a stimulus for problem-solving, cooperative drafting, and other forms of pair work and group work.

Any particular software brings with it the attributes not only of the designer, but also of the culture and society in which it was created. In this sense, every piece of software has general cultural content to which the user will be exposed in running it. Although some kinds of software or computer systems are extremely flexible in the way they can be used—e.g., in terms of participation format—each computer application, whether by design or as an indirect by-product of design features, promotes a certain type of interaction or social learning (Crookall and Oxford, 1992). In addition, some computer applications are designed to provide specific socio-cultural content, e.g., through simulations of situations in which the appropriateness of language is determined by non-universal rules of politeness and pragmatic principles. In all these ways, the computer can promote new forms of socialization and acculturation.

The computer is a highly responsive medium offering users reliable, high-quality feedback on performance, generally in a near-instantaneous manner. It is also a highly interactive medium in that the user must do something, continuously or repeatedly, in order to evoke and maintain a response from the machine. The use of the computer may therefore encourage users to develop an interactive style of learning and communication in which the computer or other learners partner their efforts and help to sustain them. In addition, the computer may provide unique interactive effects in the way of tactile, visual, and auditory feedback that sustains effort and enhances performance (Pennington, 1991c).

Through the computer, the learner is exposed to appropriate contexts for learning via such activities as simulations, which train performance for actual situations, and group interactions, which train the process of interaction and negotiation of meaning that is central to communication and language learning. The computer expands the learner's "zone of proximal development", to a virtually infinite degree, as the machine partners and supplements the learner's knowledge and capabilities, while also adding other partners and forms of supplementation to assist in building information and skills. In this way, the computer "sparks" the learning process, gives direction for it, and eventually helps the learner to gain independence in acquiring the skills modeled and trained by computer means. The electronic medium thus provides a bridge to new learning, to actualization of simulated and virtual experiences, and to real-time and real-world experiences of many kinds.

Before closing this part of the discussion, it is perhaps worth reminding the reader that not all computer potentials are positive ones (Pennington, 1991c). In addition to being a promoter of positive interactive and social experiences, the computer can sometimes encourage a form of "anti-social" behavior that amounts to working in isolation from others. Although such isolation may be needed in some cases, as when a student is performing close editing of a text in word processing, in other cases it means that the learner is working on language in a highly constrained and artificial context. There is also the potential for the student to come under the control of the machine, as often happens with commercial grammar-checking or text analysis software (Pennington, 1992a, 1993a; Pennington and Brock, 1992). This same software—and many other specific programs—simplifies the representation of the content and the structure of the task performed to such a degree as to be highly misleading. In fact, following the advice or the structure of some computer programs, a learner will end up at best wasting time and at worst being confused or led astray from his/her own learning needs and purposes. An additional problem is the failure of computer users to make full use of the software (e.g., as in some studies reviewed by Chapelle, Jamieson, and Park, this volume, and Cobb and Stevens, this volume).

In sum, while the electronic medium offers truly exciting and revolutionary opportunities for promoting and enhancing language learning, its potential may fail to be realized in specific cases due to various types of misapplication or improper use. Such misapplications include the use of certain types of software with audiences who cannot or will not take advantage of it, as the characteristics of the software do not match those of the learners or the settings of use for which it is designed (Chapelle and Jamieson, 1989; Chapelle, Jamieson, and Park, this volume), or the design of the software does not require or encourage use of its key features.

1.4. THE VIRTUAL BECOMES THE ACTUAL

New technologies put new capabilities at our fingertips, bringing about what Perkins (1985) terms "fingertip effects". Perkins describes these fingertip effects as either immediate, first-order, effects or later, second-order effects. Fingertip effects of the first order, according to Perkins, make available applications of the computer for which the medium was originally designed. By means of second-order fingertip effects, computer technology creates some new uses for the medium which were not envisioned in advance and which take human capabilities in new directions, pushing back the boundaries of our experience.

To take an example from writing, a first-order fingertip effect is the convenience for people of writing with the combined utilities of a word processor and a printer. A second-order fingertip effect, described in Pennington (in press, a), is that whereby computer-assisted writing serves as auxiliary memory and workspace for the cognitive processes involved in writing and so allows writers to venture into new territory in terms of their thoughts and use of language. We might even move beyond Perkins' conception to speak of third-order effects—effects which are "twice-removed" from the intended context of the computer's usage and which have ramifications in a totally new area of human experience. For writing on computer, an example would be the creation, along the lines discussed in Tuman (1992), of not only a new genre and aesthetic for writing involving group-produced text, but also a whole new conception of text, authorship, and intellectual property, leading to new legal definitions, new forms of sharing and international communication, and other ramifications that we could most probably not predict in advance.

As pointed out in Pennington (in press, a):

> For educational purposes, the computer can function as an added tool or resource, as a model of a real-world phenomenon or system, and as a training environment to prepare users for real-world tasks and experiences. As an added tool or resource, the computer assists humans in performing calculations, projections, graphic representa-

tions, and the like, much more quickly, efficiently, and effectively than they could be accomplished with human resources alone. In addition, the virtual world of the computer can model the actual world and provide the user with a simulation of real-life experiences. The computer experience can therefore function as a stand-in for the real thing, as when the machine provides a model of a dangerous experiment or condition such as global warming. Although the computer experiment or its projection of the future is far removed from the actual experiences represented, the user's cognition and affective experience are nevertheless expanded by these engineered pseudo-environments and experiences. (p. 183)

The effects of the computer on the human user's learning can occur at a relatively shallow or deep level. The first-order effect of a computer can be viewed as a simple additive effect which provides external processing capability, e.g., for mathematical calculation or for information storage, to complement the human user's internal (mental) processing capability. Beyond this simple additive effect, the external processor may also provide real-time supplementation of the user's limited cognitive capacity, e.g., in allowing stored information to be called up for manipulation in quantities which a human working without the computer could not manage. The machine processor can therefore aid the internal workings of the user's cognitive processor, as when the computer exhibits a mathematical calculation process as the user inputs data, or allows a writer to manipulate several written files simultaneously in developing ideas.

In extending the working capability of the human processor, the computer's relationship with the user begins to evolve towards an interactive partnership. The effects of this partnership take place not only in the amount of work produced, but also in the way the user works. With this extra capacity or ability provided by the computer, the user learns to work in different ways, directing attention to new areas which might not have been possible without the computer's aid. Thus, the work process may be changed in ways subtle or profound.

For example, with a computer, many people who formerly wrote by first developing an outline and then finding information to fill in the areas of the outline will now write in a brainstorm-revision cycle, with much more freewriting and rewriting than before, as these are part of a natural two-step input-revision process facilitated by the machine (Pennington, in press, a). Hence, the writing process facilitated by the machine both enables and simulates a simple and natural writing process. In this sense, the machine models and at the same time enacts a new type of writing process for the user, as the virtual environment for processing the writer's ideas begins to merge with the actual cognitive environment of the writer.

The more the computer and the user work as a team, the more the computer can be said to be partnering the user's cognitive processing, "shadowing" and enabling the user's processing of information. At an even higher level of effects, the computer's simulation of a human process or system becomes a virtual process or system, which through modeling and training the process or system can actually bring it into being. For example, a computer chess player actually plays chess, and in the movie "War Games", Matthew Broderick's (simulated!) playing with the computer moved a war game towards an actual war. Can one not imagine a Peace Game leading to actual peace?

To take an example of direct relevance to language learning, the virtual zero distance in time and space of communicators in e-mail "cyberspace" (Ashworth, this volume) becomes, even spontaneously for some users, a closer communication process (Hoffman, this volume; Phinney, this volume). Similarly, the kind of text manipulation described by Cobb and Stevens (this volume) virtually produces reading, i.e., *becomes*, with immediate or gradual effect, reading. In this way, the computer's *support* for work at a low or elementary level of usage becomes *partnering* and *mediation*, and this in turn is transformed into *skilled performance* in interaction with the machine, perhaps with carryover as well to work away from the machine. Thus, unlike some other environments, the computer does not merely assist in practicing and automating behavior, but develops or restructures behavior as an integrated complex of skills.

As a process in a computer-mediated environment changes, through second-order or third-order effects, to become something beyond the original process, it becomes accessible to new audiences. Accordingly, when the writing or reading process is performed on computer, new converts are won over, and whole new worlds are opened up to entirely new audiences: learners who can read interactively, creating a story as they go (Cobb and Stevens, this volume), or who can attach personal artwork, sound, or video to their stories and compositions (Daiute, 1992; Phinney, this volume) suddenly become involved in the world of literacy.

In language teaching, we want to build to real experiences from simulated and virtual ones. The first level of effects is that which facilitates or enables a process, which in turn makes possible another effect. For example, a certain computer capability makes possible a conversational simulation—e.g., using e-mail or computer-based speech equipment. When this "makes possible" effect is realized in a conversational simulation, the event in fact simulates a conversation to a greater or lesser extent. This "virtual" effect may in turn have a "grounding" or "skilling" effect in that it can build the groundwork and/or the skills for actual conversation. Eventually, a "reality" effect may be produced, either through the virtual becoming the actual experience of conversation or through the simulation laying the groundwork and developing the skills for authentic conversation to become a reality for the learner. Thus, the notion of **virtual reality**, a computer simulation so real that it mimics a human response or productive capacity to accomplish an identical result, becomes increasingly important.

1.5. CONCLUDING REMARKS TO CHAPTER 1

Much more than merely automating or facilitating various types of intellectual labor, the computer brings many kinds of resources—some of them newly conceived in a computer context and others more conveniently or differently accessed in an electronic medium—within the user's reach and helps to guide the user in accomplishing tasks. In so doing, the computer not only expands the language learner's capacity for learning and communication, but also directs and models the processes of learning and communication. Under favorable conditions, the computer model becomes equivalent to the process or capacity that is modeled, or supplants it in a new form of skilled behavior that achieves a high-quality outcome. It is at this point that the full power of CALL, as explored in the chapters of this book, is realized.

2. Elements of CALL Methodology: Development, Evaluation, and Implementation

Philip L. Hubbard

2.1. INTRODUCTION

Computer-assisted language learning (CALL) has moved in the past decade from being a mere sideshow, a curiosity, to holding a solid position in modern language teaching. As with other technological advances such as video, the number of students using CALL materials continues to increase steadily. Although there has not been sufficient study to convince skeptics of the value of the computer on research grounds, the question for many language teachers now seems to be not whether but how computers can aid in the language learning process.

Computers and accompanying software packages can be used in language teaching in a number of ways, including as creative instruments (e.g., in word processing), as references (e.g., CD-ROM encyclopedias), as communication tools (e.g., for electronic conferencing with teachers or other students), and as tools for the teacher (e.g., electronic gradebooks). However, the present work will limit itself to a discussion of methodological issues surrounding the use of software that includes content designed or adopted for language learning purposes, what Levy 1993) calls the "tutor" use of CALL, often referred to as CALL "courseware".

Because a piece of CALL courseware, like a textbook, is an instrument through which the learner is introduced to and practices the language, the focus of attention tends to be on the computer program and the materials. Courseware reviews commonly focus on technical considerations, sometimes at the expense of language teaching and learning considerations (Hubbard, 1987). Often missed is the fact that the field really involves the interplay of humans and technology and that the human end is especially significant. The choices a developer makes in how to present language and practice activities, the way the teacher utilizes the program, and the way the students interact with the program all bear on the degree of success or failure of a CALL lesson in a specific situation. It is this interplay, and not just the frozen set of instructions in the computer program, which ultimately determines the methodology of the field.

If CALL were a mature field, we could usefully define CALL methodology as the set of methods employed by CALL practitioners, where

method represents an organized set of consistent principles and their realization in a piece of courseware or in a computer-based activity. Under this conception, the present state of CALL methodology would simply be the range of methods reflected in the courseware and computer-based activities produced to date. This is the approach taken by Levy 1993) in a large-scale review of CALL methodology based on analysis of existing software and a survey of CALL practitioners. However, CALL is not a mature field. Given the high level of dissatisfaction many teachers have for much of the present courseware, it is reasonable to consider an alternative conception of methodology, one which would define it not in terms of what has been produced but in terms of what could be produced.

The rationale for such an approach is a pragmatic one. At the bottom line, courseware developers want to know, "How can I produce courseware to teach language effectively?" Teachers want to know, "What courseware is going to help the students learn some aspects of the language more independently so that teacher-student time can be spent in other areas?" Students want to know, "What courseware is going to help me learn what I need to know more quickly or effectively?" This chapter outlines a view of CALL methodology—more specifically, a methodological framework—that can lead to answers to such questions by breaking CALL down into its essential elements and describing how those elements interact.

2.2. THE CALL METHODOLOGICAL FRAMEWORK

As noted above, CALL is not viewed here as a sterile, robotic, technological enterprise but as an essentially human one. This section begins by sorting out some of the players in this teaching/learning endeavor and discussing their respective roles.

Player 1: The learner. The learner is the end user, the person who is supposed to benefit from the product. The learner's role in CALL is to accept as a working hypothesis that using the courseware as directed can help him or her increase language proficiency.

Player 2: The developer. The developer, an individual or team, designs, programs, and writes materials for the courseware. The developer's role is to produce a CALL package which will aid the teacher and learner in fulfilling broadly or narrowly defined learning objectives. In addition to the classroom situation, the developer may choose to consider the independent study situation where the learner is his/her own "teacher".

Player 3: The evaluator. The evaluator or reviewer is an intermediary between the developer and the classroom teacher. The role of the evaluator is to analyze the software package, describe its operation, pass professional judgement on the quality of the pedagogy and language materials, and determine what type of learners and teachers the software might fit. This may be done through published software reviews, by in-house evaluation for a particular school or program, or by the classroom teacher for his/her own class. The goal of the evaluation process may be to decide whether to buy a particular package or to decide whether to use one that is already available.

Player 4: The classroom teacher. The classroom teacher interprets the results of the evaluation for a particular teaching situation. The role of the classroom teacher is first to determine whether to use a particular piece of courseware, and if that determination is positive, when and how to implement it.

The methodological framework presented in this chapter consists of three components that draw respectively on the last three of the preceding roles: development, evaluation, and implementation. Previous works have discussed the rationale for such a framework and presented the evaluation (Hubbard, 1988a) and development (Hubbard, 1992) modules. The present work will review these two modules and add the final module—the implementation framework.

The expressed goal of this framework is to provide a neutral instrument for developing, evaluating and using CALL materials. Hubbard (1992, p. 42) offers a set of principles underlying this type of framework, as summarized below.

> (1) The CALL framework should be consistent with established frameworks for language teaching methodology, allowing teachers to link CALL to familiar concepts.
>
> (2) The framework should be method-neutral and flexible, describing the logical relationships among learners, teachers, and computers.
>
> (3) The framework should explicitly link development, evaluation, and implementation considerations in a consistent fashion.
>
> (4) The framework should identify the relevant elements in each area (development, evaluation, and implementation) and describe the interrelationships of those elements.

In keeping with the first of these principles, the present framework is based on that of Richards and Rodgers (1982), a framework which was derived from Anthony's (1963) conception of language teaching as definable in terms of approach, method, and technique. In Richards and Rodgers' framework, a language teaching method is described in terms of three interacting components or levels: **approach, design,** and **procedure.** Briefly, **approach** reflects the theories of language structure and language learning assumed by the method; it is by nature a relatively abstract level of guiding principles. **Design** embodies the goals and objectives of the syllabus and the roles of the teacher, learner, and materials consistent with the approach; it provides the guidelines for selecting and structuring classroom activities. **Procedure** includes an inventory of the types of exercises, techniques or classroom activities consistent with the approach and design.

Richards and Rodgers developed their framework for the purpose of method comparison, that is, to allow existing methods to be analyzed with respect to the same criteria in a consistent and insightful way. In adapting the framework for CALL, two significant adjustments are necessary. First, the CALL methodological framework will analyze not CALL methods, but individual pieces or packages of courseware. Second, it will consider not only the classroom environment but also the special qualities of the computer environment.

In accommodating the special qualities of the computer environment, the present framework draws heavily on the work of Phillips (1985). Phillips proposes a typological framework for describing the form, content, and implementation of CALL materials in terms of seven categories: **activity type, learning style, program focus, learner focus, language difficulty, program difficulty,** and **classroom management**. In his original conception, types of software can be defined in terms of combinations of these categories. For example, the activity type "text reconstruction" and the program focus "lexis", can be combined to characterize word-based reconstruction activities such as Hangman or programs which scramble the letters of a word and require the student to unscramble them. The Richards and Rodgers framework and the Phillips framework thus provide significant portions of the form and content of the present framework.

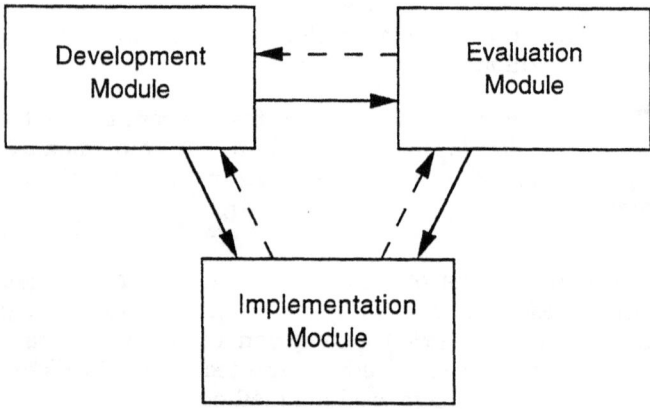

Figure 2.1. CALL Methodological Framework

Figure 2.1 depicts the relationship between the three modules of the overall framework. The modules interact in the following way. The solid

Elements of CALL Methodology

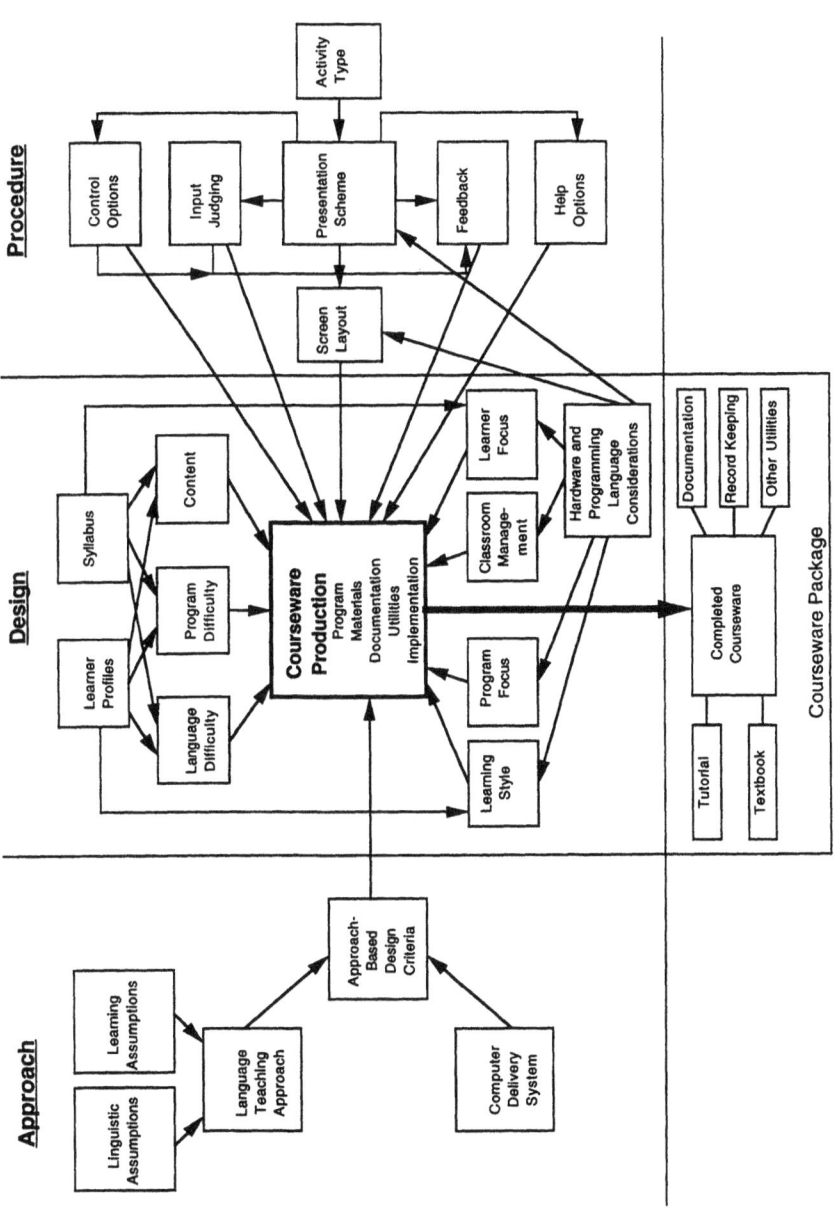

Figure 2.2. Development Module

arrows show how development necessarily precedes evaluation, while both development and evaluation precede implementation. The dashed arrows represent the fact that evaluation can inform development (i.e., the results of evaluation can lead to revisions in the courseware) and implementation experiences (i.e., actually using the courseware with students) can inform both development and evaluation.

The following section describes the development module of the framework as presented in Hubbard (1992). It introduces the elements, including those from Phillips' framework, which appear again in the evaluation and implementation modules.

2.3. THE DEVELOPMENT MODULE

Following Richards and Rodgers the development module of the framework as shown in Figure 2.2 is divided into approach, design, and procedure sections. The boxes in the diagram represent the essential elements involved in courseware development. As will become apparent as the discussion progresses, there are different possibilities for the internal structures of these boxes. Some involve a characterization of the developer's knowledge and experience within a certain area (e.g., linguistic assumptions); some involve choice within a rather fixed range of options (e.g., activity type); and others involve a consideration of a variety of factors which combine to represent that category (e.g., language difficulty). As will also be the case for the other two modules, the relations among the elements are presented as a network. The arrows in the network specify dependency relationships: the element at the tail of an arrow influences the range of options for the element at its head. Thus, all arrows ultimately converge on the large box in the center labeled **Courseware Production**.

One final note regarding the network is in order. Although some elements are of more obvious importance than others, all are treated more or less equally here. The weighting of relative importance is a task left up to the developer.

2.3.1. Approach

Within the general category of Approach, the two principal determining elements are **linguistic assumptions** and **learning assumptions**. Linguistic assumptions provide a set of guiding principles based on the developer's understanding of the nature of language and the relative importance of structural, social, and cultural aspects. Learning assumptions provide a set of guiding principles based on the developer's understanding of the nature of the second language learning process and the role the learning environment plays in that process.

These two elements combine to determine the **language teaching approach** a developer assumes for a given piece of courseware. Considering the range of choices within linguistic and learning assumptions, there are many different possibilities for language teaching approaches. However, most can be classified into a handful of categories

(Hubbard, 1987). Some of the better known are behaviorist approaches, explicit learning approaches, comprehension-based approaches, communicative approaches, and humanistic approaches. Some of these focus on language form, some on meaning, and some on human interaction. Some are more or less consistent with contemporary theory and empirical research, while others (notably the behaviorist approach underlying audiolingual methodology) are not.

Language teaching approaches have been developed for the classroom environment, but the computer **delivery system** brings in new considerations. The possibilities for individualization the computer affords are often cited as its greatest strength; however, its limitations are also well-documented. Some see the computer as a dehumanizing machine, but as noted previously, the underlying human factors are always present. Through the courseware, the computer has the capability to bring the users into contact with other humans in a more dynamic way than other media such as books or videos.

In some tutorial programs, for instance, the popular *Mavis Beacon Teaches Typing!*, the tutor is given a name, a face, and a consistent human characterization. In fact, any piece of courseware, be it for learning typing or learning a language, carries with it a "teacher in the machine", a projection of the personalities of the designers, programmers, materials developers, artists, actors and whoever else may be involved. It is this collective persona that a teacher brings into his/her class as a teaching partner when the students use CALL packages.

A piece of courseware can be tedious and mechanical and have little apparent value in helping the student learn the language. A classroom teacher can be just as boring and unmotivating. But a piece of courseware can also be engaging and provide the opportunity for the learner to absorb knowledge of the language, practice skills needed for communication, and experience aspects of the culture. Through soliciting responses from the learner and offering appropriate feedback for those responses, it can even provide a limited, but potentially valuable, simulation of communicative interaction. This possibility of "anticipatory interaction" (Hubbard, 1988b) opens the door on a new range of potentials for the CALL developer that are not available to the traditional textbook writer, the partner teachers have been bringing in as a co-instructor for many decades.

The developer's language teaching approach and computer delivery system considerations combine in forming a set of **approach-based design criteria**. Design criteria for several categories of approaches can be found in Hubbard (1987, pp. 245-247). As an example, a partial list of such criteria for humanistic (Stevens, 1989, 1992), communicative approaches could include the following points:

> (1) The courseware provides meaningful communicative interaction between the student and the computer.

(2) The courseware provides comprehensible input at a level just beyond that already acquired by the learner.

(3) The courseware promotes a positive self-image in the learner.

(4) The courseware provides a challenge but does not produce frustration or anxiety.

(5) The courseware acts effectively as a catalyst to promote learner-learner interaction in the target language.

A set of criteria such as these can provide important guidelines to a development team to assure a high degree of consistency in the final product. What needs to be stressed is the importance in the development process of making an informed decision regarding language teaching approach and then remaining true to that decision throughout the development process.

2.3.2. Design

In the Richards and Rodgers (1982) model, the purpose of the Design component is to specify the goals and objectives of a method and their actualization through the syllabus and the roles of the teacher, learner, and materials. These considerations are incorporated here primarily through elements taken from Phillips (1985). All of these elements ultimately converge on the Courseware Production box and should cohere with the approach-based design criteria.

At the top of the Design section of Figure 2.2 are its two fundamental components: **learner profiles** (called "learner variables" in Hubbard, 1992) and **syllabus**. The area of learner profiles is concerned with the intended audience for the courseware. Among the important considerations are the learners' proficiency level, age, native language, needs, and interests as well as their cognitive styles (inductive/deductive, visual/orthographic/auditory, etc.; see Brown, 1987, for a detailed discussion of these and other learner variables). The syllabus is concerned with the learning objectives and the means by which they are reached: it will be strongly influenced by the approach-based design criteria.

Considerations at the level of learner profiles and syllabus inform design decisions with respect to **language difficulty, program difficulty, and content**. The overall language difficulty is determined by a number of dimensions, such as familiarity, concreteness, length, grammatical complexity, clarity of the signal, etc. Program difficulty, on the other hand, relates to non-linguistic aspects. Phillips (1985) specifically mentions redundancy, input, and timing here, but other elements such as the complexity of the program operation, the cognitive difficulty of the task (e.g., solving a mystery), and the control options offered to the students are considerations as well. The goal here is to insure that the level of difficulty provided by a program is either neutral to or enhances learning and does not erect additional barriers to it. Content may relate to specific syllabus goals (e.g., the teaching of culture) or to perceived student needs and interests. Since the teacher may not be present when the students are using the courseware, there is a strong need for developers to consider including content that will engage the students' interest and focus their attention.

Another element that is determined by the learner profiles is that of **learning style**, which describes the type of learning supported by the activity. In his original framework, Phillips (1985) used the classification scheme of Kemmis, Atkin, and Wright (1977), who proposed five general types of CALL activities: recognition, recall, comprehension, experiential learning, and constructive understanding. Other learning style distinctions are possible as well, e.g., inductive vs. deductive task, form-focused vs. meaning-focused task, etc.

While learning style considerations account for the kind of learning the students are exposed to, two closely-related elements of Phillips' framework, **program focus** and **learner focus**, determine much of the pedagogical content. Program focus refers to the linguistic objective of the activity and ranges from phonology/graphology, through vocabulary and grammar, to discourse/text. Learner focus refers to the skill area covered by the courseware. In addition to the traditional four skills of reading, writing, listening, and speaking, this could also include sub-skills and strategies, such as the micro skills for listening described in Richards (1983) or skimming and scanning strategies for reading.

Phillips' category of **classroom management** is an element of development too often overlooked. It refers to the grouping of students in relation to the computer. Consideration needs to be given as to whether the design will support paired, small group or whole class work or whether it will only support the individual user. This is an important part of the interface with the implementation module, which I return to in Section 5.

The final element of design, which also influences elements of the Procedure section, is that of **hardware and programming language considerations**. In the area of hardware, these include questions such as the basic platform (IBM PC-compatible, Apple Macintosh, etc.), medium (floppy disk, CD-ROM, videodisc), input device (keyboard, mouse, touch screen, etc.), and so on. In the case of programming language, there are tradeoffs to consider between the ease of an authoring language such as HyperCard's HyperTalk, a popular Macintosh language, vs. the power and flexibility of a general purpose language such as Pascal or C.

2.3.3. Procedure

The Procedure section of the development module contains the elements to be considered in the actual layout of the program that presents the materials. It is important to note that a given piece of courseware may contain a number of different activities, all of which should consist of elements compatible with the determinations made in the approach and design sections.

The fundamental decision to be made here involves **activity type**, the final category from Phillips' original framework. Phillips distinguishes seven options for this: game, quiz, text construction, text reconstruction, simulation, problem solving, and exploratory. Other classification schemes that fit in the category of activity type include the common division between drill and practice activities and tutorial ones.

Following the decision to use a general type of activity, the precise **presentational scheme** must be determined. This is the specific manifestation of the activity type. It is a potentially quite complex description of how the material is to be presented, including aspects of branching and timing as well as how the learner will interact with the program. For instance, one possible presentational scheme for the activity type of text reconstruction would be a cloze where students type answers directly into the blanks. Another would be a scrambled paragraph where learners have to move the sentences into the correct order. The presentational scheme is a wide-open category, but most presentational schemes to date have been computer versions of classroom exercises. A few, however, have been developed just for the computer, such as "storyboard" programs where all of the words of a text are deleted for the learner to reconstruct. The presentational scheme as the core of the Procedure section strongly influences the remaining elements: screen layout, control options, input judging, feedback, and help options.

The **screen layout** category covers aspects of visual and auditory presentation. This includes such things as the relative positions of graphic and textual constituents and the use of color as well as the presentation of spoken language or other accompanying sounds. Where the user interface is presented on screen, it also determines the arrangement of mouse-driven control buttons.

The considerations covered by **control options** have for some time been a center of controversy in CALL. Higgins (1983) set the stage for the debate by distinguishing the opposing philosophies of the "magister", where the path and timing of the lesson is determined by the developer, and the "pedagogue", where the control is handed over to the student. Using Higgins' dichotomy, magisterial programs would be those where the student must move through some predetermined sequence (e.g., Lesson 6 must be completed successfully before Lesson 7). Adaptive programs, where the items or level of difficulty varies according to the responses of individual learners, would also fit into this category. In contrast, "pedagogical" programs would be those where the student could select the sequence, quit at will, etc. (e.g., Lesson 7 could be tried before Lesson 6, Item 10 could be tried before Item 5, or the activities could be picked from an unordered menu of titles). Research is split on this issue, with some studies showing positive results for learner control (e.g., Stevens, 1984) and others showing negative results (e.g., Pederson, 1987).

The choices made regarding control options have some influence on the areas of **input judging** and **feedback**. Input judging is concerned with the type of student response allowed by the program and the operations the program can perform on that input. In multiple choice or button-driven programs, this is a trivial matter. Lessons which allow learners to input words, phrases, or sentences via the keyboard or voice, however, must have some way to decide whether the input fits some predetermined response form. This determination includes questions such as whether there are multiple anticipated answers or just one and how misspellings, mispronunciations, and other errors in an otherwise anticipated answer are dealt with.

Once the input has been judged, there are a number of different types of feedback the program can provide the learner:

(1) an indication of the correctness or incorrectness of the answer;

(2) a comment as to the reasons for an answer being correct or incorrect;

(3) a score, grade, or other cumulative evaluation;

(4) tutorial information, such as a suggestion to review information internal or external to the program.

Besides these direct kinds of feedback, there are also indirect forms, such as the flagging of missed items for automatic review.

Help options are those portions of a computer-based activity which aid the learner in achieving a successful outcome. One type of help is a review of instructions or content. Another common form is a hint, which contains information that leads learners toward correct answers. The specific form a hint will take depends on the task demands, but as a rule of thumb, developers should try to emulate what teachers might do under similar circumstances.

2.3.4. Completed Courseware

All the elements of the development module ultimately converge on the courseware production process, symbolized by the box in the middle of Figure 2.2. Here, the program, materials (text, graphics, sound, etc.), documentation (including on-line instructions), and any accompanying utilities are created in consonance with the considerations of approach, design, and procedure. Here too, the implementation schemes, discussed in greater detail in Section 2.5, are considered. The final product is the courseware package—the courseware and anything that might have been produced to go with it: a tutorial on how to use it, a textbook, documentation, record keeping, and any other utilities, such as an authoring system or template.

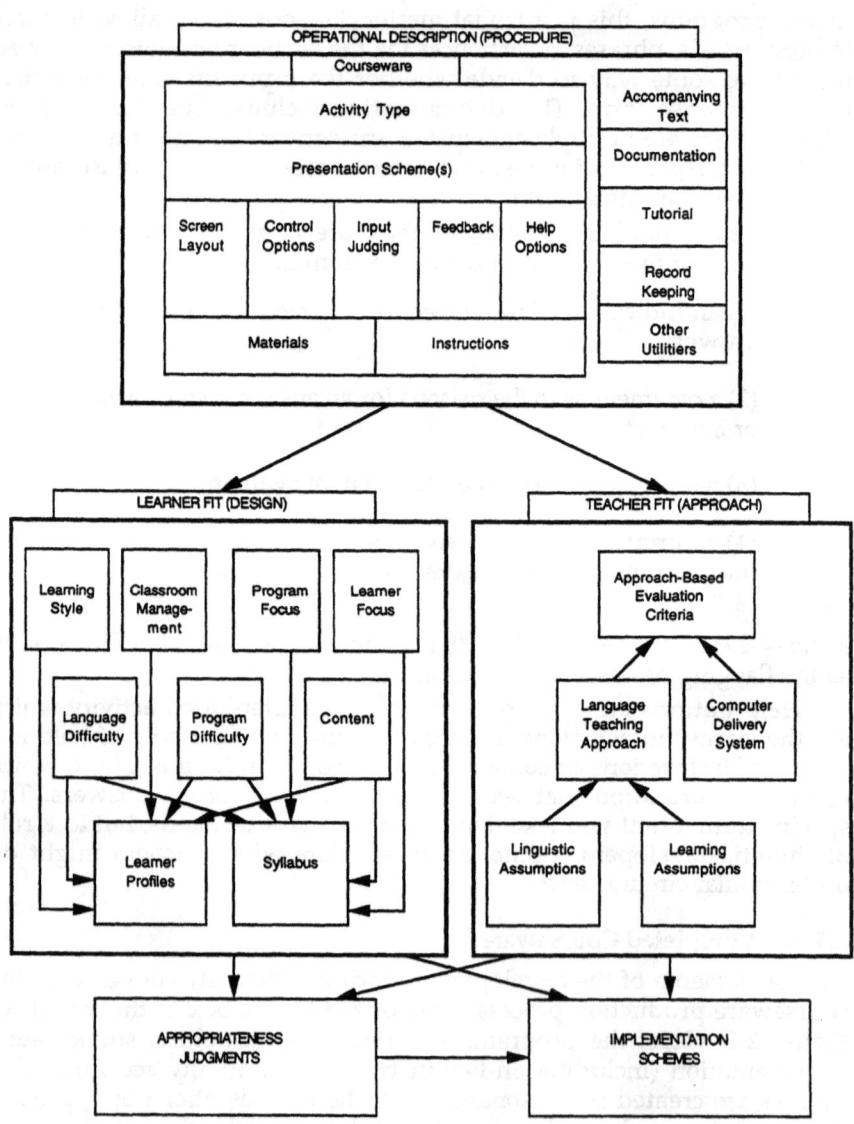

Figure 2.3. Evaluation Module

2.4. THE EVALUATION MODULE

Evaluation can in some ways be considered the inverse of development. In development we start with a language teaching approach and a target audience of learners and try to produce courseware with activities and materials that fit their needs. In evaluation, on the other hand, the courseware is the given, and the determination of fit is the goal of the process.

Figure 2.3 shows the evaluation module as presented in Hubbard (1988) with slight modifications to make it more consistent with the rest of the present framework. As with the development module, the purpose here is not to propose a specific evaluation process but rather to identify the elements involved in evaluation so that teachers and reviewers can set up their own evaluation forms and procedures. The characterization of the elements is basically the same as it was for the development module, so the discussion will center on the differences between development and evaluation. Note first that parallel to **approach, design**, and **procedure**, this module incorporates the terms **teacher fit, learner fit**, and **operational description**, respectively, as being more descriptive for the evaluator. Note also that this framework does not explicitly concern itself with a number of elements that are important in the overall evaluation process, such as include the compatibility of the program with particular hardware configurations, whether the program operates without crashing, and the cost of the program versus its perceived benefit, among others. The focus here is on pedagogical issues.

The operational description includes the elements of the procedure section of the development framework along with the elements found in the completed courseware. While the framework does not specify any particular evaluation process, the placement of the operational description at the top of the model implies that a determination of its elements is the first step, and that is essentially an objective enterprise. Once these elements are clear to the evaluator, the more subjective judgments of learner fit and teacher fit can be made in an informed fashion.

As the elements of the piece of courseware under evaluation become fleshed out in the operational description, their fit with the intended learners can be determined. Implicit within the framework are questions such as the following:

- Does the presentational scheme fit the students' learning style?
- Are the program focus (language area) and learner focus (skill area) appropriate for the learners' needs as determined by the syllabus?
- Is the language difficulty at the right level given the learners' proficiency?
- Is the feedback understandable and useful to the students?

Obviously, the number of possible combinations of elements here is quite high. In devising a practical evaluation procedure from the framework,

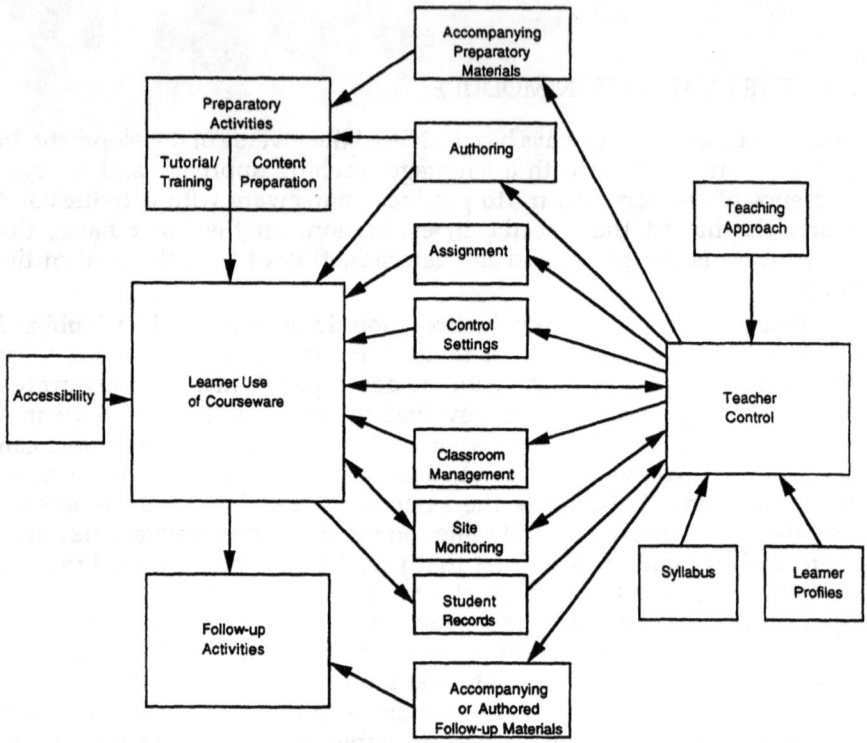

Figure 2.4. Implementation Module

it would be necessary to formulate a reasonable number of questions which highlight the most relevant concerns to guide the evaluator.

Parallel to considerations of learner fit are those of teacher fit. As with the development module, this aspect of evaluation first combines linguistic assumptions with learning assumptions into the language teaching approach. Melding the approach with considerations of the computer delivery system yields a set of approach-based evaluation criteria. These criteria can be used to judge the degree to which a piece of courseware fits within the teacher's conception of how languages are successfully learned (see Hubbard, 1987, for sets of such criteria for several well-known approaches).

The analysis of learner fit and teacher fit feeds into two distinct areas. The first of these, **appropriateness judgments**, concerns itself with whether or not the courseware is likely to be of value for a particular learning situation. In the case of a teacher doing his/her own evaluation, the assessment is likely to be straightforward. In the case of a reviewer writing for a wider audience, it represents a conclusion as to what groups of learners and types of teachers might find the courseware more or less appealing.

The second area, **implementation schemes**, depends first on a positive response in terms of appropriateness. Assuming such a positive response, a determination can be made as to when and how to use the material with the students. The elements to be considered in determining these implementation schemes are outlined in the following section.

2.5. THE IMPLEMENTATION MODULE

Using software entails more than just sending the students to the lab and waiting for learning to occur. As Keith and Lafford (1989) note, "the instructor need not feel constrained by the software developers' ideas about how the software is to be used, but might try different applications for given software which can result in an enhanced educational experience for the student" (p. 149). The framework in Figure 2.4 shows the elements that can be considered in producing an effective CALL lesson.

Beginning on the left side, the first element to consider is **accessibility**. This includes such points as the number of computers available, the time the computers are available, the setting (a computer classroom with teacher support or just a collection of computers in a room), etc.

The three large boxes to the right of the accessibility component represent the flow of a CALL lesson. The first of these, **preparatory activities**, concerns itself with what the learner does before moving to the body of the lesson. One activity that may be included is a tutorial or training module on how to use the program. Some programs are fairly complex to run at all; others are easy to use, but may require training in order to use them effectively. Hubbard, Coady, Graney, Mokhtari, and Magoto (1986) describe a vocabulary program with a number of help features; records showed that students generally ignored these features in trying to get through lessons as quickly as possible. In this case, the students were given neither the rationale for the courseware nor the training necessary to use it effectively, and the students in turn subverted the intentions of the developer. A second type of preparatory activity is **content preparation**. These activities can be of an informational nature, such as reviewing grammar rules prior to a CALL grammar exercise, or of a sensitizing nature, such as discussing the predicted content of a reading passage. This is an area all too often overlooked by both developers and teachers using the courseware.

Following the preparatory activities is the actual **learner use**, which, as Figure 2.4 shows, is determined by a number of elements. After the learner completes the main part of the lesson, there is the possibility of **follow-up activities**, an element often unfortunately neglected. One objective of such activities can be to reinforce the material learned or practiced through recapping it or reflecting on it, e.g., giving an in-class quiz on the material or asking the student to fill out a comment sheet concerning the more interesting or challenging parts of the lesson. Another objective can be to make use of the CALL material for further practice, e.g., discussing the content, using the material as the basis for a group project, or writing a composition based on it.

Moving now to the right side of Figure 2.4, we can see that the central determining element of this framework is that of **teacher control**. While not every program or teaching situation allows the teacher to control all the elements shown, Figure 2.4 captures the generalization that teachers can exert considerably more control over the learner's CALL experience than is often recognized. Three elements form the initial basis for teacher control decisions: the **teaching approach**, the **syllabus**, and the **learner profiles**. These are the main elements from the approach and design segments of the development module discussed in Section 2.3. Basically, this side of the figure reflects the view that control decisions are governed by the teacher's assumptions about the nature of language and language learning, the course requirements as outlined in the syllabus, and the teacher's perceptions of the students in the class, both as a group and as individuals.

Working from the top down in the central part of Figure 2.4, the first area a teacher can control is that of **accompanying preparatory materials**. While many courseware packages do not include these, it is important to use them appropriately if they are present. More commonly, a teacher has to produce his/her own preparatory materials or activities, an eventuality covered by the element of authoring.

Authoring is also a possibility in some programs for the CALL material itself. Many text reconstruction programs, for instance, have authoring utilities that allow teachers to type in a text. The program then automatically manipulates the text in various ways, e.g., creating cloze or scrambled sentence exercises. Some courseware packages also allow the teacher to add other acceptable answers to an item or provide additional instructions, hints or feedback. The more options for authoring a teacher has, the greater the need for incorporating the considerations of the development module in Figure 2.2.

One obvious area of control is that of **assignment**. The teacher can control which packages and lessons the students can use and when. This element also involves control of the time students spend on the task. Depending on the program, the time spent can be checked through observation, through student self-report, or through viewing student records (see below).

Some courseware allows the teacher access to **control settings**. In such a case, the teacher may be able to limit what lessons students have access to, the kind of help options available to them, the kind of feedback they receive, and what is judged as a correct answer. All of these make it possible for the teacher to tailor a lesson to his/her own teaching situation.

The most direct form of teacher control is indicated by the arrow going straight from the **teacher control** box to **learner use**. This type of direct control occurs when a teacher is working at one machine with a specific student or group of students—perhaps even an entire class. The teacher's control is then direct and immediate, and the program becomes a teaching tool somewhat comparable to a videotape or audiotape. This is a particularly useful scheme in situations where there may be only a single computer available or where the teacher wants to introduce the content and operation of some piece of courseware to a class.

Classroom management has been discussed in previous sections as an element where teachers have important choices to make. Certain programs have actually been designed to be used in pairs, and others can be used effectively in pairs or small groups. In such situations, teachers need to make informed decisions about which students are likely to work well together, who should be responsible for handling the mouse or keyboard, etc. If accessibility is limited, teachers may also make management decisions about who gets to use the computers.

Another direct form of teacher control is **site monitoring**. This situation occurs, for example, when a teacher takes a class to the computer lab and remains there working with individuals and groups of students as needed. As the double-headed arrows suggest, however, the teacher not only exerts some control over the students in this situation: he/she is also informed by it. Information and impressions gleaned from site monitoring can be used later for making other types of control decisions.

Teacher control decisions can also be influenced by reviewing **student records**. Some courseware packages include automatic record-keeping utilities, which may specify information about which lessons a student used, how much time the student spent, what scores or levels were achieved, and so on. Another form of student records is a lab log indicating when students were in the computer lab and what courseware they used: this information is particularly valuable in self-access situations or where computer use is optional. A third form of records is a feedback sheet from the student, which may be in paper form or on-line. A feedback sheet is an excellent source of student impressions and attitudes toward the courseware and is especially useful for teacher-authored courseware.

The final area of control is the selection or authoring of **follow-up materials**. As noted above, the follow-up aspect of CALL seems to be among the most widely neglected, both by developers and by teachers. The selection or production of appropriate follow-up materials to support activities allowing review, reflection, or synthesis is an important part of the learning process.

This section has looked at CALL courseware from the perspective of implementation. Developers designing courseware, reviewers evaluating it, and teachers using it all need to pay attention to the elements discussed here. The two aspects of particular note are the central role of teacher control in learner use and the importance of supporting preparatory and follow-up activities. A piece of good courseware implemented poorly can be rendered almost useless, and conversely, dull or mediocre courseware can be given greater value by informed and imaginative implementation.

2.6. CONCLUDING REMARKS TO CHAPTER 2

CALL is still a fairly new field. While the number of its practitioners is increasing, most language teachers are as yet at the stage of having only a vague notion of what the field offers. The present chapter has focused on two themes. The first is that CALL courseware is most properly viewed not as computers teaching people but as people teaching people through the medium of computers. The second is that understanding and attending to the elements involved in CALL will lead to more informed and consistent development, more informative and insightful evaluation, and more appropriate and creative implementation.

The framework proposed here represents just one of many possible conceptions of the elements of CALL and their relationships, a perspective guided by the principles presented in Section 2. Other conceptions are possible, particularly if one considers uses of the computer other than for courseware (Levy, 1993). This framework does not create methods or materials: it is a lens through which to interpret them, a tool to assist developers, reviewers and teachers in the challenging task of providing a learning environment that is enhanced rather than degraded by the use of computer courseware.

3. Second Language Classroom Research Traditions: How Does CALL Fit?

Carol Chapelle, Joan Jamieson, and Yuhsoon Park

3.1. INTRODUCTION

Early CALL researchers attempted to assess the effects of CALL on learning outcomes, but have subsequently broadened their research objectives and methods to include those of other second language researchers who investigate classroom language learning. To understand the variety of approaches used to study classroom language learning, Chaudron (1988) defined classroom research methods by dividing them into four types: **psychometric, interaction analysis, discourse analysis,** and **ethnographic**. Each of these approaches, with its own objectives and potentials for shedding light on instructed language learning, has been applied to the study of CALL. The purpose of this paper is to review the CALL research within each of the four traditions of second language classroom research. By considering CALL research within these four traditions, we identify existing CALL research findings, point out unique methodological advantages and disadvantages for CALL research, and highlight the needs for future research in this area of instructed language learning.

3.2. THE PSYCHOMETRIC TRADITION

Chaudron (1988) describes the psychometric tradition as:
> the most traditional approach to the study of second language classrooms. [It] involves comparison of the effects of specific instructional programs or methods on student learning outcomes, as measured by standardized proficiency tests or instruction-related achievement tests. (p. 28)

This approach to evaluation has been applied directly to the study of CALL.[1] When computers were a relatively novel phenomenon in language education, researchers hoped to demonstrate that students who worked with the target language on computer-based activities would show an observable improvement in their second language ability—an improvement greater than that of students who worked on other kinds of activities (Dunkel, 1990, 1991). Researchers applying this methodology have been concerned about assessing both the cognitive and the affective outcomes that can be attributed to learners' CALL use.

3.2.1. Cognitive Outcomes of CALL

The typical CALL research within the psychometric tradition provides CALL materials for an experimental group and traditional instruction for a control group, and then measures the achievement or cognitive growth of students in both groups by means of a pre-test and post-test. These types of CALL studies have yielded primarily positive results and some neutral results as well. A study in which CALL was used to teach grammar in a journalism class found that the CALL-using group made greater gains in their post-test scores over their pre-test scores (Oates, 1981). Russian translation was also found to be taught more effectively through the use of a CALL program (Van Campen, 1981). Studies in which CALL-using learners outperformed a control group receiving conventional instruction include two studies (Buckley and Rauch, 1979; Sarracho, 1982) of students learning basic language skills as well as several studies of ESL students. One group of ESL students improved their punctuation use with a CALL program (Freed, 1971), and another group made progress in writing using a text analysis program (Reid, 1986). In another study (Eichel, 1989), ESL students who worked with computerized cloze exercises scored better on classroom achievement tests than students who were exposed to traditional text instruction. In yet another study, ESL students who used a voice-interactive system for learning speaking skills had higher proficiency gains on the Basic English Skills Test than the students who had traditional teacher instruction (Peterson, 1990).

In contrast to these positive results, there are some studies that do not report significant gains in achievement. In a foreign language application, CALL drill-and-practice lessons did not effect any greater achievement than ordinary instruction in a written French course (Brebner, Johnson, and Mydlarski, 1984). In a first-language context, an experimental group of students in grades 3 to 7 who used a computerized reading program ten minutes daily made no greater reading gains than students in non-CALL sections (Lysiak, Wallace, and Evans, 1976). No significant differences were found between control and CALL treatment groups in community college English classes (Murphy and Appel, 1977), nor were any differences demonstrated in writing outcomes between students who had received computerized feedback on their compositions and those who had not (Anandam, Kotler, Eisel, and Roche, 1979). Measures of writing improvement in a computer environment have shown mixed results: students seem to write more on computer and enjoy the process (Pennington, in press, a; Phinney, this volume), but clear gains of computerized writing classes over traditional writing classes in terms of quality do not always obtain (Craven, 1988; Daiute, 1986a; Hawisher, 1989; Liou, 1993; Pennington, 1993b; Phinney, 1989).

3.2.2. Affective Outcomes of CALL

Measures of students' attitudes in relation to CALL have been less systematic than those examining student achievement, but we include this type of research focus within the psychometric approach because it assesses outcomes of CALL, often within the control-treatment paradigm.[2] For example, positive attitudes towards computerized instruction emerged from studies of CALL for written French (Brebner, Johnson, and Mydlarski, 1984), English grammar (Oates, 1981), text analysis (Liou, 1993; Reid, 1986), reading (Lysiak, Wallace, and Evans, 1976), and reading strategies (Mikulecky, Clark, and Adams, 1989). However, negative attitudes in relation to CALL were reported by Alderman (1978), and Sarracho (1982) found that students who did not use CALL had better attitudes toward it than those who did. Sarracho (1982) suggested that differences in students' response to the computer medium might be accounted for by ethnic differences in learning styles.

Anxiety about using computers and motivation are other affective areas that have been investigated. Todman and Lawrenson (1992) examined computer anxiety in elementary school children and college students; not surprisingly, they reported that younger children had more computer experience and less computer anxiety. Marcoulides (1991) reported that computer anxiety is present to the same degree in American and Chinese college students. In a study of high-risk adolescents who were given training in mathematics and reading/language arts, Christie and Sabers (1989) uncovered no difference in achievement, but rather a difference in bonding and motivation for social integration. In the ESL context, Eichel (1989) reported increased motivation of ESL students who used CALL over those who had traditional instruction.

3.2.3. Individual Variation

Although some of these psychometrically-oriented studies may indicate something about cognitive and affective outcomes of CALL, they are limited in value because they attempt to summarize the outcomes for all students from the use of CALL in general. Problems have been noted with specific studies measuring the outcomes of computerized instruction such as one in which CAI and lecture discussion sections of the same courses (composition and algebra) were compared. In this study, a significant, positive impact on achievement was reported for the computerized sections of the course; however, since the CAI groups experienced dramatic decreases in course completion rates, it may be that only good students remained in those sections of the course (Alderman, 1978). A more universal problem with studies of this type is that "the nature of the learning tasks, the characteristics of the learners, and the characteristics of the media [are] largely ignored" when the research is designed and interpreted (Jonassen, 1985, p. 30). Without an understanding of the specific attributes of the instructional environment, it is difficult to know what learning effects ought to be attributed to (Clark, 1985). To address the environmental issue, some researchers have refined their questions about the effects of CALL to consider the nature of the learners whose outcomes they investigate and the CALL features that might be responsible for those outcomes.

Individual differences have occupied the attention of many researchers in the field of second language acquisition (Skehan, 1989), and the implications of some of this work for CALL have been explored (Jamieson and Chapelle, 1988). Some psychometrically-oriented research has investigated the effects of individual characteristics or individual differences in CALL contexts. In a study of elementary school students, King (1991) reported that guided questioning strategy training on computer proved effective for fifth graders who were not naturally strong strategy users. Focusing on ability level, studies have examined the effects of software for academically talented high school students (Curtin and Shinall, 1987) as well as at-risk (in reading) high school students (Divine and Whanger, 1990). Mikulecky, Clark, and Adams (1989) found that college students needing reading remediation performed better in a computerized reading strategy group than remedial students in a control group. Rather than examining one specific group of learners, Jamieson, Norfleet, and Berbisada (1993) reported on successful, unsuccessful, and dropout students who were exposed to a series of computerized reading and note-taking lessons.

Several researchers have investigated learning style and CALL. A foreign language study which assessed students' reflection/impulsivity found that impulsive students performed better on a computerized oral sentence construction task in Spanish when the program forced them to wait before responding. This "stop and think" strategy which the program made students use improved their performance on the task (Meredith, 1978). In another study in the foreign language context, students' conceptual level was significantly predictive of their preference and need for structure in the second language learning environment, including any applications of CALL (Zampogna, Gentile, Papalia, and Silber, 1976). A study of ESL students by Abraham (1985) investigated the relationship of **field-independence** (the ability of the students to pick out a simple figure from a complex background) and **field-dependence** (the lack of the ability to pick out a simple figure from a complex background) to CALL. Abraham (1985) discovered that field-independent learners performed better on a post-test when they had been exposed to CALL grammar lessons which used a rule presentation, i.e., a deductive approach, while field-dependent learners performed better after being exposed to a CALL lesson presenting examples of the structure in an inductive approach. In another study, Chapelle and Jamieson (1986) report that field-independent ESL students tended to have a negative attitude toward the CALL lessons they investigated, while field-dependent students tended to like them.

Studies investigating individual variation and CALL include those of Blake (1992) and Viteli (1989). Blake (1992) reported on students' reading processes in learning Spanish, while Viteli (1989) investigated differences among ESL students learning idioms. Finally, Karrer (1991) investigated CAI rather than CALL, but his methodology is noteworthy.

His research investigated the interrelationships of courseware characteristics such as manner of presentation and locus of control (see Hubbard, this volume, for discussion) and student characteristics such as gender, attitude, and learning style on achievement. He reported that courseware characteristics affected achievement whereas student characteristics did not. CALL researchers have also examined some specific courseware characteristics that they believed would affect outcomes.

In the traditional psychometric framework, several studies have attempted to isolate the effects of specific aspects of CALL by comparing it to another medium of instruction with identifiable contrasting characteristics. For example, Lozano (1985) compared CALL with television and the audio lab. He then measured Spanish achievement for students using each of these media in the skill areas of reading, writing, listening, and speaking. The only difference in performance was that the CALL group did better in writing. Other studies (e.g., Doughty, 1992; Herrmann, 1991; Stevens, 1984) have examined the effects of different manners of presentation of material on computer. Still others have compared the difference in effects of different sequences of presentation on computer. For example, one study of different presentational sequences for German vocabulary items found that some sequences were superior to others for learners' long-term retention (Beard, Bar, Fletcher, and Atkinson, 1975).

Studies have also investigated the linguistic features of CALL such as the nature of the language or the degree of interactivity in a lesson. Schaeffer (1981) compared the effects of using "meaningful" versus structural German lessons. Although by current standards the definition of "meaningful" was restricted, findings indicated that students who used lessons in which they had to understand the meaning of the language to answer correctly performed better on both meaningful and structural post-tests than did students who worked with computerized lessons in which exercises could be done mechanically, i.e., without processing meaning. In another lesson strategy comparison, researchers assessed learners' retention of German based on video lessons with varying degrees of interactivity, finding that the interactive video presentation was the one for which subjects remembered the material best (Schrupp, Busch, and Mueller, 1983).

Although such studies provide some information about the type of CALL that produces the most positive effects, a more useful direction might be to note the effects of or the attitudes toward specific features of programs. Along these lines, Robinson (1986) reported that students demonstrated positive attitudes toward some features of the experimental lessons employed in her study examining specific pedagogical and linguistic features of CALL lessons. Analysis of these features reveal principles of design that may stimulate positive attitudes.

Robinson's study investigated six pedagogical and four answer-judging principles established on the basis of research in cognitive psychology and second language acquisition (Robinson, 1986). Using this foundation, experimental lessons were developed and compared to typical lessons that did not reflect such principles. For example, the hypothesis that use of a context for "introduction of discrete structural items will improve memory and subsequent learning of the items" (p. 17) was tested by providing an experimental group with a contextualized grammar lesson and a control group with a lesson containing semantically unrelated items. Although the results for each hypothesis tested by Robinson (1986) did not always favor the experimental group for short-term learning, the overall conclusion was that there was a "high level of confidence that instructional treatments did significantly favor the experimental group" (p. 35) on the post-test, which required retention of material over the course of the semester (for discussion, see Doughty, 1986, and Pennington, 1986).

The sheer number of studies using a psychometric framework points to a fundamental concern in education: Does this specific instructional approach work? Reviewing studies such as those above indicates that, first, this question cannot be answered yet. Because of the particular settings, materials, and students involved, any one study lacks generalizability. Secondly, the wide range of both CALL programs and learning outcomes examined in the past twenty-five years illustrates how CALL researchers have refined their understanding of the complex of learner and lesson characteristics which may come into play in producing cognitive or affective outcomes. As a consequence, research within the psychometric tradition should be beginning to generate results that can be aggregated, yielding patterns that can inform both instructional design and second language theory. Still, the psychometric approach to CALL research remains but one perspective. The effects of instruction in classrooms cannot be known without examining the nature of the instruction which actually occurs (Allwright, 1988; Long, 1980). To address this issue, researchers have developed methods for observing, recording, and analyzing the language and other behavior of learners and teachers in language classrooms.

3.3. INTERACTION ANALYSIS

Interaction analysis requires the classroom researcher to document specific teacher and student behaviors as they occur during classroom instruction. Second language researchers are interested in the interaction among language learners and between teachers and learners because of the hypothesized role of such interactions in language development (Long, 1985). Second language classrooms, one place where interaction can occur, differ in the degree to which an individual learner can participate in interaction. CALL classrooms have been advocated as providing a context in which each participant takes an active role, interacting with the computer program alone or with the computer and a small group of students. When students work interactively with the computer, they exhibit behavior such as the turns they take, the time they spend at various points in a problem sequence, the order in which they complete steps, and the editing they perform to produce a linguistic product. By documenting these elements of interaction, CALL researchers have begun to investigate some of the questions about CALL use which psychometrically-oriented research methods do not address. Researchers have applied interaction analysis to investigate questions with both pedagogical and psycholinguistic motivations.

3.3.1. Pedagogically-Motivated Research

In pedagogically-motivated interaction analysis, the researcher investigates how learners use software which is hypothesized to have instructional benefits. A variety of claims have been made concerning the instructional value of aspects of CALL materials. For example, CALL developers have maintained the value of offering learners environments in which they explore and call on a variety of available resources such as dictionaries and video scenes. However, the potential value of these features of CALL remain speculative until we actually observe learners taking advantage of them. Researchers with pedagogical aims have therefore begun to investigate some of the essential questions concerning learners' interaction in CALL environments.

Does the learners' interaction differ when materials are presented by computer rather than by other means? An affirmative answer to this descriptive question is important for CALL developers' arguments concerning the unique values of CALL. While one study revealed substantial differences in students' interaction on and off the computer (Mohan, 1992), another study describing differences in learning processes of students performing activities on and off the computer revealed only minor differences in the students' turn-taking behavior and in the kinds of reading strategies employed in the two contexts (Windeatt, 1986). If learners do not use the options available to them in a CALL program, then the hypothesized benefits of the computer's capabilities for interaction cannot in reality benefit them. The descriptive question of whether interaction in a CALL context differs from that in non-CALL contexts needs to be applied to a variety of computer learning environments. Only through investigations of this question will we be able to develop our understanding of the value of computer programs for improving learners' engagement with language learning activities.

Do students use the language learning strategies which the software supports? For any learning activity, instructors have at least implicit pedagogical intentions for the strategies learners will use to carry out that activity. For example, when explaining a course requirement that learners must do their writing using a word processing program, teachers often cite their intention that students will revise more—in other words, that they will use writing strategies associated with revision to improve their writing. The question for researchers is then whether learners actually do what they are expected to do. This question has been investigated through examination of the strategies employed by learners in a CALL program which allows the user to construct and edit sentences (Chapelle and Mizuno, 1989; Hsu, Chapelle, and Thompson, 1993).

The software employed in these investigations of the use of CALL in sentence construction and editing allowed learners to request reference materials (e.g., dictionary and grammar rules), a strategy believed to be positive for language learning. Such **resourcing**—learners' use of reference materials for obtaining information about the second language (O' Malley, Chamot, Stewner-Manzanares, Kupper, and Russo, 1985)—has been defined as a cognitive strategy. Consistent with this definition, researchers interpreted each request for on-line help by students using the CALL program as evidence of resourcing (Chapelle and Mizuno, 1989). The data collected as students worked on sentence construction and editing revealed that learners did little resourcing despite the availability of this option. Also using the computer-based sentence constructing and editing task, Hsu, Chapelle, and Thompson (1993) sought evidence for learners' use of another strategy, exploration, which involves experimenting and hypothesis-testing about the target language and which Higgins and Johns (1984) had hypothesized would be a valuable use of CALL. Exploration was inferred on the basis of two types of interactive behaviors, one of which revealed a large amount of variation among learners. These results are informative for software developers and teachers who need to observe the extent to which the potentials of CALL become actual benefits for individual learners.

Is learners' interaction with CALL programs related to subsequent performance in the target language? To address this important question, researchers must hypothesize and assess the specific effects of learners' interaction with software. For example, when Curtin, Avner, and Provenzano (1981) investigated students' error rate, frequency of interaction, total time, and review time on computerized Russian lessons, they found some relationships of these factors to the content of the material being used and to the subsequent success of the students in the course. Future research might focus on measuring features of interaction which reflect strategies believed to be important for language acquisition and isolating their effects.

These basic questions about learners' interaction with software in language learning activities have always been of interest. However, now that CALL includes a variety of activities and learner options, answers to questions about the user's actual interaction have become essential for understanding CALL. In some hypermedia and database environments, for example, learners can select from a large number of pieces of stored information. The question is: What do individual learners do in the face of so many options? It seems that the type of metacognitive strategies Oxford (1990) defines—e.g., organizing, setting goals and objectives, planning for a language task—would be essential for learners working in CALL environments, though individuals differ in their use of such strategies. As researchers continue to address these pedagogically-oriented questions, other interaction analysis research to date addresses psycholinguistic questions.

3.3.2. Psycholinguistically-Motivated CALL Research

Second language researchers have for some time been interested in investigating the language and strategies of learners as they develop their second language. In such psycholinguistically-motivated CALL research, learners' interlanguage is sampled as they work on a variety of experimental, classroom, and real-world tasks. Strategies have been studied through observations (e.g., Naiman, Fröhlich, Stern, and Todesco, 1978), think-aloud protocols (Ericsson and Simon, 1984), and retrospective self-reports (Cohen and Hosenfeld, 1981). The researchers conducting these investigations assume that language performance in context requires two types of capacities—language knowledge and linguistic processes—and that interesting aspects of that knowledge and those processes can be inferred on the basis of learners' performance. Traditional observational and introspective methods can now be complemented by computer-assisted methods to collect data which document precisely aspects of learners' interaction in CALL. Psycholinguistically-motivated CALL research has attempted to better understand both the knowledge and processes used for language performance in CALL contexts.

Language knowledge (Bachman, 1990) refers to knowledge of vocabulary, syntax, illocutionary functions, and other aspects of language pragmatics. The nature of learners' developing linguistic knowledge has been investigated by longitudinal observation of their linguistic input during computer-assisted tasks. For example, in a study observing students' use of an on-line bilingual dictionary, Bland, Noblitt, Armington, and Gay (1990) interpreted the form of students' queries as an indication of their stage of lexical development. These authors distinguished three levels of development, as evidenced by the nature of the queries learners made to the bilingual dictionary. The researchers suggested that as the learner develops, the words requested become less tied to the native language (which in this study was English), moving closer to the concepts of the second language and sometimes even to words in the second language (French, in this case). The lowest level queries, which they termed "token matching", are very English-bound, involving English inflected words, English phrases, and lexical representations for grammatical concepts (e.g., "none"). Words on the second level, which they termed "type matching", are English base forms (i.e., non-inflected words) and grammatical functions (e.g., negation and pronouns). The third level, that of "relexicalization", are words representing English circumlocutions and French words.

Processes refer to both the cognitive processes required for accessing language knowledge (e.g., recognizing lexical items) and the meta-cognitive strategies (Bachman, 1990; Faerch and Kasper, 1983) used to mediate between the learner and the environment by directing those processes. In experimental settings, the amount of time subjects take to respond to a task is often interpreted as an indicator of how automatic or automatized learning processes are. Another way that automaticity has been operationalized (Doughty and Fought, 1984) is by students' requests for help from a computer program while they were working on grammar items. In this case, the researchers interpreted requests for help as an indication of students' "controlled access of explicitly learned knowledge", reasoning that "attempts to complete tasks without any help from the program reflect automatic access to implicit knowledge in memory" (Doughty, 1987, p. 151).

Metacognitive strategies, defined as the processes learners use to regulate and control their language performance and acquisition (Bachman, 1990; Faerch and Kasper, 1983; Oxford, 1990) have also been investigated using interaction analysis. One study of ESL learners investigated **advance preparation**, a metacognitive strategy defined as "planning for and rehearsing linguistic components necessary to carry out an upcoming language task" (O'Malley et al., 1985, p. 33). Using ESL dictation tasks over a six-week semester, students listened to words (on a spelling task) and individual sentences (on the dictation task) and then typed what they had heard on a computer keyboard. In this setting, it was assumed that the time the student spent after hearing the input and before responding was spent planning in anticipation of performing. Advance preparation was therefore inferred by the amount of time which elapsed between the end of the input signal and the time that the student pressed the first key to begin to answer (Jamieson and Chapelle, 1987).

On the same dictation tasks, students were able to edit the response they had typed by deleting, inserting, and changing characters or words before the response was evaluated by the computer. This behavior, also documented in the records kept by the computer, was considered an indication of the user's monitoring of output, meaning the user's reflection on the formal aspects of a message as it is produced (Bialystok, 1981; Krashen, 1982; O'Malley et al., 1985; Wenden, 1985). The number of times a student had performed editing was divided by the total number of items the student completed to obtain the average number of times a student had edited each completed item. A third metacognitive strategy investigated using the same software was that of monitoring input, defined by Bialystok (1981) as reflecting on the formal aspects of a message as it is comprehended. The dictation tasks allowed learners to listen to the input as many times as they wanted before attempting to type it. The demands of the task required students to focus on formal aspects of the input. Therefore, when students had not comprehended a sentence or word the first time, it was presented again. In those cases where students had requested to hear it one or more times, those requests were used as evidence for monitoring input.

Other strategies believed to be revealed by students' use of software are "hypothesis-testing" and "inferencing based on the first language". Doughty and Fought (1984) operationalized the definitions of these strategies in terms of the type of grammar help requested by students while they worked on grammar lessons. When students consulted help consisting of examples, they were considered to be displaying evidence of hypothesis-testing. When they chose grammar help consisting of formal rules or chose the correct answer, they were considered to be inferencing based on the first language.

When we look carefully at pedagogical vs. psycholinguistic objectives, we see that they have in common the use of interaction analysis in CALL for better understanding second language acquisition. Through pedagogically-motivated interaction analysis of students performing CALL activities, we may better understand the features of CALL instructional contexts which facilitate language development. Through theory-oriented examination of learners' language and behavior in various CALL contexts, we may gain insights that can be attained only by considering large amounts of detailed and precise data. Future pedagogical and psycholinguistic research are likely to come closer together as researchers investigate questions about the ideal language and strategies they would like to see in carefully constructed instructional contexts.

3.4. THE DISCOURSE ANALYSIS TRADITION

Classroom research using a discourse analysis approach examines interaction as it occurs in larger discourses, or **texts**. According to Halliday and Hasan (1989), a text is "language that is doing some job in some context" (p. 10). It may be

> spoken or written, or indeed in any other medium of expression that we like to think of ... . Text is a form of exchange; and the fundamental form of a text is that of dialogue, of interaction between speakers. (Halliday and Hasan, 1989, pp. 10-11)

In classroom research, **text** refers to the actual linguistic data that results when participants interact, as illustrated in Text A below. Discourse analysis of classroom texts requires the researcher to document the linguistic data and to analyze it as functional moves which work as a part of the complete text. Discourse analysis provides a coherent view by looking at the big picture of the discourse as it structures the small pieces of interaction.

The study of texts produced in language learning contexts is important because, as second language classroom researchers (e.g., Long, 1980) have pointed out, these texts document instances of language use which are intended to facilitate acquisition. CALL texts are produced in any language learning context where the student interacts with the computer. Such contexts may be comprised of learners working individually with a computer, working in pairs or larger groups with a computer or multiple connected computers, or working with teachers or other experts. In each of these cases, the participants—one of which is the computer—contribute to an emerging text. This emerging text is affected by the nature of the context and at the same time both affects and provides evidence for the quality of the learning experiences that occur in that context. CALL researchers (e.g., Hoffman, 1994) have begun to examine the discourse that occurs among students in computer-based activities as well as the

Text A. From an ESL classroom

	Linguistic Data	**Functional Moves**
Teacher:	What kind of time are we talking about here?	Initiation
Student:	Happening now.	Response
Teacher:	No, we don't know if it is raining right now.	Feedback [evaluation] [comment]

(Johnson, 1992, p. 507)

discourse between student and computer, and in doing so have begun to apply principles of second language research to discourse in the CALL context.

3.4.1. Discourse Among Students

Research describing the oral discourse of students working on computer-based activities has shown that the number and types of discourse functions students produce in these activities depends, in part, on the type of programs they work with (Abraham and Liou, 1991; Mohan, 1992; Piper, 1986; see also discussion in Pennington and Esling, this volume). Abraham and Liou (1991) examined the number and types of functions of spoken language used by pairs of ESL students as they worked on three different types of programs: (1) ELIZA, a program which simulates a conversation by reflecting back key words from the user's statements into question frames; (2) a commercially successful simulation involving problem-solving; and (3) a traditional grammar drill on definite and indefinite articles (Liou, 1986). Liou's (1986) analysis revealed that, for the three pairs of students working on the three different types of programs, the simulation program "elicited the most talk and provided the most practice with language functions" (p. 45), while the drill on articles "prompted consideration and discussion of language forms, [and] elicited the largest variety of functions" (p. 46). On the basis of this analysis, the ELIZA program elicited the least language. Piper (1986), in contrast, found that the language functions learners used while they worked in groups on several different CALL activities were very restricted in range and number.

Later research by Mohan (1992) reflects both the positive and negative findings of these earlier studies. Mohan (1992) reports that ESL student pairs spoke more and negotiated more input in conversation off the computer than they did in working with a business simulation, word processor, or grammar program, while the computer context elicited a more cognitively demanding form of discourse that often involved explicit reasoning. Thus, in Mohan's (1992) view:

the computer can offer communication tasks with high cognitive demands and high contextual support. To say this is to begin to see computer use as an activity that relates action, knowledge and discourse. (p. 124)

In a similar vein, Esling (1991c) observed that student communication over a computer network produced discourse characterized by certain linguistic features such as a high frequency of explicit nominal reference (see discussion of the Victoria Project in Hoffman, this volume), and Phinney (this volume) reports that a collaborative writing program promoted student comments which were more specific and detailed than those given off the computer. Given current optimism concerning the use of the computer as a participant in group activities intended to provide oral practice, the question about the amount and functional types of discourse produced in various activities remains important.

3.4.2. Discourse Between Student and Computer

It is also useful to apply methods of discourse analysis to the texts produced when student and computer interact in CALL activities. If we consider the computer program to be a participant in a conversation with the learner, as some other software researchers have, we can investigate questions about the nature of specific examples of student-computer discourse. The example in Text B illustrates the type of text that resulted from a student working on a particular computer program and the analysis of functional moves comprising it.

Text B. Student working on an ESL "conversation" exercise (TERRI)

There is a picture of various sizes and shapes of blocks on the computer screen and the student knows from previous instructions that she can move the blocks around by typing directions.

Computer:	What should I do now?	Initiation [open solicit]
Student:	set the wedge behind the spool	Response
Computer:	I'm thinking ... You have an unclear noun phrase.	Follow-up [identify error]

(Coleman, 1985, p. 250)

When we look at student-computer interaction from the perspective of discourse functions, we can begin to pose questions about the benefits of interaction with the machine for language learning. Moreover, we can make hypotheses on the basis of other second language research which has investigated the value of particular types of interaction for language learning. Of course, since this research has been conducted by examining the texts produced by human participants, we must be tentative in applying the same principles to computer-student discourse. Nevertheless, as a starting point for discourse-oriented CALL research, we might focus on what researchers have discovered about positive aspects of human discourse. In the area of language learning, it has been maintained (Krashen, 1982) that the input learners receive in the second language promotes language acquisition if it is both comprehensible and contains linguistic material which is new to the learner. In CALL texts, then, we should be concerned with the nature of the computer's input to the student, as Underwood (1984) pointed out. The best way for the researcher to assess whether input is comprehensible for an individual learner is to observe how the learner responds to it.

Long (1985) has hypothesized that the learner's process of interaction with second language input to make it comprehensible is a key factor in language acquisition. In his view, the learner needs to receive the input, be confused about some aspects of its meaning, and therefore request a repetition, clarification, restatement, or other type of modification. According to Larsen-Freeman and Long (1991):

> Modification of the interactional structure of conversation or of written discourse during reading ... is a [good] candidate for a necessary (not sufficient) condition for acquisition. The role it plays in negotiation for meaning helps to make input comprehensible while still containing unknown linguistic elements, and, hence, potential intake for acquisition. (p. 144)

In CALL texts, then, we would like to see moves by learners which request modifications of the input they receive. We would like to see, for example, learners requesting clarifications, restatements, definitions, and explanations—all of which are intended to help them understand the meaning of the input they receive.

A third type of text that is believed to be important for acquisition, particularly acquisition of grammatical competence, is what Swain (1985) calls "comprehensible output". Because of the numbers and the dynamics involved in classroom learning, "comprehensible output is, unfortunately, generally missing in typical classroom settings, language classrooms and immersion classrooms being no exceptions" (Swain, 1985, p. 252). Is comprehensible output present in texts produced in CALL contexts? Texts in which learners initiate or respond by producing language can illustrate production of comprehensible output. Again, the value of comprehensible output can be observed in a sequence of text—in this case consisting of a learner's unsuccessful attempt to express something, another participant's communication of misunderstanding or lack of understanding, and the learner's correction of his/her previous utterance.

The work on second language discourse described above provides clear directions for CALL research. By investigating the effects of different types of discourse generated in a CALL environment, we can begin to test in CALL contexts the hypotheses of classroom researchers about the positive effects of particular types of interaction. As we pursue such research, we will, however, undoubtedly wish to consider other features of CALL contexts as well. The context refers to features of the activities, topics, and participants, in addition to the cultures in which CALL activities take place. To investigate these important contextual features and their influence on CALL texts, researchers need to adopt ethnographic approaches to CALL research.

3.5. ETHNOGRAPHIC RESEARCH

Chaudron (1988) defines the ethnographic approach as "a qualitative, process-oriented approach to the study of interaction" (p. 45) and aspects of the context of interaction. An ethnography investigates both the "micro" context of participants' interaction and the "macro" context of the socio-cultural setting (Cazden, 1985; Van Lier, 1988). For some time, educational researchers have argued that in order to understand "the contingent nature of interaction" (Mehan, 1979, p. 10) and the complexity of classroom life, classroom research needs a holistic and ethnographic approach which "considers the classroom situation in its totality and places it in a wider social context" (Mehan, 1979, p. 14).

The ethnographic perspective on classroom research is consistent with current views of language as a resource for social interaction which must be studied in context (Hymes, 1974) and of language learning as a process of socialization (Watson-Gegeo, 1988). Moreover, because second language acquisition is a complex process involving socio-cultural, psychological, affective, and personal variables, ethnography has been advocated as providing a unique and important perspective on the second language classroom (Breen, 1985; Chaudron, 1988; Larsen-Freeman and Long, 1991; Long, 1980; Nunan, 1991; Van Lier, 1988). In attempting to understand the various impacts of the computer in second language contexts, it seems that ethnography could play an important role. We will consider here how ethnographic research might increase our understanding of CALL, beginning with a brief overview of the principles and methods used in ethnographic research.

3.5.1. Principles and Methods of Ethnography

Despite the variety of theoretical perspectives that have shaped current views of ethnography, all ethnographic approaches to research are ideally holistic, process-oriented, and emic. Ethnography's holism refers to the principle that any aspect of culture or interactional behavior—among students, students and teachers, or students and CALL materials—should be described and explained in relation to the whole system of which it is a part (Erickson, 1981; Heath, 1982; Hymes, 1981; Mehan, 1979; Van Lier, 1988, Watson-Gegeo, 1988). The process orientation of ethnography attempts to reveal how and why social events occur rather than documenting only what occurred. By examining the process dimension of events, the researcher can explore "the intersubjective and context-dependent nature of [interactional] events as they occur, noting the regularities and idiosyncrasies in the events" (Chaudron, 1988, p. 48). The emic nature of ethnography requires the researcher to consult the viewpoint of an insider or "native" to the situation under investigation in order to refine and sharpen research questions using the insider's perceptions and cultural knowledge (Spindler and Spindler, 1987). The ethnographic researcher should not be restricted by "pre-established views, standards of measurement, models, schemes, and typologies" (Van Lier, 1988, p. 55).

Consistent with these principles, ethnographies are typically based on combinations of research methods such as interviews, observations, and examination of relevant documents. Data are usually collected over a long period of time with a few subjects in order to perform an in-depth investigation and analysis. Observation methods can be either "participant observation", in which "researchers take part in the activities they are studying" (Larsen-Freeman and Long, 1991, p. 15) or "non-participant observation", in which "researchers observe activities without engaging in them directly" (Larsen-Freeman and Long, 1991, p. 16). As we look toward applying ethnography to CALL, we find examples of both participant and non-participant research which have been used to investigate second language acquisition as well as computer use in monolingual English classrooms.

The diary study is one type of participant observation used in the context of second language research (Bailey, 1980, 1983; Schumann, 1980; Schumann and Schumann, 1977). Bailey (1980) kept a detailed journal of her observations of fellow students and the teacher while studying French as a researcher-student. On the basis of the daily journal documenting her learning experience, she was able to reflect on competitiveness and anxiety in adult second language learning. In a monolingual English setting, Herrmann (1987) conducted an ethnographic study through participant observation as a researcher-teacher to determine the effects on student collaboration and social relationships of using the computer as a writing instrument in a high school writing class of eight students over a year-long period. Participant observation can provide valuable insights about personal and affective factors which influence learning and interaction but may at the same time be limited by its subjectivity and anecdotal nature (Van Lier, 1988) as well as by problems associated with dividing the researcher's attention between observing and participating. Because of these limitations, Schumann (1980) claimed that it is necessary to develop methods for aggregation of journal data across many studies.

Using non-participant observation, Cohen, Levin, and Souviney (1986) conducted an ethnographic study of six exemplary elementary classrooms to explore the grassroots implementation of computers in classrooms. Four interviews with teachers, eight observations, and follow-up interviews of administrative personnel were carried out in each school. Findings of this study showed that successful implementation of computers was the result not of a traditional top-down hierarchical approach, but of the combined efforts of an enthusiastic teacher, who became the "computer expert", and a supportive principal, who in most cases did not know about computers but recognized their potential. Also using a non-participant observation technique, Cullen (1988) conducted a case study of six developmental writers who composed with a word processing program and a set of computerized prewriting and revising aids (*WANDAH*) over a nine-month period. Cullen (1988) used a stimulated recall method which asks the writer to "relive" the composing experience and to verbally describe it while replaying a videotape of the composing session immediately after it is completed. In this way, the attempt is made to overcome the limitations of non-participant observation.

3.5.2. Ethnographic Research Questions for CALL

Computer use in second language learning has raised controversial questions and issues concerning the value of various computer activities. Can the technology be used to improve language learning, or does the technology actually isolate students from meaningful learning contexts and opportunities (Johnson, 1991; Pennington, 1991c)? Can CALL help to create an empowering environment for language learning, as many CALL developers and teachers have suggested, or does the computer act as another foreign element in an already foreign environment? To address the complex issues surrounding computer use in second language classrooms, ethnographic research can help researchers to discover and investigate the many relevant and interrelated variables holistically and with a sensitivity toward the perspectives of the learners.

With its emic and flexible perspective, an ethnographic study in a CALL context could help to identify some of the significant features of how learners participate in interaction with the machine. An example from a non-CALL learning context can give an idea of how such a study might progress and what sorts of findings might emerge. Acting as a participant observer, Freeman (1992) used ethnographic methods to identify significant aspects of interaction in a French class. The data he considered included lesson transcripts, field notes, and interviews with students and the teacher. He began his study by asking how the teacher defines what can or cannot go on in a lesson and how these boundaries of acceptability are constructed or negotiated through the teacher's talk and activity. During the investigation, he realized that the initial research question was premature and that he could not examine the teacher's boundaries on acceptable classroom behavior without first gaining some understanding of the classes under study. His shift in focus is reflected by an interaction between data and analysis which amounts to an interaction between the participants in the research and the researcher. The research question, now with a focus on the nature of the French classroom, became how authority and control were distributed, through pedagogical approach and interaction, to build a shared understanding of French. The results of the study highlighted "social and interpersonal aspects of language learning" (Nunan, 1991, p. 265) and described not only the nature of the interaction in the classroom studied, but also how that interaction was achieved. In addressing the "how" question, the findings of this ethnographic classroom study helped to define what learners would need to know in order to be able to participate appropriately in the types of interactions observed.

With its process-oriented perspective, an ethnographic study in a CALL context could help to describe the process of learning that takes place within a complex interaction carried out in a specific setting. As a CALL example, Bueno and Nelson (1993) conducted an ethnographic study in two elementary Spanish classrooms to investigate the classroom discourse and interactions among the participants in the setting as well as the interactions of the participants with specific software (*Salmanca*) in a contextualized computer environment. They employed various data collection methods: participant observation, ethnographic interviews, oral proficiency interviews, writing samples, and data collected by the computer during students' interactions with the software. The interactions involved negotiating a number of features of the context, including: the role of the computers in the setting, the role of the computer laboratory, the nature of the computer-based lessons, and the nature of communication with peers within the computer environment. Based on the analysis of the field notes from participant observations, Bueno and Nelson (1993) developed three qualitative concepts to describe the interactions that take place in a contextualized computer environment: the notion of experts (in this case, children), the role of gatekeepers (here, the teacher), and the negotiated nature of all endeavors within a community of learners.

With its holistic approach, ethnographic studies of CALL can provide evidence about students' interaction and learning in view of the complete context. This holistic view is necessary to provide a thorough and meaningful understanding of how learning takes place. For example, Cazden, Michaels, and Watson-Gegeo (1987) investigated how the use of writing software in a sixth grade classroom affected the teaching and learning process. To obtain a holistic view, they conducted classroom observations, ethnographic interviews, naturalistic experiments, and discourse analysis of classroom texts. This method allowed them to see that the computer was not a single innovation but instead affected the entire system of writing in the classroom. Another ethnographic study obtaining a holistic view of teaching and learning is Park's (1994) research investigating the introduction of multimedia ESL software into a classroom in an intensive English program. By observing both the details of the learners' interaction with the multimedia software and the larger context of the ESL classroom and the intensive English program, Park was able to interpret the observed interactions in view of the larger culture.

Many researchers have suggested the need to combine ethnographic approaches with other research methods in order to gain a broader perspective of second language classrooms and CALL contexts (Dunkel, 1991; Erickson, 1981; Larsen-Freeman and Long, 1991; Long, 1980; Van Lier, 1988). This need for combining research perspectives seems particularly relevant to CALL research, which has been conducted primarily within the psychometric tradition, despite the fact that within such a paradigm any observed learning gain or achievement cannot be unambiguously attributed to the computer (Clark, 1985). Pa–pert (1987) strongly argued that educators have to center their attention on the culture and context of learning because

> the context for human development is always a culture, never an isolated technology. In the presence of computers, cultures might change and with them people's ways of learning and thinking. (p. 23)

As Levine (1990) argues, "any technological innovation [such as] the implementation and instructional use of microcomputers" (p. 462) must be understood as part of "a complex system of social, political, and cultural values, priorities, and relations" (p. 462). Such a "macro-contextual" view of CALL is required, given that "the effects of microcomputers on education depend on the social and educational contexts within which they are embedded" (Sheingold, Kane, and Endreweit, 1983, p. 431).

Some researchers believe that an ethnographic perspective can enhance the generalizability of CALL research based in other traditions. In order to generalize the results of a research study, i.e., to answer the question of what relevance findings concerning the influences of the variables of one study have for other instructional contexts? (Chapelle and Jamieson, 1991, p. 49), the research report should describe the classroom context and the factors of the research setting as clearly as possible. To this end, a CALL research report should describe "(1) the elements of the target language context, (2) the characteristics of the subjects, and (3) the CALL materials used" (Chapelle and Jamieson, 1991, p. 49), in addition to the empirically based or linguistically grounded findings discovered by psychometric tradition, interaction analysis, or discourse analysis. Such careful reporting can bring about a more thorough understanding of the generalizablity of findings which can contribute to the future development and use of CALL materials.

3.6. CONCLUDING REMARKS TO CHAPTER 3

Examining CALL research from the perspective of other classroom researchers brings into focus a number of important research questions that might be investigated in a CALL context as well as the methods CALL researchers might use to investigate them. It is clear that the uncharted territory in CALL research lies in the process-oriented domain, a domain investigated through interaction analysis, discourse analysis, and ethnographic methods. The range of process-oriented research questions in CALL become more interesting as our understanding of second language acquisition increases and as technological developments expand the range of potential computer uses in second language classrooms. Through continued CALL research, we may begin to understand how software can be developed and used to best facilitate second language acquisition.

NOTES TO CHAPTER 3

1. This research approach is not unique to CALL. Many researchers have tried to determine whether students learn as well or better using computer-assisted instruction (CAI, the experimental group) rather than some other type of instruction (the control group). Over the past twenty years, meta-analyses (which attempt to aggregate and summarize research findings across many studies) have consistently reported three findings for CAI: students using CAI have performed moderately better on achievement measures, have slightly better attitudes, and take about 30% less time to complete their tasks (see, e.g., Kulik and Kulik, 1986, 1991; Kulik, Kulik, and Bangert-Drowns, 1985; Kulik, Kulik, and Shwalb, 1986; Roblyer, 1988; Roblyer, Castine, and King, 1988).

2. For example, Dixon (1981) reported that ESL students were "happy" and usage was "high so something must be right" (p. 105) with the ESL CALL lessons on the PLATO system at the University of Illinois. Reid, Lindstrom, McCaffrey, and Larson (1983) reported that all of the ESL students who used a text analysis program for composition "enjoyed the cultural experience" (p. 41). Questionnaire results typically—but not always—indicate favorable attitudes toward CALL.

4. Computer Networks: Webs of Communication For Language Teaching

Robert Hoffman

4.1. INTRODUCTION

In the Information Age **computer networks** are spinning webs of communicative relationships among language learners and teachers. These electronic networks can support the teaching and learning of language, realistic practice of language, and research about language and the teaching of language.

Computer networks can broaden interaction among language learners and teachers by providing them a channel of communication free from the restrictions of time and distance. Learners can access a wider variety of teachers—and other learners, both native and non-native speakers of the target language—throughout the world. Collaborative projects can bring together native speakers and second language learners for the achievement of complex and communicatively demanding tasks. Over networks, learners have access to real audiences with authentic needs for information and authentic reactions to the quality of the communication that takes place.

Networks can deepen communication, too, allowing learners to work through complicated tasks in which the development of the message is recursive. Such tasks can range from basic assignments that lead learners through the writing process to the negotiation of meaning required for consensus on texts in international negotiation simulations. Learners involved in collaborative local and international projects have a reason to reflect on the success or failure of their language as they negotiate meaning in support of common goals. The anonymous quality of network communication can be face-saving as well, relieving learners of the inhibitions associated with face-to-face communication and allowing them to express themselves more freely as they develop their proficiency.

This chapter explores some of the creative ways in which teachers and learners are using computer networks to enhance language learning, by enriching their physical and personal networks of communication. The distances encompass rooms, buildings, campuses, countries, regions, and the world. Communications can be interactive—simultaneous or delayed—and can involve pairs, small groups, and very large groups of groups. Much development in the use of networking for language learning has taken place in first language teaching. However, every day more projects in networking are emerging as the technology develops and language teachers perceive an ever increasing number of ways in which telecommunications can contribute to their methodology.

Also, this chapter, while recognizing the obstacles, pitfalls, and drawbacks of the use of computer networks in language teaching and learning, is unabashed in focusing on examples of successful implementations of network technology as a part of CALL. Here readers will find an overview of electronic networks in action, with many ideas for the use of a technology that is becoming a fact of life.

Computer networks essentially give teachers and learners the capability to exploit communication more fully in support of language learning (see Phinney, this volume, for examples). The networks themselves—the hardware, software, and connections that form the webs of communication—are quite complicated, although technological evolution is working to humanize them. Nevertheless, thinking about networks requires a basic understanding of their terminology. The next section attempts to demystify this terminology for the less than fully initiated reader.

4.2. DEMYSTIFYING THE "NET"

A computer network is a linkage of two or more computer workstations for the sharing of software, data, and peripheral devices. A network also provides communication among the workstations, a key to the use of computer networks in language teaching and learning. Networks can be so small as to fit in a single room or large enough to interconnect with other networks and encircle the globe. The past decade has seen a wave of network development that has percolated up from the strata of highly technical specialists to the business and academic communities, and from there to the general public. In the academic community, network use has extended from faculty to graduate students, and then down to students in their first year of study. Electronic networks support a wide range of information exchange, collaborative work, research, and recreational activities. All of these uses can serve the goal of developing language proficiency.

Computer networking and telecommunications are replete with terminology—connectivity, coaxial cable, optical fiber, netware, servers, modems, **LANs, WANs, BITNET, Internet, Usenet, World Wide Web (www), NREN, e-mail, asynchronous** and **synchronous communication, virtual reality,** the **"Information Superhighway"**—and the list goes on. These terms—referred to by some as "computerese"—attempt to describe the foundation and girders that support the potential uses of computer networks for language learning. As the technology becomes more transparent and user-friendly, the terminology may become more accessible as well and give way to the more important issues of designing learning activities which will exploit this technology and expand the repertoire of the language teacher. For the time being, though, it is useful to have at least a nodding acquaintance with these terms and the general principles of computer networks.

4.2.1. Technical Connectivity

Connectivity refers to the fact that in a network, workstations are linked together. The basic components of a network include the workstations themselves, either terminals of mainframe or personal computers, the cable or radio waves and attendant hardware (**modems, multiplexers**) that join them, and the computer (**server**) and software (**netware, communication packages**, e.g., Crosstalk or Telix, etc.) that manage the connection. Incidentally, connectivity can also refer to whom and what is connected—the people who are put in contact with one another and the information that they can access (this illustrates the natural development of multiple meanings of terms in this field).

Network systems can include large mainframe computers, personal computers (PCs) in all their variety, and combinations of these. These can be linked one to another by common coaxial cable, which provides acceptable performance in communicating large amounts of data very quickly, or by the newer technology of fiber optics that offers a further significant improvement in speed over coaxial technology. "Cableless" communication by radio waves is a variant form of network connection, usually found in small networks confined to a single room. Through modems, devices that enable computers to communicate over telephone lines, networks make use of existing telephone systems and satellite enhanced telecommunications systems forming a worldwide web. Development is continuous in telecommunications.

4.2.2. LANs and WANs

A **LAN** is a Local Area Network, a collection of PCs or terminals linked together, usually in a single room, building, or institution. LANs can be linked to other LANs and to **WANs**, Wide Area Networks, which can cover large geographical areas such as large institutions, communities, regions, countries, and continents. WANs can also be linked into a virtually global network in which the interconnections between countries and regions are all but transparent to users (Howard, 1992), who interact with a common interface. To send electronic mail to the room next door or to send it to a discussion list of 350 participants around the world requires the same basic actions.

An example of a LAN is a departmental network that connects faculty computers to share a central software library and centralized peripheral devices, such as laser printers. A LAN might link computers in a writing lab or a CALL center to support the sharing of data and computer functions, e.g., student writing in process, CALL software, and printing.

A WAN might link all the departments of a university and provide electronic mail service, access to larger WANs, and the sharing of mainframe computer resources. Such a network would support internal communication and provide a gateway to the greater collection of networks throughout the world.

Large-scale WANs that enable global communication are many and are under constant development. BITNET, the "Because It's There" or "Because It's Time" network, links educational institutions around the world. The Internet brings together educational institutions, governmental agencies, and other kinds of organizations for educational and research purposes. The Internet, which has grown from 2,000 participants in 1981 to 15 million in 1993 (Eckhouse, 1993), is intended to be replaced in 1996 by the high speed National Research and Education Network (**NREN**) (Howard, 1992). Many tertiary educational institutions and an increasing number of secondary school systems have access to the WANs, opening the door for quick and efficient world-wide communication, with all of its positive implications for language learning.

The WANs described here have been established to foster the exchange of research and to support education, but proprietary products for information distribution and sharing that run on WANs also exist, such as **Prodigy** and **Compuserve**. Subscribers to these products pay a fee for access to communication and databases, including connection to BITNET and the Internet as well as access to financial information, up-to-date news, electronic journals, special interest discussion groups, gaming, and even "tele-shopping" for a variety of mail order items.

The **World Wide Web** (WWW) is a refinement of the Internet that provides multimedia access to an enormous number of archives of information throughout the world. Multimedia means exactly what it says—users can access and receive information in text, graphic, photographic, sound, or moving picture and animated formats, depending on the nature of the equipment available to them. Multimedia computer workstations are becoming the standard for new personal computers on the market. These archives include such resources as huge institutional databases at universities and research organizations and at public and private, profit and non-profit, organizations. Also, users of the WWW can reach the personal archives of all kinds of people who are willing, whether for profit, altruistic, or other motives, to make information available.

The WWW uses the concept of hypertext to allow users to follow their intuition as they seek information. As detailed in Ashworth (this volume), Hypertext is a method of organizing information in which specific parts of that information are highlighted on the screen. When users select a highlighted item, they penetrate further and further into the information available. Users can search for information, access "homepages" (WWW sites that relate or link to specific information), view and search through the contents, follow links to other associated homepages, download or save information, interact with people throughout the world via built-in e-mail, and generally "travel" electronically throughout the world via the WWW.

WWW "readers" are application programs that offer interfaces or user-friendly displays that enable people to command operations on the WWW. Typical examples of these are the popular *Netscape* and *Mosaic*

Web readers. Web readers provide access to a variety of search "engines" or programs that catalog the topical areas available on the WWW.

It is almost impossible to visualize how much information is out there on the WWW and how much is being added every day. All such information is a potential gold mine for the language teacher who seeks to unite learners in the use of a common language, find matter for the design and production of relevant learning activities, or find vital contact with current research and researchers.

4.2.3. Network Communication at Work in Language Teaching and Learning

To contextualize the above description of the technology and to illustrate how transparent network technology can be, two examples of networking in action follow.

Jim, a lecturer in a university program in English as a Second Language, powers up his home computer, selects his communications software, and dials up access by modem to his university's mainframe and WAN. He logs on to the VAX electronic mail system and reads a message from Vivian, a non-native student who enquires about a point of language and a question of content in some writing she is doing. Jim extracts her message into his reply and writes his comments at appropriate places within her original text. Thinking that the comments might also be useful for other students in the class, Jim asks Vivian if he might share his comments on her paper with others. Jim then sends the message to her and goes on to other business. Later, when Vivian has logged into her e-mail account and reads the response, she replies in the affirmative to Jim's request. When Jim next checks his e-mail, he reads Vivian's message and then retrieves from disk his earlier message to her, edits it to provide a meaningful context for the class, and posts it to the class electronic bulletin board.

Later that day, Vivian completes a draft of her contribution to a communication project in English that she is working on with a team of two other classmates. She e-mails her draft to her team for their review and commentary. That evening, at home, she logs into e-mail and reads their comments. Sunny, one of her teammates, working from home over his modem, tells her that he does not understand a point she is making and asks her to include an example. Mei, who is writing in the university's computer center, replies that Vivian's writing has prompted her to change her "reporting" verbs to past tense. Vivian sends a message to Sunny asking him to help her devise an effective example to illustrate a point she wants to make. The students continue communicating back and forth in this manner until they complete the project, accessing the teacher's e-mail address periodically to inquire about content, organization, and grammar in their evolving report.

In the next example, the participants reach beyond the confines of their department and their university, using WANs to interact with other learners globally. Two students studying English for Professional Communication in Hong Kong are working on an international negotiation simulation problem. They prepare a position statement in English and then log into **Telnet**, a system that enables them to use the resources of a mainframe computer at another university halfway around the world. Although neither of these students are native speakers of English, they interact with the remote computer in English. Using specialized communications software, the students distribute their position statement to teams in Finland, Russia, Chile, Japan, and the United States. Before the day is over, this diverse audience will read the Hong Kong students' communication with care, because they need the information to reach consensus on an international treaty they are drafting as part of the simulation exercise.

In the evening, a teacher and a group of students log into Telnet again, this time to participate in a synchronous or real-time conversation in which learners in several different countries explore their views on the text of the treaty they are writing. Although the real-time conversation taking place over the network flows more slowly than spoken conversation—because of the different keyboarding speeds of participants, the amount of time required for conceptualizing and expressing themselves, and the awkwardness of turn-taking—the students are deeply involved in the developing discussion that is led across the screen by the dancing cursor. Their teacher stands behind them watching developments, and the students appear to be unconscious of her, at least as a teacher. They chat with her briefly about ideas or joke about the language that emerges on the screen, then they return to speaking among themselves in English as one of them enters their contributions.

In these examples, the communication and its impact on language learning dominate the impression; the technology seems merely instrumental and practically transparent. In reality, the network processes vary from being easy and convenient, e.g., e-mail communication over a sophisticated user-friendly interface, to the more problematic synchronous interchange of ideas among participants in six or seven countries. The important point is that in each case, computer networking enriches and expands the opportunity to learn and use the target language naturally and with communicative purpose. The following sections describe how computer networks can add flexible communication channels to expand the language resources existing among teachers and learners.

4.3. THE LAN: SUPPORT FOR THE INTERACTIVE PROCESS-BASED LANGUAGE CLASS

The uses of the LAN for language learning can range from a file server (a separate computer linked to and controlling other computer work stations) that enables learners to share resources such as CALL software, to a true network that brings together teachers, resources, and learners in a dynamic interactive language learning environment. The impetus for evolution of LAN technology as a foundation for collaborative language learning came from the process writing movement in English composition.

Daiute (1984) extended her vision of computers and writing beyond the single workstation to networks that enabled the fulfillment of the writing process as a recursive and collaborative endeavor. The most common uses for LANs thus far have been in the interactive writing lab, but the potential for the local area network to support a variety of other exciting language teaching activities is considerable. These include shared exercise and project work, and multimedia exercises that combine reading, writing, speaking, and listening skills.

Since the time of Daiute's first vision, there has been an exponential increase in the number of articles devoted to networked writing environments in the field of first language composition. Of late, the interest in networks to support communicative process writing has spread to the field of foreign and second language learning (Clifford and Warren, 1993; Hoffman, 1991, 1993; Kalaja and Leppänen, 1991; Phinney, this volume). The bottom line is that a LAN in a writing lab can support a class in which all of the strata of the writing process can be exploited, i.e., prewriting and invention, collaborative drafting and peer review, efficient revising and editing, and the sharing of texts with a variety of real audiences.

Table 4.1 below contrasts characteristics of an early interactive environment for developing literacy, QUILL (Rubin and Bruce, 1990), with those found in a traditional classroom and serves to illustrate how computer networks can realize the concept of writing as a process.

QUILL (an Interactive Writing Environment)	Traditional Classrooms
Pre-writing	Sit and write w/minimal planning
Topic choice	Designated topic
Multiple genres	Mostly narrative
Multiple real audiences	Teacher as audience
Real purposes	Writing for a grade
Conferencing	Red marks as response
Revision	Editing
Collaboration	Hidden papers (solo work)
Sharing writing	Isolated writers
Writing across the curriculum	Writing in *language* class

Table 4.1. Contrasts between QUILL (or an Interactive Writing Environment) and Traditional Classrooms (adapted from Rubin and Bruce, 1990)

The gist of the table is that in the traditional classroom, writing is undertaken to fulfill an assignment and earn a grade, is narrowly planned and developed in a linear fashion, is directed toward the teacher, is performed in isolation, and receives a restricted response. In an integrated writing environment, writing is driven by the writer's ideas, is creatively and expansively planned, addresses multiple real audiences, is collaborative, is shared, and receives a variety of responses. In the remainder of this section, I describe how the process approach can be supported by a LAN and examine the implications for second language teaching and learning.

4.3.1. Interactive Invention

Writers in a first or second language need to write with a purpose in mind and need to organize their thoughts around that purpose. Language learners are faced with an additional hurdle—the problem of expressing their thoughts in appropriate and linguistically accurate language. The idea of process writing addresses these problems by leading novice writers through heuristic activities aimed at helping them to align their thinking and to shape their expression with regard to the needs of an audience and the requirements of a particular topic. The LAN allows learners to manage these activities efficiently and to share key stages of the process with peers and teachers.

Heuristic activities use a set of prompts or questions to guide the writer in the choice of a topic and in the selection of things to say about it (Phinney, 1989). Teachers and learners can choose among prompts provided by the software in a variety of packages or can invent their own sets of prompts tailored to the requirements of the course or the special needs of the learners. The individualized prompts can then be added to the invention or pre-writing module of the package.

The LAN aside, all the mechanics of invention carried out on software could be managed with paper and pencil. But because the process is computerized, the learner can save and recall preliminary ideas, lists, and phrasings efficiently, branch to new ideas without losing old work, and integrate ideas into an outline that can later be expanded into a complete text with a word processor.

Invention, however, is often the loneliest part of any writer's task, and some might say it is better for novice writers to face their topics alone and find their own voices. Perhaps the most powerful enhancement to process writing brought about by the LAN is found more readily in the drafting and revising stages of the process, where the writer needs to assess the quality and expression of ideas and the mechanics of the language used by viewing work through the additional lenses provided by collaboration with peers and teachers.

4.3.2. Collaborative Drafting, Revising, and Editing

Software intended to fulfill the idea of writing as a process uses the LAN to allow for the quick and convenient sharing of drafting with a set of guiding questions to evoke useful commentary from peers or teachers. Again, these prompts can be modified to reflect the needs of the assignment or of the learners.

Harnessing the power and appeal of the computer, and the ease with which it allows users to interact, the LAN provides a web over which the critical activities of collaborative writing can be conducted. Networked computers allow the writer to display work in progress or even final work to a selected audience who are then prompted to express their critical reaction to the writing. The critical remarks of reviewers can be saved by all stakeholders involved in the evolution of a piece of writing.

Again, nothing is being done here that cannot be done *sans* computer network: in a process writing class, teachers prepare copies of guiding prompts for reviewers, writers copy and distribute drafts, reviewers write responses and copy them for future reference. What the computer and the network bring to the process are immediacy, convenience, a saving of time and paper, greater objectivity (and the face-saving inherent in this), and the potential attraction and motivation of using appealing state-of-the-art technology.

4.3.3. Messaging and Real-Time Conferencing

In addition to offering structured drafting and critical response capabilities, ideally, a writing lab LAN should allow spontaneous and collaborative discussion about writing, about assignments, and about the process of communication. A feature found in well-designed integrated network writing packages is a user friendly messaging module that allows asynchronous and, possibly, synchronous communication. Asynchronous communication, typical of electronic mail systems, gives second language learners time to digest the messages they receive and time to develop their ideas and express them as clearly as possible in their replies. Synchronous, or real-time, conferencing can promote quick and spontaneous interchanges, and at the same time preserve anonymity, depending on how the interactions are set up and managed by the teacher in regard to the identification of participants.

Useful multi-user communication modules include the capability to post messages either privately or publicly, allowing learners to confer on a one-to-one basis or to publicly discuss issues related to topics and assignments. A good integrated communications package for novice writers should allow the writers maximum latitude for revision, improvement, and reuse of even casual messages posted through the network. Such a feature supports the learners' developing awareness that good communication, even casual communication, is processed to some degree and needs to be as accurate in form and as clear in expression as possible.

A user-friendly and multi-featured messaging module supports collaborative teaching, too. Teachers working together can access the communications of several classes to find examples of common linguistic errors present in the students' work, or to remark on positive developments in their class skills and understanding of each others' communication or of course material. General issues related to topics and assignments can be shared among a number of classes.

Synchronous communication, similar to computer bulletin board **Chat Mode**, enables learners to participate in a real-time discussion.

Communication software commonly uses split screens to allow each participant in a chat session to compose messages while viewing other messages that are posted to the list in the order in which they were sent. Learners quickly adapt the written medium to what is, in fact, a new style of conversation by use of non-verbal symbols called "emoticons" or "smilies" to denote a variety of reactions. Typical smilies (viewed horizontally) are :-) to show good feeling, :-(, the sad face, and the winking smilie ;-) to indicate a risqué remark. Inventive networkers have built up a collection of hundreds of smilies to enhance the conversational style of e-mail and the chat mode. Also, participants use a range of non-lexical devices such as *errr...* (to preface a doubt or gentle disagreement), **gulp**, **gasp**, **sigh**, *grrrrr !!!* (a growl of displeasure), ZZZZzzzzzzz (nodding off). A range of acronyms has also evolved in network communication, including *BTW* ("by the way"), *IMHO* ("in my humble opinion"), *TTYL* ("talk to you later"), and many others.

Participants in synchronous communication over a network simulate—or indeed, emulate—many of the other behaviors of conversation as well, including turn-taking, leadership, digression, politeness—and impoliteness, called "flaming" in net terminology. Conferencing sessions can be managed to provide anonymity among the participants, thus encouraging shy learners to "speak up" and "speak out" in the target language. Such interchanges can bring about a radical change from the often passive behavior of many language learners and can diminish the effect of dominant personalities in face-to-face communication.

Additionally, the logging of synchronous sessions allows teachers and learners access to machine readable transcripts that can be used for research, in-class analysis of language and communication exemplified by the stored texts, or the development of language exercises based on authentic communication. Such archives are easy to build and convenient to store by computer means.

4.3.4. Sharing Work

Finally, an effectively networked writing lab enables novice writers to share their finished work conveniently, i.e., to have their writing read by people other than teachers and collaborators. The posting of finished products to an electronic bulletin board on the LAN network gives learner writing validity. Content, style, and linguistic accuracy can be put on display before a variety of audiences, some of whom might be personally interested in the topics and others of whom might actually need the information for assignments in the class. The writing that is shared becomes more than a demonstration of learning for a teacher: it is communication.

Electronic sharing is not intended to replace hard copy in all situations, for example, in assignments simulating real-world communication that would not normally be distributed electronically—e.g., resumes, business letters, reports, proposals, and the like. What network distribution can do is quickly and conveniently make appropriate samples of learner writing available to inform or to edify an authentic audience.

A powerful rationale for using LAN communications for language learning is offered by Kreeft Peyton (1986) in a description of LAN use at Gallaudet University:

(1) Students read and write using language that is meaningful, functional and comprehensible;
(2) a non-threatening environment can be created for using English;
(3) students are engaged in using written language for a wide range of purposes (such as joking, complaining, and requesting information) in a wide range of contexts;
(4) students are motivated to write in English by communicating with real and present audiences.

As these observations on computer use by deaf students implies, the LAN provides a medium that allows for authentic, purposeful communication in a structured environment.

4.4. A SMALL WAN: E-MAIL IMPROVES MANAGEMENT AND LEARNING IN AN ENGLISH COMMUNICATIONS SKILLS COURSE

Elsewhere (Hoffman, 1993) I have described the integration of a school-wide electronic mail system into courses in technical communication skills offered to Cantonese-speaking students studying for a B.A. in Information Science. This network communication channel was used to disseminate course material, to receive and respond to short written assignments and draft portions of longer assignments, and as an additional channel for interaction with students.

Students and teachers involved in the courses said that network communication added a further dimension of warmth and humanity to the repertoire of feedback channels they had experienced before. Electronic mail provided students with more timely, more complete, and more usable information about their writing and assignments than written comments on work returned to them. They also found, on occasion, that e-mail feedback was more face-saving and less stressful than face-to-face communication. Four teachers who used e-mail with their students and whom I studied, found that network communication was efficient and flexible.

One of the greatest advantages of improved communication using e-mail was that teachers could offer students more scope for participation in developing the course during a term. There are risks in managing assignments and simulations in an open-ended and loosely structured course that evolves in response to the needs perceived by the students and the dynamics of the real world. Presentations by guest speakers or interviews with experts may be postponed or prove to be fruitless; topic ideas may fail to mature or prove to be too complicated as they develop; group dynamics within student teams may require frequent intervention from the teacher; and so on. But the risks can be justified and the problems diminished when timely and efficient communication is available for teachers and students to cooperatively negotiate the course in response to circumstances as they arise. In fact, the very management of the risks and problems becomes a secondary learning path and so a secondary agenda for the course curriculum.

4.4.1. Managing the Risky Course

The use of e-mail makes it possible, as I reported (Hoffman, 1993) in relation to the technical communication skills course described above, to implement an open-ended course design. Such a course aims to activate the students' academic knowledge of the target language by forcing them into situations where they frequently have to communicate in that language with each other and with the teacher if they are to fulfill the course assignments. In teams, the students work on tasks in which there are no guarantees of straightforward success. They research self-chosen topics in their major field, with the requirement that they obtain information from a variety of sources, including fieldwork. If they meet with problems of team management, availability of information, or scheduling of appointments with those who act as information sources, they have to communicate with their teacher and their peers promptly to resolve their difficulties.

Students are given minimal classroom input on the communication events around which the course is organized, including written summaries for later presentation of technical proposals to clients, briefing meetings through which each team shares its findings with a partner team, simulated investigative interviews on information systems, and presentation of proposals. This motivates them to design their own strategies for dealing with these tasks and demands that they query the teacher on their developing plans of action. Also, each team has to coordinate meetings with its partner team. The course goes on with ever increasing mutual involvement that would be difficult—logistically, at least— without the resource of electronic mail.

The teacher and the students in this case communicate with each other on matters of logistics, strategy, and team management (Hoffman, 1993). Each semester, unique issues impact the course, as students choose topics on the cutting edge of their major field of study as the focus for their work. The computer network enables these classes to cope with unpredicted problems. Thus, the content and activities of the course can be adapted to respond to new issues, and changes can be communicated to the students in broadcast e-mail messages. The teacher can respond promptly to student questions and concerns, motivating students to take risks in the second language, by using their emerging communication styles and strategies.

4.4.2. E-mail Feedback

E-mail can also be used to augment a teacher's feedback repertoire. As illustrated by my application of e-mail in writing instruction (Hoffman, 1993), the teacher can receive and comment on assigned short writings, such as summaries, and on drafts of portions of longer works over an e-mail network. Using this capability, the teacher is also able to respond to ad hoc requests from students for comments on work in progress.

When student submissions are quoted electronically into e-mail replies, the teacher has virtually unlimited space in which to give feedback. The restrictions of narrow margins, lack of space between the lines of a student's writing, or the amount of blank space at the end of the paper do not exist. Nor are the students handicapped by having to read deteriorating handwriting as their teachers work through long sessions of giving feedback.

Giving e-mail feedback makes it possible for a teacher to develop ideas, ask more and better questions, give examples, and offer more positive remarks in the same amount of time formerly reserved for handwritten marking. As described elsewhere (Hoffman, 1993), in the case of ad hoc requests for commentary, students receive answers to their queries often immediately and usually within an hour or two of the time they post their messages. Assignments submitted in batches are returned to students one by one, as soon as they are read. Students feel free to extract and query or seek elaboration of the teacher's comments on their assignments by return mail. This use of the network disregards traditional restrictions such as scheduled course days and hours and the physical availability of the teacher.

4.4.3. The "Warm" Network

In another context (Hoffman 1994), I have reported the unexpected "warmth" to be found in the putatively "cold" computer network environment. Students in that research noted that they often communicate with the teacher in a light-hearted or humorous way, that they sometimes forget they are "talking" with a language teacher when they use e-mail. They see the teacher's use of the network connection as evidence of a concern for their individual needs and a willingness to become personally involved with them. Students find that the "faceless" medium of network communication makes it emotionally easier for them to ask questions, e.g., to query their teacher's comments and to ask for reactions to their work in progress. A number of students have reported that their teachers' helpful attitude in e-mail communication made them more inclined to interact comfortably on a face-to-face basis.

Communicating by e-mail over an institutional WAN provides an additional communication channel which prompts students to use the target language more, use it more communicatively, and helps them establish ownership of the language they are learning. Similar results can be found in other aspects of computer networking in support of language learning, such as those described above.

4.5. BIG WANs: NATIONAL AND INTERNATIONAL NETWORKS AND LANGUAGE LEARNING

Possibly the most compelling appeal of computer networks is their ability to link language learners with native and other non-native language users. This dimension of networking can offer learners the exposure to authentic communicative language use that is so often missing in the micro-world of the classroom. Students learning a language can experience the satisfaction as well as the frustration of communicating with people for whom the target language is their mother tongue and other people who, while not speaking the language as natives, use it as a "bridge language" to facilitate intercultural communication. While network communication cannot replace the marvelous experience of actually immersing oneself in a language by living in a place where it is spoken, it offers an economical and convenient alternative to travel. Large WANs can connect language learners and teachers in geographically distant places throughout the world and unite them in authentic communication or in tasks that simulate a range of complex communication events.

This section will look at four examples of language learning dependent on large WANs connecting regions or nations. The simplest kind of network connection in support of language learning is the use of **pen pals**, an activity that can be utterly unstructured or progressively structured to meet specific objectives. A more defined program for communicative language learning within a set of task-specified activities is exemplified by the **Victoria Project**, initiated between two Canadian universities in 1986. Two international networking projects, **ICONS** and **IDEALS**, facilitate global negotiation simulations in which language learners from many different countries interact in English to achieve consensus on mutually constructed texts of treaties, position papers, and policy documents. QUILL, a large scale computer-assisted literacy project connected teachers spread throughout Alaska and project developers in "the lower 48" states in a cooperative effort, between 1983 and 1987, to implement an innovative approach to reading and writing. In each example mentioned above, computer networks have been instrumental in connecting learners and teachers, often widely separated in terms of geography, and enabling a learning experience that would be difficult or impossible to achieve by other means.

4.5.1   Electronic Pen Pals

Anyone scanning the archives of the Teaching English as a Second Language e-mail discussion list (**TESL-L**) would find many requests for e-mail pen pals from ESL teachers on behalf of their students the world over. A glance through the directory of **soc.culture.penpals**, a popular electronic **newsgroup**, would reveal a large number of requests for networked international pen pals from teachers, students, and a variety of other network users in business, research organizations, and educational institutions. It is evident that teachers and learners alike view computer networks as a good medium for exchanging information and establishing relationships across languages and cultures.

Some teachers are looking to structure formalized assignments in which learners in different places might cooperate on joint tasks. Other teachers simply want to put their learners in touch with native and nonnative speakers from other parts of the world. In published accounts, teachers have been reporting a mixed response to the efficacy of e-mail pen pal relationships as a language learning device. However, the preponderance of reports suggest that these relationships produce positive results, if certain pitfalls can be avoided.

Upitis (1990) draws a distinction between contrived and "real" uses of electronic mail in elementary schools. She contrasts electronic applications that replicate traditional activities with those that are prompted by a real need to communicate which springs from the participants themselves. Describing a project that involved elementary school children at Canadian and American schools in contact with children from as far away as Australia, she contrasts the uninspiring effect of the generation, over e-mail, of round robin stories—a typical classroom exercise which elicited little enthusiasm from the learners—with the marked excitement that arose from the very fact that the students were in contact with other children at a distance. When questioned, the students revealed that they were most interested in communicating with children on the other side of the world; they had questions, curiosity, and a need for information and sharing.

While it is reasonable to believe that language learners around the world will be excited by the opportunity for authentic "conversation" with native speakers or other non-native speakers, sometimes such contacts fail to endure or to produce the outcomes which teachers would like. Merely putting language learners in contact with one another is no guarantee that learning will occur.

Pitfalls can be found in the technology itself. If the systems falter in delivering the prompt communication they promise, correspondents can easily become discouraged. If the systems are difficult to use, the technology will overshadow the communication, sometimes blocking it altogether. In addition to the need for the technology to provide an efficient channel for communication, the learners themselves must be interested to communicate often enough and in sufficient depth to establish a substantial interaction.

Reports garnered from browsing over TESL-L tell of cases in which pen pals failed to respond to the initial introductory messages or, having replied to a message or two, lapse in their correspondence. Reasons for such communication breakdowns can range from conflicts with other activities to frustration with language proficiency, a correspondent's own or that of the distant pen pal. More often, though, pen pals establish satisfying and motivating social relationships, for the duration of the activity at least, and cooperate in shared projects that enrich their linguistic performance and their appreciation of other cultures.

Loosely structured e-mail exchanges can produce a volume of interaction, but the results are often predictable. Upitis (1990) gives examples of the simple exchange of personal information in response to exercises that ask students to tell about where they live, what famous person they would like to invite to their homes, their interests in music, their birthday, their favorite TV show, and so on. The content of these messages lacks depth, and the style is lifeless, as shown in the excerpt that follows:

Dear Pen Pal,

How are you? If you could invite a TV star home for a day who would you invite? What do you like to do in your spare time? I like dominoes and swimming and drawing. My birthday is on June 13 1978. When is your birthday. What are your favorite TV shows? My favorite TV shows are... .

Yours truly,

(Upitis, 1990, p. 236)

As teachers in the project reported by Upitis took less time to work with the students and no longer routinely read the writing that flowed over the network, the students began to share messages that were more authentic. Students' creativity led them to ask humorous questions, e.g., "Do you like chairs?", and to adopt the role of extra-terrestrials (Upitis, 1990, pp. 236-237). However creative these efforts may have been, Upitis suggests the learners are only making the best of contrived assignments.

Upitis contrasts the communication generated from contrived assignments with that which flows naturally when students have a genuine need to communicate, to deal with real issues, or to solve technical problems. In cases where students sent messages internationally to report their success at sending messages via computer or to describe their trials and triumphs with the technology, Upitis finds a freshness and originality which is missing in the stilted language that characterizes more structured pen pal communications (Upitis, 1990), as the following example shows:

Dear Miss Upitis,

We received your letters....and guess what, Miss U? We got stuck in the command center while writing our letter. Soooooo we still have more. Did you get our test message? We hope it was not a mess. I (Sonya) accidentally hit a wrong button and then pushed ENTER! I (Carina) was just wondering when you are coming back for heavens' sakes! We all miss you, Miss U. Excuse the pun....

(Upitis, 1990, p. 239)

A structured but still creative, task-based electronic pen pal project, **Computer Pals Across the World**, has the following language learning aims, among its overall goals:
- to provide students with a real context in which they can improve their written communication skills;
- to provide an opportunity for cultural exchange through reading and writing;
- to motivate the linguistically less interested student... .

(Beazley, 1989, p. 599)

The Computer Pals project connects students from North America, France, England, and Australia, truly encompassing the globe. Pen pals are matched according to age and special interest for regular and somewhat structured relationships—e.g., introductory exchanges, reporting on aspects of regional or national culture, exchanges of poetry, news, dialogues on social issues, and sharing of myths and legends. The sensitive structuring of the sequence of exchanges leads to development of reading and writing skills, as well as raising the cross-cultural awareness of the participants (Beazley, 1989).

While traditional pen pal relationships, using paper and the postal service would support the same kind of activities as appear in the Computer Pals project, Beazley (1989) argues convincingly that the intrinsic motivation of using high technology plays an important role in generating learner interest in the activities. Also, the speed with which messages are exchanged helps keep learners focused on the point of the lessons, and the speed with which messages appear on the screen develops the learners' scanning proficiency. Working in pairs before the screen, students negotiate meaning as they process incoming text and compose their outgoing messages.

These cases and others reported in the literature show that the use of computer networks as channels for "pen pal" language learning activities can increase motivation for learning and increase students' enjoyment of the learning activities. Requisites, however, are smoothly functioning and user-friendly technology, commitment on the part of the learners to involve themselves in the regular exchange of messages, and, above all, a clear sense—on the part of all participants—of the objectives of the experience. Finally, teachers should strive to exploit the unique power of computer-mediated communication and go beyond simply replicating paper-and-pen tasks.

4.5.2. The Victoria Project

Esling (1991c) reports on the Victoria Project, which integrated computer networking into an ESL program that included word processing, other computer-based composition tools, and the exchange of messages and reports through electronic mail. Among the functions that Esling attributes to the use of the computer, two stand out:

> ... it created an enjoyable and novel workshop activity for students, and it supplemented pen-and-paper composition work. The networking yielded an activity that was content-based, student-focused and amenable to evaluation using discourse-analysis procedures.
>
> (Esling, 1991c, p. 125)

The content of the exchanges between the language learners described by Esling centered on their experiences in learning to use computers for text editing, i.e., the messages had "real" purpose in language use beyond that of language learning. This result reflects the value of authentic communication in language teaching and the creative exploitation of computer networks to foster such communication, as discussed above.

The results of the research conducted by Esling demonstrate that partners in exchanges work hard to develop intimacy and affiliation through extensive self-disclosure. This sharing of information about oneself, one's locale, local events, and one's current situation—e.g., other classmates' actions in class—serves to flesh out for participants what they would be aware of immediately in face-to face interactions. Not only do the learners produce a substantial quantity of writing in the target language, but the network medium, in conjunction with a specific task, serves to focus learners on a variety of linguistic functions. For example, an implication of the findings is that networking, as a form of CALL, could be an efficient way of "introducing and eliciting discourse containing a high proportion of nominal reference to persons, institutions, places, times, and events" (Esling, 1991c, p. 127).

In the networking model, the interactions can be authentic, as in the case of the Victoria Project, in which the learners needed to communicate with one another if they were to master the technology they were using. The "information gap" that may promote real communication is widened in network communication by the perceived distance—the physical gap—between the learners and by the lack of visual and aural cues. CALL activities designed to exploit the qualities of computer networks can enable and stimulate learners to practice more realistically—and more intensively—more types of language than they can in the classroom, as discussed in the next section.

4.5.3. ICONS and IDEALS

The International Communication and Negotiation Simulations (**ICONS**) and Promoting an International Dimension in Education via Active Learning and Simulation (Project **IDEALS**) both seek to put language learners from around the world in contact as they labor to reach consensus on documents relating to significant and timely topics, such as world trade, ecology, human rights, drugs, and others.

ICONS was first developed for students of international studies but has also been exploited within a language learning curriculum to give students new kinds of complex and purposeful communication experience (Tammelin, 1991). IDEALS, a simulation that centers on the drafting of a global treaty on the use of the ocean's resources, likewise allows for the internationalizing of the educational curriculum and the concomitant development of thinking skills, literacy, language development, leadership, teamwork, and cultural awareness (Crookall, 1991).

Both of these international negotiation simulations use **Telnet** to enable distant participants to access the specialized **POLNET II** communications software package at the home university of each project (the University of Maryland for ICONS and the University of Alabama at Tuscaloosa for IDEALS). The POLNET II package contains a module for the sending and receiving of asynchronous messages and another that supports real-time synchronous conferencing. Asynchronous communication allows for the careful development of a variety of position papers and other texts where real-time interaction is neither necessary nor desirable. The real-time conferencing mode enables participants to negotiate meaning, strategy, and position as final drafts of documents are compiled.

Simulations of this kind demand commitment on the part of the learners—and their teachers—as all parties build up a sense of community and involvement over the long-term experience. Real-time conferencing can impose an additional burden on participants, as they have to make themselves available in what are often narrow and inconvenient "windows of opportunity", times when interactants in far places are awake and able to access their equipment. Communication through these windows can often find participants awake and at their terminals into the wee hours of the night. The payoff, however, appears to be well worth the commitment and sacrifice: "[S]tudents are reading and writing in English as part of a negotiation process so enthralling that they forget they are using a foreign language" (Drave, 1993, p. 15). Both the ICONS and the IDEALS simulations engage language learners in communications that stimulate their interest in the purpose of the interactions and give them a real reason to use the target language as a currency of exchange among their peers around the world. The sense of reality engendered by these factors is of inestimable value in building positive motivation towards language development in learners who otherwise might feel that use of the target language is restricted to class or some unimaginable future.

Participants in these and other international simulations can observe the effect of their language use in achieving the goals and objectives of the simulation. When inaccurate language or inept expression interferes with progress, the learners can see and feel the impact of the breakdown. Simulations such as ICONS and IDEALS provide a reason for learners to be reflective about their language use and the language use of their peers around the world. Additionally, learners become sensitive to the intercultural mix they experience as they use a single language to interact with people from a variety of national and cultural backgrounds.

Simulations such as these are experiences that are readily available through the computer network and the big WANs, but rarely available to language learners by any other means. Large-scale international simulations build on the principles that have been identified above as critical for language learning to be fostered even in such simple interactions as computer pen pal relationships. These include:

- A successful initial contact;
- The novelty and excitement of quick and efficient global communication;
- The need for a common purpose to facilitate a depth of authentic communication that includes creativity and originality;
- Commitment to the "network community"; and
- Students' guided reflection, aided by the teacher, on their performance as individuals and as members of the group.

4.5.4. QUILL in Alaska: Networking Language Teachers

Language learners are not the only people who can benefit from computer network communications. Language teachers, too, have a strong need for community, especially if they are involved in innovative projects or working in isolation from their peers. Communication over networks can enable teachers to find support for their work by the sharing of experiences, ideas, problems and problem-solving, and even through the catharsis of ordinary conversation. An example of how teachers who worked very remote from one another to implement a complex innovative program of literacy development follows.

QUILL, the early computerized interactive environment for developing literacy mentioned above combined process writing pedagogy with software that enabled the effective realization of that pedagogy. It was used in Canada and the United States in the upper elementary and middle school grades between 1983 and 1987.

Four perspectives informed the design of QUILL in respect to the role computers could play:

> (1) Individualize instruction, provide learning material at a controlled pace, and record student progress.
>
> (2) Make the regularities, the beauties, and the difficulties of language something that students could examine and interact with in new ways.
>
> (3) Aid in reading; allow students to produce and format texts easily; facilitate revision of texts; check for spelling errors; and store in a compact ... form ... information that learners need.

(4) Permit new forms of meaningful communication in a new social realm.

(Bruce and Rubin, 1993, p. 21)

The software made possible text production, storage and retrieval, invention and planning, collaborative drafting and revision, and a degree of messaging between teachers and students and among peers. The program was supported by a rich variety of materials, a workshop for teachers, and learner materials.

One of the underlying principles of QUILL was the sense of community its use instilled in teachers and learners. Central to the effective implementation of QUILL was "the intimate connection between community and communication" (Bruce and Rubin, 1993, p. 146). While the logistics for wide-area networking of students were beyond the resources of the many schools that implemented QUILL, the software did support messaging within individual schools, at least, using the Mailbag feature.

However, teachers also had a great need for contact with one another if they were going to integrate QUILL into their teaching. Nowhere was this need more dramatic, perhaps, than in Alaska, where QUILL was introduced to promote literacy among the geographically diffuse and culturally diverse population of the state. Teachers working in isolation measured in very long distances and exacerbated by extremes of climate and weather needed to stay in touch with others on the project if they were to bring about the innovation made possible with QUILL. In 1983, though, the conditions for development of a teachers' network were daunting in respect to the availability and reliability of telecommunications, the money available to cover long distance phone charges, and the impact of the rugged wilderness environment on equipment. Yet, because of the perceived need to develop a community among QUILL teachers, the Alaskan implementation included a long distance network, despite the problems that it would entail (Bruce and Rubin, 1993).

The network that finally evolved seems remarkably primitive and cumbersome in view of what teachers and learners are enjoying now, but it served to connect the teachers scattered over the state and fostered their sense of community as intended. To enable teachers in the large communities served by the University of Alaska Computer Network (UACN)—which did not charge for network services—and those in small communities not served by the UACN, as well as the QUILL developers—who were outside the state—to network without significant cost, the UACN was joined to The Source, a national consumer data bank and mail system. While The Source charged for subscription and connect time, this was far less expensive than the cost of standard long distance charges. The portaging of messages between the two systems was complex, but in time the QUILL participants responsible for coordinating traffic over the network became adept at keeping the traffic smooth.

The QUILL network carried a variety of messages among the participating teachers and the QUILL developers, including new materials, student projects, newsletters, and personal and professional messages. The network worked in conjunction with postal mail to bring the far-flung teachers into the QUILL community and to support their innovation in using computers. The evolution of the network occurred in four phases:

- Phase One comprised greetings and the resolution of hardware problems;
- Phase Two saw an increase in messages relating to the curriculum;
- Phase Three was characterized by a broadening of the topics of messages;and sharply increased density of message traffic;
- Phase Four focused on future developments.

(Bruce and Rubin, 1993)

Communication among the teachers comprised a rich mix of professional and personal exchanges, enriched with the same paralinguistic features (e.g., emoticons and typographical variation simulating nonverbal communication) common to network communication as noted above. People exchanged views, problems, solutions, and jokes about the weather. They supported one another and helped each other develop the language teaching innovations inherent in QUILL. Bruce and Rubin (1993) report that some of the connections were maintained even after the project ended, which is to say that the community developed an existence apart from the day-to-day implementation of QUILL. Cohesive computer network communication seems to engender a feeling of being part of a community and all of the implications of community participation for language learning.

4.6. THE FUTURE: NET BENEFITS

To adapt an analogy from Wells (1993):

> Mapping the domain of computer-mediated communication in distance education is like trying to count the whales and fish in the oceans. Despite the most careful observation, only a relatively small number of individuals is ever identified. Yet the oceans swell with activity that is sensed yet never completely apprehended by researchers. (p. 79)

Even as these words are written, the reach of the networks extends, the quality of the interfaces improves, and the creative ways language teachers and learners use the networks grow apace.

In the next decade, the quality of network communication will be enhanced by greater standardization and far more user-friendly interfaces. Text is already being enriched with multimedia that enables the convenient transmission of sound, images, and moving images over a network. Network access to databases for research will become more readily available and more easily navigable for students and teachers. Distance learning will reach into more homes through widespread use of modems and more accessible long distance communication.

For language teachers and learners, navigating the web of network communications is not without problems. Major concerns for those who wish to exploit networking are the following:

- The need to provide convenient and cost-effective access for language learners and teachers;
- The need to develop user-friendly technology, in particular, interfaces which allow teaching and learning to dominate within a technology that should be largely transparent to the users;
- The need to continue to evolve a pedagogy that exploits the strength of network communication to enhance language learning, not merely to replicate other media and forms of instruction.

Nonetheless, the obstacles inherent in these needs are being chipped away daily by technological development and the increase in computer literacy among language teachers.[1]

4.7. CONCLUDING REMARKS TO CHAPTER 4

Superficially, it would appear that computer networks are best situated to serve the needs of language learners in a traditional distance education environment. However, the information presented here clearly shows that the distances bridged by computer networks can be geographically far or near; can be a measure of time rather than space; or can encompass a hiatus of culture, based on age, gender, ethnic, political, or status factors. Communication over networks will put language learners in contact with learning resources, increasing opportunities for intercultural collaboration and dramatically improved global communication (Wells, 1993). Networks connect language learners and language teachers and empower them by expanding and deepening their opportunities for communication in a range of contexts which support the learning and use of language, and which make possible the exchange of ideas on a scale far beyond that imaginable in the traditional classroom.

NOTE TO CHAPTER 4

1. A new book by Mark Warschauer explores many of the topics in this chapter in rich detail (Warschauer, 1995).

5. Hypermedia and CALL

David Ashworth

5.1. INTRODUCTION

Hypermedia is a major new resource for education and for communication more generally which also puts users in touch with other resources. This chapter discusses the concepts related to hypermedia and the possible value of hypermedia to CALL. It also offers several programs and ideas for programs that aim to take advantage of the medium, focusing on second and foreign language applications.

5.2. HYPERMEDIA AND CALL

Hypermedia is conceptually very simple but allows for a very high degree of complexity. A computer is used to control and link together various types of media resources: text, graphics, animation, sound and video. Emerging technologies of mass storage and devices for compression and decompression of very large files (in the gigabyte range) are making it possible to include full motion video, including full-length movies, as resources. Its complexity stems from the ability to link the various resources, traverse many different paths among them, and thus assemble "hyperdocuments" (Martin, 1990) that consist of combinations of these resources. Consider a hypermedia-based encyclopedia: one searches for *Mozart*, finds pictures of the composer, descriptions and scores of his major works, and by clicking the mouse on one of the scores, can play the selected work, view an animated display of the score showing what part is being played, and perhaps call up video clips from the movie, "Amadeus".

In a recent example of a hypermedia encyclopedia, Microsoft's *Encarta*, a Windows CD-ROM application, the user can look up *American Indians: Navajo*, hear and see examples of the language, view typical Navajo dwellings, listen to Navajo music, jump to a linguistic description of Amerindian languages and see how Navajo fits into that classification. A Spanish language tutorial using a videodisc as resource includes a dictionary of all the words in the script, which can be "played back" exactly as they appear in the movie, with cultural notes in English that appear in windows when certain frame sequences of the film are played.

The ability to display such a variety of resources, to link them together, and to combine all of these resources with tutorial programs on the computer provide a highly sophisticated, yet potentially easy-to-use and easy-to-author medium for developing educational materials in any subject. The number of presentations on hypermedia and CALL (and on multimedia, with these terms often used synonymously) at recent annual meetings of CALICO overwhelms all other topics. The CALICO '92 Outreach conference (CALICO, 1991), for example, listed 39 hypermedia topics out of a total of 73 (somewhat more than 50%), with titles ranging from "Pedagogical Models for Multimedia Language and Culture Applications" to "Putting the 'Multi' into Multimedia".

Because hypermedia is a new medium, it has suffered from the same problems as all new media in the beginning—unbridled development with little attention to quality of content. The linking of resources in hypermedia provides such a wealth of opportunities for creative expression that this creativity still outruns the concern for sober, well-founded educational applications based on research findings. Software houses advertise hypermedia and multimedia products for language learning that differ little in quality from the first products that appeared on the market when language laboratories first became popular: gadgets and gimmicks to make language learning quick and easy. The strong appeal of the new medium also motivates development of software that differs little from the old drill and practice programs, except that they now add sound and video. However, the recent emergence of a *Journal of Educational Multimedia* and *Hypermedia* and the serious treatment of CALL software in mainstream journals such as the *Modern Language Journal* augur well for the development of high-quality programs based on sound rationales.

5.3. HYPERMEDIA AND OTHER TERMS

> If you can figure out what they mean by multimedia, please send us a note because it's not clear that there is a universal definition. (Schwerin, 1993, p. 15)

Conventional text exists mainly on paper. Some documents, such as a sentence, a paragraph of text, or a novel, are "linear", in the sense that one reads them from beginning to end, while others are usually read in non-linear fashion. In a newspaper, for example, the articles are displayed together on a page, and the reader chooses where to begin. When tracking down information in an encyclopedia, one proceeds from item to item depending on the topics being investigated, in non-linear fashion, e.g., Ronald Reagan -> Reaganomics -> supply-side economics -> Laffer.

Hypertext exists only in electronic form. Since it is read from a monitor rather than from a paper page, the methods of accessing the information are different. Pressing F1 for Help or selecting[1] a topic from a menu screen represent primitive examples of linking to information related to the program or text one is viewing on a computer screen. In hypertext, one can link one piece of text to any other piece of text and display the latter as a separate page (screen), or as a pop-up window. Basic hypertext-producing systems include *Black Magic, Hyperwriter,* and *Hyperties* for DOS, *KnowledgePro* for Windows, and *Guide* for both Windows and Macintosh. In a foreign language tutorial, for example, a glossary or translation of a non-English text can be displayed in a window that is called up by clicking on the word in question. Hypertext can also include graphics. One could, for example, select the phrase suspension bridge in a piece of text and display a picture of the bridge in a window or on a separate page (screen). In a "haunted house" game, one could select a door in the picture of a house to bring one inside, show a goblin, a warning sign, etc.

Hypertext may also allow for display of animation. Clicking on a door in the above example could result in the door opening and the goblin coming out. However, the computer allows us to go much further than merely linking texts to each other and to graphics. We can consider the types of items that can be linked to each other as "resources", which currently include text, graphics, digitized sound, video (e.g., from a videodisc), and video clips (e.g., Apple's *QuickTime* for the Macintosh and for Windows, and Microsoft's *Video for Windows*). Since any resource can be linked to one or more of the same or other resources, one has, in effect, the equivalent of an "audiovisual library in a box", a library that allows much richer displays of information than would be possible without the computer.

The term **hypermedia** is thus usually used to refer to electronic documents that can access and link together a rich collection of resources in various media, while **hypertext** may refer to the simpler linking of text to text and/or to graphics. In current jargon, **(interactive) multimedia** is used synonymously with "hypermedia", although "multimedia" is also used to refer to presentations of information such as a combination of slide projection, movies, and sound that might not be controlled by computer—for example, an on-location "packaged" real estate presentation to attract investors in a new resort complex. For the purposes of this chapter, "multimedia" refers to combinations of sound, video, and other resources, "hypertext" to the linking of text to text, and "hypermedia" to the linking of all media. The term "multimedia" as used here does not include the assumption of linking.[2]

The simplest use of hypermedia is for **annotation**, i.e., footnoting or expanding on a piece of information, such as calling up a footnote (text annotation) in a separate window or screen, or an annotation in the form of digitized sound, a movie clip, or playing a movie from a videodisc player. Annotation is a fairly linear mode of interacting with the medium—in which the user goes through a text and calls up annotations (text, sound, video) as desired, where they are marked as such on the screen.

The *Voyager Expanded Book,* a Macintosh hypermedia format developed by the Voyager Company is a good example of an authoring tool that primarily uses annotation. It is designed for "reading" materials on a laptop, such as the PowerBook. The authoring system, called the

Expanded Book Toolkit, allows for easy creation of hypermedia materials. Since it is based on *HyperCard*, it can be extended through programming in *HyperTalk*.

5.4. INTERACTIVITY

> Optimizing frequency and range and significance in human choice-making will remain inadequate as long as we conceive of the human as sitting on the other side of some barrier, poking at the representation with a joystick or virtual hand. (Laurel, 1991, p. 21)

Interactivity is a key term in hypermedia, especially as it relates to CAI applications. It is extensively used but rarely well-defined. In general, it refers to the degree to which a user of a program is involved in, or has control over, that program. In *Computers as Theater* Laurel (1991, pp. 20-21) struggles to define it in terms of (a) **frequency** ("how often can you interact?"), (b) **range** ("how many choices are available?"), (c) **significance** ("how much the choices really affected matters") and (d) **participatoriness** ("the feeling or not that one is participating in the ongoing action of the representation"). In a CALL application, one could use these definitions to assess the degree of interactivity.

If the user merely clicks a button to go to the next screen, interactivity is minimal—about as interactive as reading a book. If the user has many choices with various possible effects of those choices, there is a high degree of interactivity. The most interactive program would be "first person virtual reality," i.e., a three-dimensional virtual world which changes as one moves one's head around, reaches out and "touches" virtual objects or interacts with them in some way. In such a case, one does not feel that the computer is separate from the person, but that it provides a separate world for exploration.

Hypertext and hypermedia allow for efficient access to multiple views of a topic or problem. It is "efficient" because one does not have to traipse to the library for references or dictionaries, or to a media center to view a videotape or videodisc. The author of a hypertext can treat aspects of an issue in separate files and call these up in windows as necessary. A simple mouseclick can call up the text or video of the reference and place it on the display screen.

5.5. THE STRUCTURE OF HYPERMEDIA

As suggested by the above definitions, a hypermedia document consists of a collection of **nodes** that are linked together in various ways. The structure can range from strictly linear (one proceeds through the document along a single path from node to node) to highly non-linear, in which some nodes are connected to many others, while others may be linked linearly. For example, using *HyperCard* or other hypermedia authoring tools, one could completely "scramble" the movie on a videodisc by writing instructions to display frame sequences in any arbitrary way; to link and display the frames that deal with a particular topic, regardless of their sequence in the movie; to display all and only scenes with velociraptors in "Jurassic Park", etc. The nodes may contain any type of resource: text, graphics, audio, video.[3] This freedom of connectivity poses a danger in designing an application, however, since one does not want the user to become hopelessly lost in working through it.[4]

5.6. USES OF HYPERMEDIA IN CALL

It is convenient to distinguish three basic uses of hypermedia in CALL: reference, instruction, and research, although as will be seen below, the flexibility of hypermedia makes it possible to combine these functions.

5.6.1. Reference

Hypertext has revolutionized the dictionary and the encyclopedia. The electronic version of the *Oxford Dictionary of the English Language* (or of any dictionary, for that matter), enables the user to locate and view every word in the dictionary in all of its occurrences, whether as the main entry, as a synonym, or in example sentences. In language learning, this is especially important, since the language learner using a monolingual foreign language dictionary, for example, may need to "look up the definitions in order to understand them". New encyclopedias, such as Microsoft's *Encarta* on CD-ROM, contain hundreds of sound bytes, movie clips, and other resources, plus the ability to roam through the encyclopedia in any manner. One can imagine a dictionary for ESL in which words are pronounced with a dramatic reading, e.g., "REALLY?" as an expression of surprise, or "Waiter! Check, please", under *check* in the meaning of 'bill'. It is interesting to speculate whether a dictionary containing such affective embellishments could facilitate the learning of pronunciation and listening comprehension. Alternative pronunciations (different sexes, dialects, registers) are also possible.

The interactive nature of hyperdocuments suggests that reference materials such as encyclopedias can have learning built into them. Following is an example of an interactive dictionary of notions and functions along the lines of the *Longman Interactive Dictionary* on CD-ROM.

An Example: An Interactive Dictionary of Notions and Functions
There is no necessary clear delineation between reference and instructional tools. Let us consider an instructional, interactive dictionary of notions and functions in ESL. It allows the user to find any word or notional-functional category, with definition and examples, and also to interact with words/categories to see animated and audio representations of them. The structure of such a dictionary includes the following:

> (1) **Conventional text and graphics.** Conventional "linear" text and graphics are used whenever deemed the most appropriate for explanation. However, some

concept exploration and testing can also be incorporated here (see below).

(2) **Animated or video illustrations.** These resemble definitions found in existing multimedia encyclopedias (employed to the extent that such resources are useful for defining notions and functions).

(3) **Phonological variation.** Phonological applications include digitized sound examples of the pronunciation of words in context, especially words that tend to be abbreviated or assimilated in speech. For example, *you* is pronounced [juw], [ji], and the like. Phonological variation is included for those entries where such variation is common, using the voices of several speakers. The screen shows a list of phrases or sentences which contain these examples and which, when selected, will cause their pronunciations to be played.

(4) **Concept exploration.** Concept exploration allows the user to explore concepts by manipulating objects on the screen. Consider, as a simple example, learning how to express notions of spatial relations in English, i.e., terms such as *this side, the other side, the left, the right*. Here is a crude illustration of exploring spatial concepts in English, where the user selects "inside of the box". First he/she sees a screen like this:

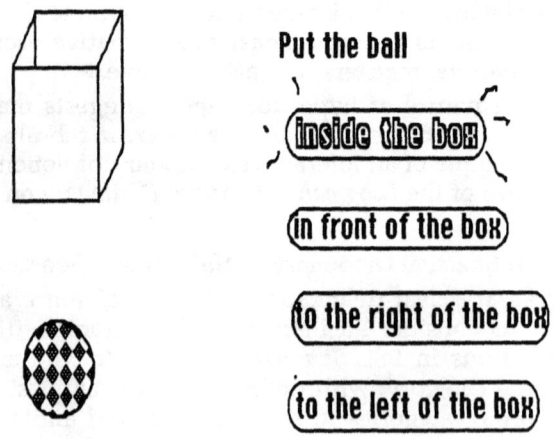

Figure 5.1. Initial Screen in Explore Mode

On selecting the first button, the result is displayed thus:

Figure 5.2. Result of Selection

Clicking on the other commands will result in them being similarly executed. Although a simple graphic was used for illustration here, video clips using *QuickTime* or animation sequences could be used when feasible.

Speech functions can be similarly explored. For example, in a foreign language application, making an invitation in Japanese can be illustrated in concept exploration mode by showing the reactions of an addressee to appropriate and inappropriate forms of invitation. For ESL students, the same principle can be used to compare/contrast forms of invitation in English with those in the native language.

(5) **Concept Testing.** Concept testing allows the user a way of checking his/her understanding of the entry, by way of roleplays or games and by providing evaluative feedback. For example, an entry on invitations could contain a roleplay test in which the user, a student of Japanese, is presented with a video clip of her teacher and his wife. The teacher invites the user to his home for dinner. The screen presents the user with a set of choices for expressing acceptance of the invitation, ranging from very polite to very casual. If he/she selects the correct polite expression, the computer displays a video clip in which the wife smiles and the husband says they will be happy to see her. If he/she selects a too casual expression, the wife will look somewhat miffed, and the husband will act embarrassed when he responds. An opposite scenario, one with a Japanese ESL learner, can be imagined as well, i.e., one in which an overly formal response elicits a blank look or perhaps a giggle from a native English speaker.

The incorporation of such a variety of activities and of access to information was unthinkable without the computer.

5.6.2. Instruction

As the above example illustrates, with regard to CALL applications, it is perhaps convenient to incorporate learning/instructional components in reference hyperdocuments, e.g., by including both interactive exploration of concepts and concept testing. I present here several existing and proposed means of instruction in a second or foreign language using hypermedia. The potential to link resources is so compelling that as I write, I realize that for any language application, a reference tool such as the dictionary described above could easily be linked to any reading or comprehension exercise.

Reading

Hypermedia has the obvious advantage that its linkages can be used to support reading in a foreign language. Words or larger pieces of text can be glossed in pop-up windows, the text can be pronounced in digitized voice; and meaning can be illustrated with pop-up graphics, animated sequences, and video clips. Different "views" of a text can be provided: outlines that unfold into full text by clicking the mouse on the headings, opposite points of view on a controversial subject displayed next to the main text, contents displayed in tabular or list form, and so on. Many of the CALL hypermedia reading programs offer these kinds of features. *Chinews*, a hypermedia program for the Sun computer used for listening and reading comprehension of Chinese news, and the newspaper component of *Kanji City* for Japanese utilize hypermedia in this way.

Chinews provides extensive support to the student for listening and reading comprehension. It allows the student to select news items by topic, listen to recorded broadcasts of the topic, vary the speed of playback, view the transcript, consult vocabulary in context, and hear and view all instances of a word in a particular text or all texts. It has also been expanded to include television news broadcasts with hypermedia support for the student.

Kanji City, a hypermedia program for studying Japanese at various levels, uses outlining as a means of supporting reading comprehension. In the illustrations below, the contents of a newspaper article are displayed first by expansion in non-linear form, and finally, an original sentence, paragraph, or entire article is displayed in a window. The non-linear form allows the student to seek answers to the questions appearing on the screen in any sequence.

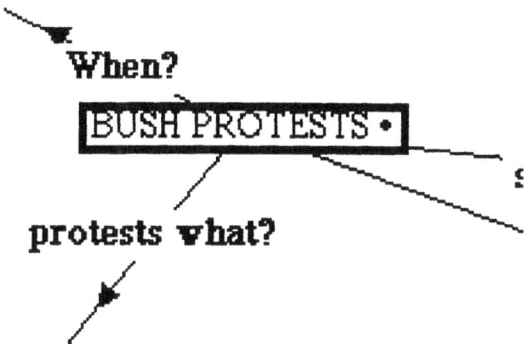

Figure 5.3. Newspaper headline, before expansion of information.

The student can expand on either or both questions by clicking on the arrows.

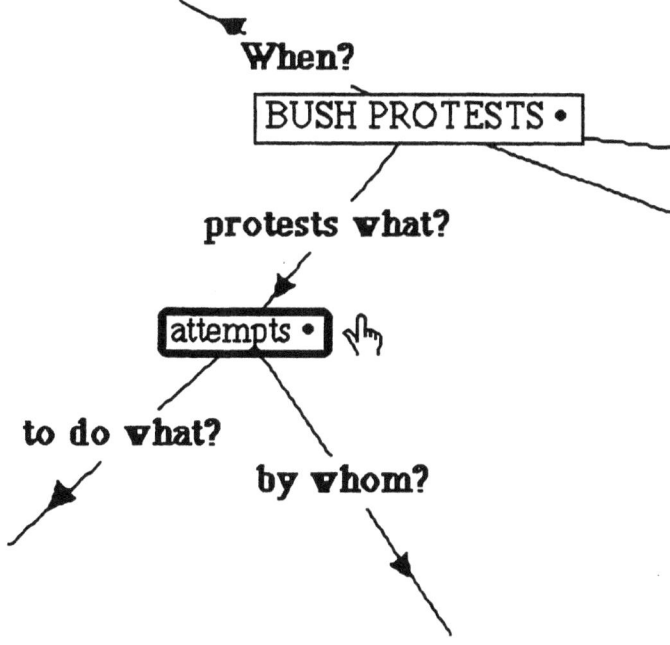

Figure 5.4. After first expansion

The outliner program for creating this type of software allows a hypermedia author to produce both linear and non-linear outlines and expansions for various purposes. Expansions include both text and other media such as video clips, animations, or sound.

Pronunciation
Hypermedia may also be used in pronunciation training. In many programs (e.g., *MacEnglish*), students can record their own voice and compare it with the sample on disk, or compare the waveforms of their own speech with that of the sample (see Pennington and Esling, this volume). In such applications, the students themselves remain the judges of their own behavior: the computer does not provide feedback. For the productive skills, i.e., speaking and writing, in which the computer has to judge the well-formedness of the student's input, it is necessary to rely on artificial intelligence (natural language processing and speech recognition), which still has many weaknesses. Recent advances in speech recognition may overcome these weaknesses. The new Macintosh Centris 660 and Quadra AV series allow for extensive use of spoken commands in place of the mouse and menus.[5] Such a development has obvious application to pronunciation training: one can create interactive CALL ESL programs based on the pronunciation problems of, say, Japanese learners of English, in which the learner must pronounce a command properly to get the computer to perform the desired action.

Thus, hypermedia circumvent some of the problems of other approaches to CALL, and in that sense may make more appropriate use of the medium (Pennington, 1991d).

Writing
Hypermedia can be employed to facilitate the writing of text by presenting the content of a report or article first in a form that is relatively easy to understand, e.g., an interactive paraphrase in simple sentences based upon which students write their own versions of the content. The program illustrated here is based on the notion that, at least for newspaper reports, any given report can be considered as potentially representing one of any number of paraphrases of the content of that report. The paraphrase given in the hypertext format is simple and atomistic, i.e., it represents the information as individual propositions. The students absorb the content of the simplified text and then proceed to write their own version of it. Certain constraints may be incorporated into the instructions for writing, e.g., "avoid the copula (for writing in e-prime[6])", "use (a particular grammatical pattern)", and the like.

In this program, the user opens a page that is blank, except for the headline at the top. The headline acts like a button that expands the content of the report in an outline fashion. The parts of the outline in shadowed rectangles themselves serve as buttons for further expansion. The original text is as follows:

Rioting against Saddam Hussein is increasing despite a ruthless crackdown by his loyal Republican Guard in which thousands have been killed, opposition sources said travelers from Iraq reported Saturday ...

The text is non-linear in the sense that any outline part appearing on the screen can be expanded, as shown in Figure 5.5.

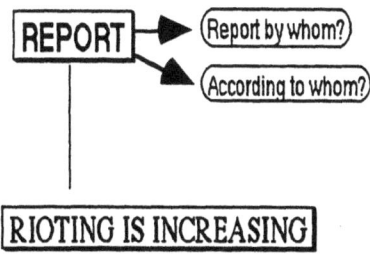

Figure 5.5. Beginning of interactive paraphrase

By clicking on one or more of the pieces of text on the screen, the display in Figure 5.6. is presented:

Although the program shown here is basically hypertext, it could be extended to hypermedia by inserting video clips or sound bytes of the news reported in it. If a sufficient number of multimedia resources are available, students can produce a simulated video news program of their own (see, for example, Campbell and Hanlon, 1988). Once students study the contents of the report, they write their own full-text versions (paraphrases) and compare and evaluate them. If the original article is available, it is compared with the students' versions for comment. In a journalism or language class it would be interesting to conceal the origins of the versions and try to guess which is the original.

This kind of program may also be useful for reading comprehension. It was developed originally as a tutorial for learning to read Japanese and Korean newspapers in the applications *Kanji City* and *Hangula Express*. The students become familiar with the content of the articles via hypertext and then in a conventional class study the originals, analyzing the grammar and the relationships of content to style, grammatical structure, and lexicon. In the application described by Campbell and Hanlon (1988), students study multimedia resources on the Great Depression, including newspaper texts and other documents,

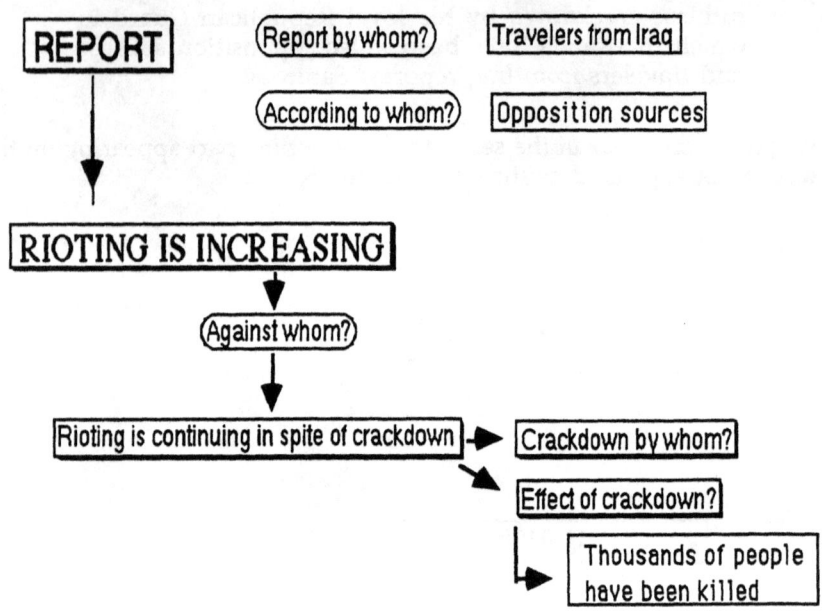

Figure 5.6. Expansion of paraphrase

video clips of newsreels, and sound clips of radio news and speeches, and then create their own hypermedia documents which are shared and reviewed electronically.

Conventional CALL programs are text-based and may include graphics. However, the development of computer networks is accompanied by the increasing incorporation of sound and video in messages sent over a network, and many word processing programs now include facilities for attaching both voice messages and video clips. It is possible that in the future, documents will be distributed primarily in electronic form and that both "writing" and "reading" a document will involve graphics and sound as well.

5.6.3. Hypermedia and Research

The above sections describe how hypermedia may be used in language instruction. However, many of the available programs have neither been tested nor even presented explicitly in the form of testable hypotheses about what can be taught and learned by using them. They are simply presented as new ways to learn language, on the assumption that the medium and the methods involved will work.

Computer logging, i.e., recording the actions which a user performs when using a computer, makes it possible to study exactly what the user has done, for example, in writing a composition electronically. Until recently, the usual actions performed and then analyzed in computer logging were the steps involved in typing text into the computer and the various actions associated with editing the text. A recent study (Hulstijn, 1993) goes a step beyond this form of analysis by logging the interaction of subjects with on-screen reading exercises that contain links between the words in the text and a pop-up glossary window. The goals of Hulstijn's (1993) study were:

> (1) to assess the influence of some task variables on [foreign language] readers' look-up behavior ... and (2) to determine the relationship between word look-up behavior on the one hand and two learner variables: readers' vocabulary knowledge and their ability to infer the meaning of unfamiliar words from information contained in the context. (p. 140)

Since hypermedia involves a larger number of types of interaction between user and computer, and a richer variety of tasks that can be performed in comparison with the more conventional programs, it is desirable to be able to both log and play back the actions. One such program for analysis and playback developed at the University of Hawaii is *The Observer*. This program records all keyboard activity of the user, including mouseclicks and cursor movements, as well as keyboard activity in the form of both a log (text) and a script which allows the investigator to play back and view all actions of the user. It was first used in conjunction with listening comprehension exercises in Japanese called "Eavesdropping" (Jorden and Noda, 1986), in which subjects listen to conversations spoken at normal speed and transcribe them.

In designing the study by *The Observer* of the actions of a user in transcribing natural conversation, the conversations were recorded using *QuickTime*, so that the user can control the play and replay of any segment of the sound file. The spoken language is represented at the top of the screen in the form of an oscillogram, along which a cursor travels across a marked slide rule. The subject can control movement of the cursor with start and stop buttons and select any section of the oscillogram for replay. He/she types the transcription in a window (field) below the oscillogram display. *The Observer* logs all actions, including control of the cursor and the typing and editing of transcription, and creates a script that enables the investigator to play back and observe all actions of the subject. In this way, the investigator can view a subject's actions, identify what problems the subject had in listening comprehension, and what strategies the user used in attempting to transcribe the conversation.

Although *The Observer* has so far only been studied from a feasibility point of view (i.e., "Can such a program be developed and used?"), it shows promise for conducting various types of studies. In listening comprehension, for example, the behavior of both native and non-native speaker subjects doing tasks involving digitized voice files of various native speakers should help to pinpoint the phonological behavior of both populations of subjects. Studies for listening comprehension can be conducted similar to those done by Hulstijn (1993) for reading comprehension. As another application, in studying the composing process, subjects can be given an assignment on a particular theme, which they type on the computer in a field (such as in *ToolBook* or *HyperCard*), and have access to on-line dictionaries and thesauruses and other reference works to help them in writing. *The Observer* can unobtrusively observe and record all interactions with the computer for later playback and analysis.

5.7. THE FUTURE

5.7.1. Hypermedia and Communications Technology

Hypermedia refers to a medium, not a method of teaching or learning, though some seem to treat it as a method—as if CALL had simply extended itself to a new way of drilling and exercising. One of the difficulties in discussing hypermedia and CALL applications lies in the emergent nature of hypermedia as an electronic medium for communication. It is just as prone to MacLuhan's "rear-view mirror" phenomenon as the cinema was when it first began to portray drama in the medium of the film, i.e., putting a camera in front of the stage. In the case of CALL, one tends to think of (and to develop) programs that incorporate sound and video into existing applications: a "flash card" program that includes digitized voice, a multiple choice quiz that is based on video clips, a calligraphy tutor that includes animated brush writing. All of these, to be sure, can fall within the definition of hypermedia, but represent mainly enhancements of the earlier medium of text.

The immediate pedagogical impact of hypermedia stems from the ability to link multimedia resources and to control access to them for pedagogical purposes through programming or, in a more limited way, through authoring systems. Generally, educators think of hypermedia CALL as existing on a single computer or, at most, on a file server for access by a group of students. Language is conveniently divided into four skills on the assumption that they are largely separate from each other. Hypermedia, however, has a much broader significance, linked to the trend towards computer networking that includes multimedia resources. Microsoft Word for the Macintosh, for example, allows a writer to include voice annotations and *QuickTime* video clips as part of a document that is shared over a network. While it is premature to predict that in the future most documents will be produced, distributed, and "read" on a computer, the development of hypermedia and the parallel development of sophisticated networking suggests that in the field of languages at least, whether language learning or language services such as translation and interpretation, the electronic document—sometimes referred to as a **hyperdocument**—may become a widespread phenomenon.

With electronic networking, all four skills may come into play at once. More and more, "reading a document" involves viewing and listening to it as well (as also noted by Cobb and Stevens, this volume). For example, in collaborative work over a network, participants communicate by video conferencing, by displaying text and graphics, as well as video and sound clips, so that all skills are used integratively in ways not foreseen a decade ago. For translation and interpretation services, the distinction between translation and interpretation is blurred as the "language worker" deals with all of these forms of language.

5.7.2. Cyberspace and Virtual Reality

Cyberspace is another term that, because of its currency, has become quite ambiguous. I will use the term to refer to electronic as contrasted to physical space. In this definition, one occupies cyberspace when talking to another on the phone. A conference phone call is a virtual conference occupying cyberspace. Corresponding by e-mail or engaging in computer video conferencing over the Internet is likewise a form of cyberspace communication. One enters cyberspace when donning a virtual reality helmet and gloves, and interacts with the objects therein. Electronic environments such as Compuserve and Internet are becoming increasingly familiar (see Hoffman, this volume). Virtual reality, which until recently has been prohibitively expensive to develop, and has been confined to military and astronautical training, is beginning to see development in commercial fields. It is reported that the number of Internet nodes has been increasing geometrically over the past three years and within a decade, if the increase continues at the same pace, their number will exceed the human population.

While virtual reality will continue to be limited for quite some time because of development costs, one type of interactive program of considerable interest for language learning is *Habitat*, a cyberspace "community" originally developed by Lucas Film and then purchased by Fujitsu, Ltd. of Japan. It is now available over Niftyserve, the Japanese counterpart of Compuserve. *Habitat* is an on-line, real-time interactive community. One purchases software and CD-ROM disk (Fujitsu or NEC versions) and subscribes to Habitat on Niftyserve. One can access Niftyserve from the U.S. via Compuserve, but the user must have a Japanese computer (Fujitsu FM-TOWNS or NEC computer) and software to enter the program. All menus, system messages, etc., are in Japanese. It is possible to communicate with others in English, however, via e-mail and in any text field.

Upon entering the city of Habitat, subscribers choose a new identity, in the form of a two-dimensional cartoon character, and interact with others on screen by typing in greetings or whatever one wishes to say. The words appear in speech balloons above the characters' heads. Objects can be moved about by typing in commands (in Japanese), members can go to "meeting rooms" to hold meetings, and the like.

Habitat presents an interesting possible environment for language learning and for research. Since members "speak" to each other by writing, they have more planning time for producing language, and since someone could be identified as a language helper—for example, as an English-Japanese bilingual tutor—this tutor could (1) facilitate interactions and (2) download all interactions for analysis. Since the interaction is in real time rather than asynchronous as in e-mail, the pragmatics should be closer to spoken than written communication. Of course, the structure of this kind of discourse will evolve in its own way and may also differ from both conventional spoken and written discourse (see Hoffman, this volume, for discussion).

5.8. CONCLUDING REMARKS TO CHAPTER 5

Hypermedia represents both a new medium for developing instructional programs, providing immediate access to multimedia resources, and a new communications medium in its own right. People will communicate in real time over a network, supporting their arguments and illustrating their points with video clips, sound quotes, background music, and the like. As sufficient bandwidth[7] becomes available at reasonable cost, the communications network can become vastly enriched, enabling people with computers and video cameras to hold a video conference from any two or more points on earth, conduct teleclasses, exchange digitized movies, and the like.

Hypermedia CALL applications thus constitute a realistic part of the future of communications, and will have to be designed to meet the needs of people communicating through this medium. As large bandwidth networks grow, e.g., by the spread of fiber optic cable, it is not beyond the realm of possibility that certain nodes on the Internet will become media servers. For example, a program on public radio concerning *Hybrid*, a multimedia network on the West Coast of the U.S., demonstrated access to a music server in Michigan. Instructional resources can also be stored on such servers and be made available for various purposes. One could create a hypermedia application by drawing on these resources directly—a CD-ROM or other storage device would be replaced by calls to a server in Schenectady[8] rather than to tracks on a disk. This marriage of hypermedia and electronic networks suggests the unlimited possibilities of CALL as we move into the twenty-first century.

NOTES TO CHAPTER 5

1. "Select" refers to placing the cursor at a sensitive location on the screen by keyboard or mouse. It may also involve pressing the return key or clicking the mouse button.

2. Some authors, however, fail to distinguish between the terms "hypertext", "hypermedia", and "multimedia".

3. A new type of software, *CUSeeMe*, allows for video conferencing over the Internet (Utsumi, 1993).

4. Presumably, when someone authors a hypermedia document, the intention is to give the user choices in navigating through it. At the same time, the author faces a natural dilemma in wanting the user to access and appreciate all of the program. For this purpose, the author might create interactive "hyperstories", with various outcomes, depending on the paths followed, using such tools as *HyperCard* or *StorySpace*. While this way of proceeding has the benefit of providing a guaranteed form of full access to the options contained in the software, it may inhibit some users from further exploration on their own.

5. The speech recognition software is based on a very large sample of spoken English, obviating the need to train the program before using it.

6. E-prime is a "dialect" of English created by the S.I. Hayakawa semanticists in which use of the copula in any of its forms is prohibited for any purpose. It is used by some psychotherapists for assertiveness training and can also have some value in teaching writing.

7. I.e., as the means for very rapid transmission of large quantities of information, in the range of gigabytes per second, becomes available.

8. This kind of utilization of remote servers on the Internet is already happening. NTT in Japan, for example, has basic lessons in Japanese, including sound, that are available over the Internet through the World Wide Web, using a graphical browser such as *Mosaic*. It is accessible at the following address:

http://www.ntt.jp/japan/japanese/essential.html

Similarly, one can "go to Uganda" (to a server there) to listen to Ugandan folk music and read text about it.

6. Concordancing In Language Learning

John Flowerdew

6.1. INTRODUCTION

Concordancing is a means of accessing a corpus of text to show how any given word or phrase in the text is used in the immediate contexts in which it appears. By grouping the uses of a particular word or phrase on the computer screen or in printed form, the concordancer shows the patterns in which the given word or phrase is typically used. Figure 6.1 shows a concordance for the word *down* from a short text of radio interview data (source Longman *Mini Concordancer* Text Files).

```
, what, two or three days of your week   down here and the rest of the tim
       rest of the time..? Redhead: I come  down fr-...I live in just outsid
 d Macclesfield in Cheshire, and I come    down usually on a Monday eveni
   might sort of whittle the instruments   down a bit umm but basically tha
    der and you just listen and you write  down answers, things like that,
  ng so that we knew there was nobody    down the slope because that was
    top of the mountain and we were going down. He was just int front by abo
       put my skis on, pushed off and I went down and off, you see, and I thou
```

Figure 6.1. Concordance of *down*
(Source: text of 5371 words from the text samples accompanying Longman *Mini Concordancer*)

Concordancing has a variety of applications. One of the earliest of these was in the field of lexicography and dictionary making. This work has resulted in the *Collins Cobuild* dictionary, in which the entries make use of authentic concordanced examples. Concordancing has also been used in the field of stylistics and literary research, as well as in purely linguistic research. Typically, these applications to depend upon large corpora of text, which in many cases run to millions of words. This paper will not concern itself with these areas, but will focus on the application of concordancing in language learning, where smaller corpora can be employed, with particular emphasis on classroom teaching, learning, and curriculum design.

To date much of what has been written about concordancing in language teaching has been programmatic or has described experimental applications which have not been widely replicated. However, there are signs that concordancing has reached the stage where it is about to have a significant impact on the organization and practice of language teaching. This development is likely to come about for three main reasons:

> (1) The experimental studies are building up a literature indicating the ways in which concordancing can be used in teaching and curriculum development;

> (2) The software has become much more "user friendly" and is now capable of handling large amounts of text very quickly and easily, whereas in the past large amounts of data could only be handled by software which was slow and difficult to use;

> (3) The large publishers, such as Oxford University Press, Longman and Cambridge University Press are creating corpora of data which are being made available for use with concordancing software by the general public.

6.2. SOFTWARE AND CORPUS

6.2.1. Software

The best available software for language teaching applications has until recently been the Longman *Mini Concordancer* (Higgins, 1991b). This software has the advantage of being very easy to use—with limited instruction students can very quickly start to use the program themselves—and very quick—the concordances are presented almost instantaneously. However, the one serious drawback of this program is that it can only handle a maximum of about 45,000 words of text. For this reason, the Longman *Mini Concordancer* is likely to be superseded by the Oxford *Micro-Concord*, which can handle much larger amounts of text in a similarly convenient fashion. The reason for the greater amount of text that can be handled by the Oxford program is that the Longman program holds all of the corpus in memory when it runs, while the Oxford program stores in memory only pointers to where data required at any given moment physically resides on disk. Corpus size with the Oxford program is limited only by the size of the hard disk, while for the Longman program, it is limited by the amount of working memory (RAM).

Although the example in Figure 1 shows the concordanced word (referred to also as **key word** or **search word**) in one line of context, many concordancers can also provide a greater amount of context if required. In addition, the concordance lines can be ordered according to different criteria (this is often referred to as **sorting**). In Figure 1, the key words

Concordancing in Language Learning

are sorted in the order in which they occur in the text, but they could alternatively be sorted alphabetically, from the right or from the left, i.e., according to the first letter of the word which follows or precedes the key word. Figure 6.2 shows the same data as Figure 6.1, but sorted from the left and from the right, respectively.

```
d Macclesfield in Cheshire, and I come  down  usually on a Monday eveni
       rest of the time..? Redhead: I come  down  fr-...I live in just outsid
    top of the mountain and we were going  down. He was just in front by abo
      might sort of whittle the instruments  down  a bit umm but basically tha
  ning so that we knew there was nobody    down  the slope because that was
  , what, two or three days of your week    down  here and the rest of the tim
    put my skis on, pushed off and I went   down  and off, you see, and I thou
        der and you just listen and you write  down  answers, things like that,
```

```
      might sort of whittle the instruments  down  a bit umm but basically tha
      put my skis on, pushed off and I went  down  and off, you see,a nd I thou
        der and you just listen and you write  down  answers, things like that, a
       rest of the time..? Redhead: I come   down  fr-...I live in just outsid
    top of the mountain and we were going  down. He was just in front by abo
  , what, two or three days of your week    down  here and the rest of the tim
   ing so that we knew there was nobody   down  the slope because that was
d Macclesfield in Cheshire, and I come    down  usually on a Monday eveni
```

Figure 6.2. Concordance of *down* sorted from left and right, respectively (Source: text of 5371 words from the text samples accompanying Longman *Mini Concordancer*)

The ordering which has been found to be most useful is from the first word to the right of the key word, because it shows up phrases and typical collocations which begin with the key word. Other functions available on most concordancers include a list of all the words in a corpus and their frequencies, ordered either alphabetically or by frequency (useful when deciding what to look for with the concordancer), a "wild card" symbol generated at the keyboard which can stand for any letter or combination of letters (useful in finding both singular and plural forms of the same word, different forms of the same verb, or words from the same family but with different affixes), among many others.

6.2.2. Corpus

Type of Corpus

As mentioned in the introduction, the major publishers are now starting to make available corpora of text for concordancing purposes. Oxford University Press, for example, is making available million word corpora made up of text from the different language media—e.g., books, periodicals, unpublished written discourse, scripted and unscripted spoken discourse—divided according to genre (imaginative, informative) and subject area (pure science, applied science, commerce, arts, leisure, etc.). The availability of different types of corpora allows users to select the particular type of language they wish to base their concordances on. This feature is important because work in linguistics has shown that the use of language varies according to the different type of spoken or written text one focuses on (see, e.g., Biber, 1988).

As well as using published corpora, users may wish to create their own corpora. A purpose-designed corpus will have the benefit of suiting the particular target learning group it is designed for. Purpose-designed corpora are particularly suitable for use in ESP (English for Specific Purposes) situations. Johns (1988), for example, used a corpus of text from the field of plant biology for ESP students from that discipline, and Tribble (1990) created a corpus made up of articles from the journal *Historical Review* for use with a group of his EAP (English for Academic Purposes) students.

Corpus Size
Regarding the question of corpus size, writers are unanimous in arguing that in principle bigger is better (Sinclair, 1991). The more text there is in a corpus, the more likely it is to give an accurate representation of the language and an adequate number of examples of a given key word.

There is a large imbalance of word frequency in text (Sinclair, 1991). Grammatical words (articles, prepositions, auxiliary verbs, etc.) will be the most frequent in any text. Indeed, in any sizable text, it can be predicted that the definite article will be the most frequent word, occurring approximately every 10 words, followed by *of* and *and*, which will both occur approximately half as frequently as the definite article. Content words (nouns, adjectives, adverbs, etc.), in contrast, have a much lower frequency. About half the words in a text will occur only once (these are all content words), and this does not take account of different uses or meanings of the same word.

For concordancing purposes, it follows that where the aim is the study of grammar, a relatively small corpus can be used, as a representative sample of the more frequently occurring grammatical words can be assured. Where the aim is the study of lexis and collocation, however, a larger corpus is required to be sure of a representative set of examples of these less frequently occurring items.

General English vs. ESP Corpora
The preceding statement may be more true for General English applications, however, than for ESP. The frequency of content words, unlike that of grammatical words, depends upon text type and subject matter. A **dedicated corpus**, i.e., made up of specialist texts, can therefore be expected to provide a representative set of concordances for important

content words without having to be so big as an equivalent General English corpus.

This means that if a corpus is designed for General English purposes, it is necessary to make sure that the corpus is made up of a wide variety of texts. If, on the other hand, the corpus is designed for ESP purposes, then it needs to be made up of texts specific to the field. This greater specificity of the ESP corpus means that a smaller corpus is more likely to be adequate for ESP applications. Table 6.1 shows the size of corpora used in various ESP concordancing applications (not all of which were for direct classroom use, it should be noted).

King, 1989	Academic lectures and tutorials	155,000
King, 1989	Scientific and technical journals	114,000
Tribble & Jones, 1990	ELT Text Pack Corpus	45,000
Tribble, 1990a & 1991	English Historical Review Corpus	104,555
Tribble, 1990a & 1991	Longman Corpus of Learners' English	54,861
Mparutsa et al., 1991	Economics Corpus	20,749
Mparutsa et al., 1991	Geology Corpus	33,687
Mparutsa et al., 1991	Philosophy Corpus	6,853
Johns, 1988	Transportation and Highway Engineering	100,000
Johns, 1988	Plant Biology Corpus	100,000
Johns 1991a	New Scientist Corpus	760,000
Johns 1991b	Byte Corpus	1,000,000
Johns, 1991b	Corpus of Academic Papers	250,000
Roussel, 1991	New Scientist Corpus	760,000
Flowerdew, 1993a	Biology Lectures and Readings	104,483
Ma, 1993b	Direct Mail Sales Letters	16,345

Table 6.1. Size Of Small Corpora for Concordancing as Reported in the Literature (adapted from Ma, 1993a)

6.3. APPLICATIONS

Higgins (1991b) points out that classroom concordancing tends to have two characteristic objectives: "using searches for function [grammatical] words as a way of helping learners discover grammatical rules, and searching for pairs of near synonyms in order to give learners some of the evidence needed for distinguishing their use" (p. 92). Let us take one example of each of these applications for illustrative purposes. First, to derive grammatical rules, suppose we are interested in the grammar relating to the word *like*. A concordance will reveal a variety of meanings and patterns attached to this function word. Figure 6.3 shows at least eight different semantic uses and syntactic patterns, based on a very short text for illustrative purposes (a larger text would, of course, provide more examples on which to base generalizations and on which to base teaching and learning activities).

```
          Britain, describes what she doesn't  like about modern T.V. I
       expected. Interviewer: What do you     like about the job? I like
         like about the job? Diane Abbott: I  like the opportunity to put
           usic more and umm they like a they like a good tune, and if
                  principles into practice, I like meeting people, and I'm
              in my case I can sleep as long as I like the rest of the time.
         had an idea of what being an MP was  like. i had been on a local
           of 'clubby' atmosphere, it's a bit  like a gentleman's club, and
       ntails xylophone, marimba which is     like a xylophone except
             call kitchen sink things which is like woodblocks and casta=
           know about Stravinsky or something like that then they're quite
          and you write down answers, things  like that, and umm well I
              nterested me was polite violence, like on The A-Team...Mrs
```

Figure 6.3. Concordance of *like*
(Source: text of 5371 words from the text samples accompanying Longman *Mini concordancer*)

The second example, presented in Table 6.2, shows the use of pairs of near synonyms in a corpus of biology lectures and readings, concordances of which were used for teaching and learning activities in a content-based language program (Flowerdew, 1993a).

The following section of this chapter will now look in more detail at a variety of teaching and learning activities which can be developed around the kind of concordance data exemplified above.

1. occur/happen/take place
2. include/contain/consist of/be composed of/be made up of
3. be situated/be found
4. is shaped like/is ... in shape/has a ... shape/is -al
5. prevent/not allow
6. made of/made from
7. is used for/is used to/the function of ... is to/
8. filled with/full of
9. joined to/connected to/attached to

Table 6.2. Near Synonyms for Concordancing in a Biology Corpus

6.3.1. For the Teacher

As a Linguistic Informant
One important application is to use the concordancer as a resource tool to inform teachers' appreciation of linguistic usage. This use of the concordancer as a linguistic informant has not been emphasized in the literature. Especially where non- native teachers are concerned, but also for native speakers, this use is a significant one. Native speaker intuition (termed **introspective data** in linguistics) and native speaker judgments about the acceptability of grammatical and vocabulary usage (termed **elicitation** in linguistics) are notoriously unreliable (Stubbs, 1983). Non-native speakers are even less able than native speakers to trust their intuitions and are unlikely to have access to native speaker judgments when they want to test their intuitions concerning rules and examples in grammar and vocabulary use. Native speakers who want the added support of an objective linguistic informant to reinforce and corroborate or refute their intuitions and their grammaticality and vocabulary usage judgments, as well as non-natives who lack the confidence to trust their linguistic intuitions can thus turn to a concordancer to provide them with reliable, objective data on grammatical and lexical usage. The relative merits and demerits of the three possible sources of linguistic information, introspection, elicitation, and corpus-derived data, are summarized in Table 6.3.

As can be seen in the table, corpus-based data has many more advantages than the other two types of data. Positive attributes of corpus-based data are: information on frequency, objectivity, large amounts of data, accessibility for non-natives, information on style and register, no risk of hesitation or fatigue, the possibility of diachronic information, and the fact that the data is authentic in the sense that it is not produced artificially. Even where corpus-based-data is given a negative rating, for "simplicity, speed and cost" and for "attitude to usage", these ratings are questionable. For "simplicity, speed and cost" it can be argued that with present-day technological advances, these three factors are all being reduced very rapidly, to the extent that they are becoming less of a consideration. For "attitude to usage", although it is true that with introspective and elicited data the attitude of the informant can be ascertained, corpus- derived data, in not allowing room for personal attitude, ensures objectivity.

Features	I	E	C
1. simplicity, speed, cost	+	-	-
2. attitude to usage	+	+	-
3. frequency information	-	-	+
4. objectivity	-	+	+
5. large data quantities	-	+	+
6. non-native access	-	+	+
7. style and register range	-	-	+
8. risk of hesitation and fatigue	-	-	+
9. diachronic dimension	-	-	+
10 actual, non-artificial production	-	-	+

I = introspection
E = elicitation
C = corpus based

Table 6.3. Merits and Demerits of Sources of Linguistic Information (Svartik, cited in Yang, 1991)

How might teachers go about using a concordancer as a linguistic informant? As a first example, suppose a teacher was planning to teach the use of sentence connectors to students of English for Science and Technology. As a first step, he/she could consult the vocabulary frequency list of a scientific corpus to see which connectors are commonly used in scientific writing and their relative frequency. Next, concordances could be run of the most frequent connectors to find in what way they are used, both semantically and syntactically. The considerable list of concordance lines for each connector would give a good indication of the semantic relations which the connectors express, and a comparison of the concordances of connectors which are close in meaning would allow any semantic distinctions to be teased out. A study of the syntactic patterns of the concordance lines would indicate how many connectors are typically not used in sentence-initial or clause-initial position as might have been thought, but more commonly occur following the subject.

To take another example, suppose this time a teacher wanted to refresh his/her memory on the use of *for* and *since*. Concordances of the two words would quickly reveal that for is typically followed by a period of time (*for three years*, etc.) while *since* is followed by a point in time (*since 1987*, etc.). Such a statement, of course, might be found in a grammar book, but the concordancer will give a much greater range of examples and nuances and will show the preferred collocations these two items enter into. For example, the concordancer is likely to show that *since* is typically followed by a time expression, *since Friday, since 1945*, but also, less frequently, by a noun referring to a person or thing, *since Margaret Thatcher, since the budget*.

As a Source of Input for Teaching

In using the concordancer as a source of input for teaching, as opposed to simply as an informant on usage, teachers can generate authentic instances of usage to present to students when teaching a particular language point. Thus, for example, when teaching the contrasting uses of the present progressive and the present perfect tenses, instead of teachers trusting to their intuitions and making up examples to illustrate contrasting uses, these can be derived from a concordance. Similarly, in presenting new vocabulary, concordances can provide examples of authentic contextualized language.

If the concordancer is kept in the classroom, then the teacher can run a concordance when a problem of usage arises during teaching. For example, if a student is having difficulty with distinctions of meaning involving the modals can and could, then the teacher can call up, or have the student call up, instances of usage of these two modal forms and by means of the examples conduct an analysis of the differences.

As Input for Materials Development

One potential problem with using concordances directly as described above is that not all of the examples might be appropriate for teaching purposes, or some may illustrate a certain usage more clearly than others, or there may be not enough or too many examples based on the text sample used, or the language of the examples may be beyond the proficiency level of the target learners. This is where there is an advantage to be had in preparing concordance-based teaching materials in advance. In this way, for example, inappropriate examples can be deleted, or all of the examples illustrating one particular usage of a word can be grouped together. This sort of editing can easily be done by converting the concordance file into a word processing format.

An extension of this editing facility is the production of exercise material based directly on a concordance. Figure 6.4 is an example of this type of material—an extract from a gap-filling exercise—from the manual for *MicroConcord* (Murison-Bowie, 1993), based on the difference between *interested* and *interesting*:

Focus: The difference between *interested* and *interesting*.

After you have studied Worksheet 7A, complete the following concordance lines with either *interesting* or *interested*:

1. When I heard Celtic were   I decided Scotland would be muc
2. ugh it might make for a more   evening dramatically. <p> most
3. rning up late and being more   in fishing and shooting than
4. she said, was the reason why   parties had come together to
5. moured yesterday to be still   but his family's interest in

Figure 6.4. Extract from Gap Filling Exercise (from Murison-Bowie, 1993, p. 91)

Gap-filling is an obvious type of exercise to base on concordance printouts. Honeyfield (1989) has developed a complete exercise typology based on concordance material, of which gap filling is only one of seven types:

(1) Filling blanks in concordance material;

(2) Completing, or guessing the wider context of, concordance material;

(3) Using concordance materials as a reference tool for various exercises focusing on grammar, usage, vocabulary, etc.;

(4) Discourse-oriented exercises involving the use of concordance material, e.g., the use of discourse markers;

(5) Comparing the meanings or uses of expressions in different types or samples of writing;

(6) Exploring emotional tone or style, e.g., comparing the tone of certain concordanced items between different genres;

(7) Freely using a concordancing program to assist writing, correction, or comprehension.

6.3.2. For the Learner

Error Analysis
A guided use of the concordancer by the learner is in error analysis and correction. In this activity, the teacher indicates errors in student writing which can be investigated and corrected with the help of the concor-

dancer. This is a good activity to begin concordancing with, as it gives learners specific language items to investigate, but at the same time allows them to work out how their use of language differs from that of the concordanced material.

Serendipity Learning

The easiest, most obvious, and most autonomous learner application of concordancing is to allow learners to use the concordancer as and when they wish for whatever purposes they wish. This type of usage has been referred to as "serendipity learning" (Johns, 1988). A typical type of serendipity learning might be as follows. A student decides to look at some examples of the present progressive. He/she accordingly uses the wild card function, followed by *-ing* to find instances of the present participle which the student knows is used in the present progressive. The concordance reveals, however, that the *-ing* form can also be used as a noun modifier and as a non-finite verb, something the student might have been only half aware of. This newly acquired awareness perhaps leads the learner to look up these other uses in a grammar book or to ask the teacher about them.

To take another example of serendipity learning, here a student starts by browsing down the word frequency list which most concordancers provide: this is rather like browsing the pages of a dictionary. The student notices that the word *experience*, which had been learned as a non-count noun (and hence should always be singular), occurs in the plural as well as in the singular form. A concordance run on the plural form of *experience* reveals that this word also has a countable use and that when employed in this way the word has the meaning of something like 'salient events which occur in someone's life'.

Serendipity learning has at least three obvious benefits:

> (1) Learners are truly autonomous and responsible for their own learning;

> (2) Because searches are learner-initiated it can be guaranteed that the learning corresponds to learner needs and/or wants;

> (3) By researching into language use this way learners develop what James and Garrett (1991) refer to as "language awareness".

Inductive learning

One issue in the use of concordance-based materials is that of the application of inductive or deductive reasoning. Concordance material can be used in both ways. If a teacher explains that he/she is teaching the contrast between the present continuous and the present perfect tense, explains the difference in meaning, and presents concordances to illustrate both, this is a deductive approach. If, on the other hand, the learner is told to work out a rule to distinguish between the two tenses, using concordance printouts, then this is a more inductive type of activity. Where learners use the concordancer themselves, as opposed to being exposed to pre-edited printouts, it can be argued that concordancing is inherently inductive. The serendipity activity just described is clearly inductive in that it leaves the learner to ask and answer all the relevant questions about usage, but the error analysis and correction technique just described also, although guided by the teacher, still requires inductive thinking on the part of learners in diagnosing how their usage differs from that of the concordancer.

Johns (1986) has written of the inherently inductive nature of concordance-based learning as follows:

> [A] concordance occupies an intermediate position between the highly organised, graded, and idealised language of the typical coursebook, and the potentially confusing but far richer and more revealing "full flood" of authentic communication. By concentrating and making it easier to compare the contexts within which a particular item occurs, it organises data in a way that encourages and facilitates inference and generalisation. Such generalisations may leap out of the contexts in an obvious fashion (for example, the word before "same" is almost always "the", or may require a good deal more work on the part of the user ... . (p. 159)

For Johns, the sort of inductive learning encouraged by the concordancer is actually a stage beyond what is normally accepted as inductive (Johns, 1991a). Noting that the inductive learning of the "examples first, rules second" type is really a case of "rules hiding" rather than the encouragement of truly inductive thinking—because the teacher knows all along where the learner is being led—Johns proposes a role for the learner in which the teacher does not in fact know where the analysis will lead and in which the linguistic data is primary. In this "data-driven" learning approach, the initial problem, instead of being teacher-initiated, is likely to come from a student query. Johns (1991a) gives two examples of how such student queries have been exploited in his own teaching: the contrast between *persuade* and *convince* (a lexical application) and the uses of *should* (a grammatical application). Johns describes concordance-based worksheets designed to provide sufficient data to allow students to work out their own answers to the questions they pose. In both cases, Johns claims the answers provided by the students were superior to the answer provided by the teacher.

Honeyfield (1989) has proposed a four-step procedure for encouraging students to use concordance material in the sort of inductive way envisioned by Johns (1991a, p. 44)

> 1. The student becomes aware of a need for data, for information about how the language is used. Such awareness may arise from a more communicative task,

such as writing a report, or from a more language-oriented exercise, e.g., a vocabulary or grammar exercise.
2. The student consults relevant concordance material, either through direct access to a computer or by using concordance material supplied by the teacher.
3. The student analyses the data and draws conclusions.
4. The student applies the insights gained to the task in Step 1.

Notable in this procedure is the possibility of students themselves accessing the concordance data from the computer in order to answer specific questions. Here learners become true researchers, initiating the research question and seeking out the answer themselves.

A number of writers have suggested a use such as that just described. Pickard (1993), for example, has described an EAP course entitled "Learning from Expert Writers", in which learners are trained to use the concordancer independently outside the classroom as a tool for enhancing their writing. Similarly, Ma (1993) has described a course in EAP writing where learners are shown how to use a concordancer and then access a corpus made up of computer manuals as an aid in their own writing of a manual.

Both these applications fit in with a suggestion by Levy (1990) for the concordancer to be available on-line with a word processor in the same way that it is now becoming possible to access a spellchecker, dictionary, thesaurus, and grammar checker on-line. Levy proposes that these applications be integrated in such a way that the student might ask a question of the dictionary or thesaurus and then supplement the limited examples provided in these sources with authentic examples from the concordancer.

Levy (1990) proposes that the learner might use the concordancer in the following ways:
- Checking meaning
- Checking general syntax
- Checking usage
- Exploring special lexis, especially ESP vocabulary
- Checking derived forms
- Checking collocates of words
- Exploring set pieces, e.g., phrasal verbs, clichés

Both Ma (1993) and Pickard (1993) stress the need for learner training in both the mechanics of concordancing and the sort of questions that can be asked of the concordancer, if concordancing is to be integrated successfully in applications such as these.

6.3.3. Other Curriculum Applications

In addition to use by classroom teachers and by learners, a number of other concordancing applications related to various aspects of curriculum development have been made. One such application is in syllabus design. In line with ideas set out by Sinclair and Renouf (1988), Willis and Willis (1988) have developed a complete general English syllabus and set of course books based on concordancing. The theoretical basis for a concordance-based syllabus is set out in Willis (1990). The database from which these materials were developed was the one used for the *Cobuild Dictionary* and was thus very large.[1] Flowerdew (1993a, 1993b) has described how a much smaller corpus can be used to assist in developing a syllabus and teaching materials in an ESP setting. The basic idea is that where the target ESP situation is known, a corpus of data made up of language collected from this situation (e.g., lecture transcripts and reading material in Flowerdew's case) will provide the basis for concordancing. A concordance of such material reveals the most frequent lexical items, significant syntactic patterns, and important functional/notional areas which are needed for the target situation and which can be incorporated into the syllabus and teaching materials.

Another area of the curriculum where it has been suggested concordancing can play a role is that of testing. Butler (1991) has promoted the idea of cloze tests based not on complete texts but on single-line concordances. Each question in such a test would consist of a number of concordance lines with the same word deleted. Butler claims that such tests, although not based on complete texts, meet the sort of contextual and discourse criteria for what Oller (1979) calls "pragmatic" tests.

A further application of concordancing is in error analysis or interlanguage studies. Concordances based on corpora of learner data can reveal the typical features of learner language for those of different language backgrounds and at different stages of linguistic development. A project along these lines is currently being developed in Hong Kong, where a corpus of text has been created which is made up of the essay answers to exam questions in the Hong Kong Certificate of Education Use of English examination (Milton, undated). Information culled from such data will be available to inform curriculum design for English teaching.

6.4. SOME CAVEATS

The introduction to this chapter mentioned the fact that much of what has been written about concordancing in language teaching has been programmatic or has described experimental applications which have not been widely replicated. As a result, not much has been written about some of the problems encountered when working with this new and exciting medium. This section, accordingly, will list some of the problems which can arise.

6.4.1. Problems with the Corpus

Two major problems are associated with the choice of corpus. First, there is the problem of size. This question was discussed earlier in the present chapter, but it is important to emphasize the need to guard against using a corpus which is not large enough to provide representative data. Second, there is the question of specificity, also touched upon earlier. If learners are aiming to acquire a certain type of English, then a general corpus will not be appropriate, and a specific corpus of the target variety must be created or sought out. If, on the other hand, the target is General English, there still remains a problem; for there is no clear definition of what constitutes general English: what is general for one person is not general for another. Most "general" corpora are made up of samples from a range everyday genres. In practice, this has meant mostly newspapers, periodicals, novels, and other mainly written media. But the most typical everyday genre is casual conversation, and most available corpora are notable for their lack of spoken data, due to the difficulty of collecting and transcribing it. A lack of spoken data for concordancing is thus a serious drawback for learners wanting to acquire colloquial spoken English.[2]

6.4.2. Usefulness of the Data

A number of problems attach to the use of concordance data. These were mentioned earlier as problems when using a concordancer directly in the classroom, but they are repeated here, as they actually apply to any concordance application. First, if the concordance is to be used for teaching purposes, it is quite possible that many of the concordance lines will contain language which is beyond the proficiency level of the learners (even though the teaching point which the concordance illustrates may be at their level). Of course, the teacher always has the option of editing the concordance on a word processor in order to simplify it, but then the authenticity of the concordance is reduced. Second, if single-line concordances are used, not all concordance lines may provide enough context to make the meaning clear. Third, depending on the size of the corpus and the frequency of the item chosen for concordancing, the concordancer may provide too few or too many examples of the particular usage to be illustrated. Learners will quickly become frustrated if they cannot find enough (or any) examples of items selected for concordancing; they will equally quickly become frustrated, on the other hand, if they are overwhelmed with too many examples. Finally, even where a manageable number of concordance lines are found, if a certain item has a variety of usages, then some usages might be better represented in the concordance than others. None of these problems associated with concordance data is irremediable, but together they pose a significant challenge to the successful application of concordancing in the classroom.

6.4.3. The Need for Learner Training

In a study referred to earlier, that of Ma (1993), possibly the only detailed evaluation conducted to date on concordancing, ethnographic data was collected on a course in which students used concordancing as a tool in academic writing. Observation of students, questionnaires, in-depth interviews, student diaries, and analysis of student writing led to the conclusion that one of the main requirements for successful use of a concordancer was learner training. Learners in this study were severely limited in the use of concordancing as an aid in their writing because they were unable to make use of many of the search techniques which can be performed with a concordancer. If concordancing is to achieve optimal results, adequate time must be devoted to familiarizing learners with the kinds of information they can discover and the different techniques for discovering it by means of a concordancer.

6.5. CONCLUDING REMARKS TO CHAPTER 6

This chapter has considered various aspects of concordancing for classroom language learning. It has considered the question of software and corpus; it has considered a range of applications, both for the teacher and for the learner, and for wider aspects of curriculum development; and it has considered possible problems in using concordancing.

On this last point, under the heading "Caveats", potential problems in applying concordancing were described, in order to redress somewhat the paucity of critical perspectives in a perhaps over enthusiastic concordancing literature. In this "Caveats" section reference was also made to the study by Ma (1993) as one in-depth evaluation of the use of concordancing. Given that concordancing is likely to become more and more widely applied in the future, for the reasons mentioned in the introduction, it is perhaps appropriate to conclude this chapter with a call for more evaluative studies.

As with other new technologies before it, such as the language laboratory and other audiovisual media, there is a danger of the enthusiasm for concordancing being inflated to such an extent that concordancing is seen as a sort of language teaching panacea. Carefully conducted evaluative studies will ensure that such an inflated view will not prevail. Instead of concordancing being promoted as a panacea, considered evaluative studies will allow concordancing to be incorporated appropriately into the teacher's battery of reference and teaching resources as the useful additional teaching and learning tool that it undoubtedly is.

NOTES TO CHAPTER 6

1. This same database is also being used in the development of a series of grammatical reference books (e.g., Cobuild, 1990).

2. Publishers are trying to remedy this problem by creating corpora of naturally occurring spoken data.

7. A Principled Consideration of Computers and Reading in a Second Language

Tom Cobb and Vance Stevens

7.1. INTRODUCTION

It has often been noted that CALL lacks a solid research base (Dunkel, 1987, 1991; Roblyer, 1988). The problem lies mainly in two areas: inadequate reference to theories of language acquisition (Hubbard, 1992, this volume), and inadequate description of what students actually do, if anything, with specific CALL programs (Chapelle, 1990; Chapelle, Jamieson, and Park, this volume). The arguments made in this chapter in favor of using text manipulation activities to develop reading skills in a second language will attempt to address these problem areas. Evidence from research on student use of text manipulation will be presented.

7.2. WHAT IS READING COURSEWARE?

It is not at all clear what language teachers expect reading skills development courseware to do. While making insightful predictions concerning the impact of CD-ROM and laser printers, two devices neither widely used nor understood when his article was written, Wyatt (1989) placed use of computers in reading on a continuum constrained by development of orthographic recognition skills at the low end and mechanical/meaningful tasks such as comprehension exercises at the other. "Revolutionary" applications extended only to annotation (i.e., hypertext), modeling of productive reading strategies, and interactions with branching plot and adventure/simulation programs. While extolling the "raw potential" of the medium, Wyatt (1989) noted that "almost none of the existing courseware for second and foreign language reading skills has moved beyond the stage of directly paralleling the activities found in printed textbooks" (p. 64).

Teachers often assume that reading courseware might do something similar to what they do as a reading class activity. Indeed, much reading courseware does attempt to emulate what might be done in a classroom; hence the "reading comprehension" approach, where a passage is presented on screen followed by questions. In such courseware, computers can make existing techniques more efficient for the learner, in that feedback is immediate and interactive, possibly highlighting areas of the text where attention could be most productively directed. The main drawback regarding the "efficiency" of this approach is the inordinate amount of time needed by developers to prepare each CALL lesson. For example, software which highlights context clues assumes that help has been set up for "*every* relevant word in every reading passage" [italics in original] (Wyatt, 1989, p. 73). Adding to the frustration is the work wasted if content which the software is tied to (e.g., in textbooks) is later deemed inappropriate and replaced in the curriculum. For these reasons, tools for producing this type of courseware are prone to lie fallow on developers' shelves after only one harvest.

More recently, computers have been used in reading in ways which do not emulate traditional methods of teaching and learning reading. Development along these lines has been directed not so much at the creation of new courseware, but at devising ways of making connections between an emerging battery of software tools and the proliferation of machine-readable text. One focus of this chapter, then, is to examine such connections in light of recent thinking on how reading skills are developed in a second or foreign language.

Hypertext is one means of making such connections. In its simplest form, hypertext allows annotations to on-screen text to be displayed on request. In more sophisticated implementations, hyperlinks can be developed to almost anything imaginable: e.g., video or sound segments, pathways into reference databases, annotations made by other readers, etc. These links might give students access to background and reference information, e.g., on-line access to tools such as dictionaries and encyclopedias (see Ashworth, this volume, for examples).

An example of the evolution of such courseware can be seen in the development of *Where in the World is Carmen Santiago?* and its offshoots (*Where in Space..., Where in the USA...*). In these programs, users try to solve a crime by discerning clues that enable them to track down a criminal moving freely throughout the virtual world (or space, or the USA). Solution of the mystery depends on "world knowledge" which, if lacking, may be augmented from a database of information supplied on a disk that contains appealing sound and animated graphics. More recently, CD-ROM versions of the program have come out, greatly increasing the amount of information and imagery that can be made available to crime-stoppers, as well as enhancing the sophistication with which this information can be accessed. In the CD-ROM version, the screen becomes a mouse-driven console providing a video telephone, a computer sub-screen for database access, a notepad, and a video window where pictures are displayed. The program produces a plethora of spoken discourse via the sound card, and whatever is spoken is generally printed out on the computer sub-screen (giving students who read it the benefit of vocalization). Many other CD-ROM-based multimedia packages offer similar rich mixes of reading and sound. *The Animals!*, for example, offers hyper-linked video and still-image tours and explorations of The San Diego Zoo. Authentic, native-level instructional text is spoken to users and also printed on the screen for those who prefer to read it or who may have difficulty in following the spoken discourse (the category into which many second language learners would fall). Similarly, hyperlinked resource packages such as Microsoft's *Encarta* can immerse students into media-enriched target language environments, in which the comprehension of authentic written discourse is both encouraged and facilitated by sound and image.

Thinking along these lines, we might envision students solving similar language-enriched learning tasks by accessing authentic real-world databases over local or global networks, exploring the databases via hyperlinks, and annotating the materials or reading the annotations of others to achieve some result or resolution. The potential of these media in providing both a text-rich substrate for second language learning and the means and motivation for these materials to be used is becoming more apparent to those engaged in teaching and learning languages, as these powerful tools become more readily available and commonplace on networked microcomputers and stand-alone PC's.

When readers have widespread access to such tools, the concept of reading itself may change. Tuman (1992) argues that an "on-line literacy" is emerging which, while empowering some readers by allowing them to interact in compelling ways with text and with each other, will also lead to the demise of the author as the qualified and ever-present guide to a reader's private, sustained, and critical reading experience. Reading could soon be characterized by zapping one's way aimlessly around the "docuverse" of available materials. Thus, as with any application of technology to pedagogy, researchers will need to characterize the nature of the reading that takes place when learners are granted access to corpora and databases[1] and assess what affect this might have on second language reading in particular. Our own experience suggests that there is no guarantee that making large and varied amounts of on-line text available automatically promotes particularly deep processing, even when the task is in a motivating, pleasurable game format and other types of information are on offer. So, before we turn our students loose to cruise the information highway, we need to decide what they can use there and roughly to what effect.

Having speculated about on-line reading in the not-so-distant future, we would like to step back to a point where we are more certain of our position. The remainder of this chapter will suggest how students can be presented with copious amounts of text, along with exercises which we believe train strategies in comprehension of that text for language learners. In developing a theory supporting such implementation, we expand somewhat Wyatt's notion of courseware for reading, taking the concept beyond what is typically done in classes where reading is "taught". In particular, we support the text manipulation concept as a second language reading activity, as it is readily implementable on most present-day computer-based learning configurations, and as it is of particular value to students learning to read in a second or foreign language. Moreover, it can make use of the large amounts of text now becoming available without departing totally from a pedagogy that we at least know a little about.

7.2.1. Access to Text, the Computer-Based Reading Advantage

One of the most significant recent developments which impacts computer-based reading is the proliferation of and improved ease of access to machine-readable text. Text comes in over e-mail, is scanned from printed documents, is downloaded from CD-ROM databases in university libraries, is purchased as huge corpora from commercial suppliers, or is captured in endless streams from close-captioned television broadcasts. Consequently, experienced as well as less-skilled readers can anticipate increasingly wider access to text in a format which can be exploited in computer-based programs of reading instruction.

One of the most interesting aspects of computerized text is that almost all of it is authentic discourse. In light of Higgins' (1991a, p. 5) definition of authentic text as "anything not created by a teacher for the purpose of demonstrating language at work", the question then arises whether second and foreign language learners can cope with real-world written discourse. Happily, indications are that they can.

Bacon and Finnemann (1990) examined perceptions of general language learning (as reflected in attitudes, motivation, and choice of strategy), gender, and willingness to deal with authentic input for first-year Spanish students at two U.S. universities. They wanted to know whether these perceptions could be associated with comprehension, satisfaction, and strategy use in situations of authentic input. The results suggest that students perceive the value of authentic text to their learning and that they are not unduly constrained in processing it.

Similarly, Allen, Bernhardt, Berry, and Demel's (1988) study of 1500 high school foreign language students indicates that subjects were able to cope with all authentic texts they were presented with at three levels of difficulty. In an offshoot of that study, Bernhardt and Berkemeyer (1988) found that secondary level learners of German could cope with authentic texts of all types, and "that target language and level of instruction was a more important correlate of comprehension than was text difficulty" (Bacon and Finnemann, 1990, p. 460). Finally, Kienbaum, Russel, and Welty (1986) found from an attitudes survey that elementary level foreign language learners express a high degree of interest in authentic current events materials. These results all suggest that use of authentic text in second language reading can be motivating and not unduly daunting to second language learners.

The foregoing is of particular interest in light of Kleinmann's (1987) suggestion that reading courseware rarely provides adequate amounts of comprehensible input. Kleinmann found no significant differences in learning when a selection of twenty computer-based reading programs was used to teach reading compared to conventional reading materials, and he reasoned that the drill-and-practice nature of the CALL material prevented greater strides in learning by failing to address higher order reading skills, hence the need for more text. In his words:

If we accept the notion that comprehensible input in the form of text material that is interesting, relevant, and at an appropriate level of complexity is crucial to second language development (Krashen & Terrell) then the nonsignificant findings with respect to the effect of CAI compared to non-CAI in the present study are easily understood. Very little of the available reading skills software meets these criteria of comprehensible input, especially for more advanced learners ... . Moreover, it will be necessary to develop software that stimulates general learning strategies that have been correlated with successful language learning, e.g., guessing, attending to meaning, self-monitoring (Rubin, Stern), as well as more specific strategies relating to particular skill areas. For reading skills development, strategies such as skimming, scanning, and context utilization will be important. (Kleinmann, 1987, p. 272)

So there is a prima facie case for channeling appropriate parts of the text stream through reading courseware designed for language learners. However, if beginning or intermediate learners are to be exposed to large amounts of authentic text, clearly they will need something to do with this text besides attempting to read or use it in their academic courses as if they were native speakers. Intermediate learners may be able to search through various on-line textbases, perhaps seeking answers to questions on a worksheet. However, because scanning for specific information requires only a modest degree of engagement with either high-level themes or low-level details of a text, this is not the type of reading development most beneficial to second language learners.

This chapter argues that TM (text manipulation) templates can engage students at higher cognitive levels while presenting them with virtually limitless amounts of comprehensible input in the form of authentic texts. Although scanning is not a skill that cloze activities encourage (Alderson, 1980; Feldmann and Stemmer, 1987; Nunan, 1985; Windeatt, 1986), work with text manipulation such as on-line cloze exercises may promote awareness of contextual help in restoring degraded messages (Bachman, 1982, 1985; Jonz, 1990) while exposing learners to a considerable amount of comprehensible input, assuming that learners take advantage of the amount of text that can be made available. And it appears from the results of the studies described above that use of authentic, ungraded text, rather than posing insurmountable problems for second language learners, might instead provide opportunities for the exercise of higher order processing skills called for by Wyatt, Kleinmann, and others.

7.2.2. Templates for Text Manipulation: Developer's Convenience or Sound Instructional Design?

It is not hard to see the attractions of linking text manipulation technology to the stream of on-line text becoming available. Copious amounts of machine readable text, on the one hand, coupled with ease of implementation, on the other, makes appealing a template approach, where the courseware incorporates an algorithm which can be applied to any text supplied, realizing quantum savings in implementation time. Indeed, the distinctive feature of TM program design is that the program is able to deal with any text whatever.

TM systems can be quite varied, although they all have in common the algorithmic deconstruction of on-screen text for a learner to put back together. Some common types are the following:

- Cloze and other systematic deletions (suffixes, auxiliaries, transition markers, all function words, etc.);
- Scrambled elements (chunks, sentences, or paragraphs);
- Sentence boundary identification;
- Crosswords;
- Hangman or concentration-type word matching or supplying.

The developer's task is to find machine-readable features of text that correspond to something readers need to pay attention to, as indicated by either observation or theory. For example, if readers are observed to pay little heed to sentence boundaries, then an algorithm can be written to detect the surface features of sentence boundaries and then eliminate them throughout a given text so that the reader focuses on them by a process of re-insertion. Because such features are common to all text, one great advantage of a template approach is that texts of almost any genre can be shared among a set of driver TM programs.

On-line help can also be designed to take advantage of this commonalty of generic text. The only limitation is that the help must come from the text itself (or from the larger textbase from which the text derives) and be computable by an algorithm rather than coded ad hoc or "canned" (see Pennington, 1992a, for a discussion of the problems associated with "canned" CALL). Within this constraint, help can be any kind of information the text can provide which is relevant to the task at hand, from letting learners take a peek at the target reconstruction, to granting access only to that part of the context which will enable them to make inferences. One option made possible by the potentially large amount of text available is to provide help in the form of a concordance on the word the learner is trying to discover, with that word masked in the concordance output, giving learners richer context, but not the answer. The authors' present experiments are looking at user responses to on-line concordance as a help system for various word-level TM activities.

Text manipulation ideally uses any text, "raw" from its authentic source. However, the TM concept extends to cases where text is altered or annotated slightly to adhere to the particular requirements of the template, but in such a way that alterations do not render the text unusable by other text manipulation programs. For example, *Hopalong*, an implementation of the "speed read" approach to reading instruction developed by John Higgins, highlights text to guide the eye from chunk to chunk at a measured speed. All that the developer (e.g., the teacher or the curriculum specialist) must do, after selecting the text, is to denote the chunks with carriage returns (in the case of *Hopalong*, the comprehension questions must be written in as well, but as these are in a separate file, the integrity of the original text is maintained). The already chunked text can be used directly in another of Higgins' programs, *Sequitur*, which displays the first chunk of text and has the student rebuild the entire passage by discerning the next chunk in sequence from among several proposed (i.e., the correctly sequenced chunk plus two distractors taken at random from the pool of not-yet-used chunks found elsewhere in the text file). The chunked text can in turn be used in a variety of other text manipulation programs which format the text according to sentence and paragraph boundaries (sentence-ending strings and blank lines, respectively), so that the integrity of sentences and paragraphs is essentially unaffected by the chunking required by *Sequitur* and *Hopalong*. Furthermore, the text can be part of a larger corpus used in concordancing or other forms of text analysis, from which still other text-based activities may be drawn (such as the concordance help feature noted in the preceding paragraph).

Thus, a wide variety of reading activities can be performed on any text considered relevant to the learners, who might prefer to restore or unscramble components from an article in a recent issue of *The Wall Street Journal* rather than perform equivalent operations in their graded reading workbooks. Or if the students prefer the graded readers, then these can form the text matrix. Whatever motivates the students is suitable text.

From a developer's point of view, the advantages of this approach to CALL implementation are obvious. However, the history of technology in education should alert us to the potential dangers of too-easy marriages of technology and instruction, which sometimes hides the fact that one partner has been made to adapt to the other (instruction to technology in this case). Dick (1991) has noted, with regard to the development of interactive multimedia instructional systems generally, that as the technology becomes more sophisticated the pedagogy tends to become more simplistic, often becoming detached entirely from any basis in instructional research.

The question to be addressed in the rest of this chapter is whether the TM approach yields corresponding benefits to second language learners, and particularly to their skills in reading. In arguing that it does, the authors will show how the activities students perform in text manipulation exercises are commensurate with current theories regarding productive reading strategies and environments favoring the development of second language reading ability.

7.3. THEORETICAL BACKGROUND: TM AND READING THEORY

For most people, reading is more agreeable and efficient on paper than on screen (Heppner, Anderson, Farstrup, and Weiderman, 1985). However, on-screen reading has the potential for overt interactivity. A reader can send a message via the screen to a text, and then the text, properly coded, can send a message back to the reader. A paper text, by comparison, suggests a reader responding to a text whose fixed and independent meaning he/she must discover. Of course, for a skilled reader the process is interactive, whether via paper or screen text, except that with a paper text the interaction is mainly invisible, occurring in the mind of the reader.

Some notion of interactivity between reader and text characterizes virtually all post-behaviorist models of the reading process (various applications of the term "interactive" to the study of reading are discussed in Lesgold and Perfetti, 1981). In these models, the skilled reader is far from a passive responder to print stimuli, but rather a questioner, judge, summarizer, comparer, predictor, hypothesizer, and elaborator, depending somewhat on the type of text and a great deal on the reader's prior knowledge and current goals. A text's meaning for a particular reader is gradually constructed through the dynamic flow of information between reader and text, both "top-down" (reader to text) and "bottom-up" (text to reader). Of course, no two readers are likely to construct identical mental models of a given text, inasmuch as they bring to it different knowledge bases, purposes, and information processing strategies.

However, interaction with a text, although characteristic of skilled reading in the native language, is often problematic for second language readers, even those at a relatively advanced level of proficiency. The second language reader characteristically resembles B.F. Skinner's reader, passive before the text in attempting to extract its secret meaning. This characterization often holds true even for second language readers whose reading in their native language is highly interactive. The reasons for the prevalence of a non-interactive style of reading in a second language are many. Second language readers may not have automated one or more of the component processes of reading in the second language, such as word decoding and recognition, resulting in working memory overload and diversion of attention away from the construction of a text model. Or, at a higher processing level, readers may not be familiar with semantic or discourse schemata specific to the culture of the second language, so that they have no preactivated scaffolding to help them summarize and organize the details of the incoming text, and quickly face overload. For these and related reasons, many second language readers experience reading as a one-way flow of information coming from the text to them, and never send messages of the types suggested above back to the text. So one objective for second language reading courseware might be to encourage the automatization of certain controlled processes such as decoding; or it might inform the learner about certain discourse schemata or in some other way attempt to establish the preconditions for eventual interaction. Perfetti (1983) has advocated such a role for courseware with regard to young first language readers, and Frederiksen (1986) has implemented and tested related ideas in a second language context.

Text manipulation courseware attacks the problem in a different, but complementary, way. TM simulates the target activity itself, rather than giving practice in any of its preconditioning or component processes. At any of a number of levels of processing, text manipulation externalizes the otherwise invisible reader-text interaction and gives the reader supported practice in real interaction with the text. Readers faced with a text that has been deconstructed in one of the ways described above must operate on it by questioning it or hypothesizing about what it might mean or how it might fit together. Readers have no choice but to interact with the text if they want to engage in the computer-based reading activity: passive meaning-extraction is not an option. Admittedly, the simulations of interaction provided by a TM system may not be perfect ones. Many of the typical TM operations that must be performed to reconstruct a text involve cognitive processing at a level not far below the surface of the written text, whereas the target interaction is actually deeper, i.e., it is semantic. Nonetheless, we assume that a second language reader who, for example, uses the mouse to drag boxed sentences of a text into their proper place in discourse order, is doing something akin to what skilled native language readers do unconsciously when they read—such as puzzling out the logical connection between two sentences or supplying a bridging inference from memory or from the preceding text. Further, when the boxed sentence has been placed, we assume that the TM system's mechanical feedback then simulates the far more subtle confirmatory or disconfirmatory feedback supplied for the skilled reader by subsequent text itself.

How successfully TM operations simulate the high-level interactions that characterize skilled reading, and with what degree of transfer, are empirical questions. The best-case scenario is that the habit of interaction is transferable to on-paper reading regardless of the exact level of the interactions provided by a TM system. In any event, the alternative is worse—many second language readers get no interaction with text from solo reading and only second-hand and/or delayed interaction from classroom reading.

So far, then, we are arguing that TM is capable of tapping text in ways which we can currently implement and that the interactive model of skilled reading can serve to guide, control, and evaluate. However, alert readers (highly interactive ones, armed with appropriate schemata) will have noticed that this interactive-simulation idea of TM is phrased in a particular conceptual framework, that of information processing or cognitive psychology. Such readers may also be aware that adapting such a framework raises some controversies. In the battle with behaviorism, cognitivism may have seemed unified, but now that "we are all cognitivists", the subdivisions are assuming more importance. For example, even given an interactive view of skilled reading, how do we know that readers who are skilled interactants in their first language need support for a similar target interaction in a second language? It could be that higher level skills involving inferencing and integration with prior knowledge are completely transferable from the native language. If so, it would be redundant to encourage learners to practice these skills and, worse, a diversion of time and attention from where it is needed—such as at lower levels of cognitive processing involving lexical knowledge and lexical access, where positive transfer is generally low or nil. A good deal of first language research locates the typical source of reading deficit at the lower rather than the higher level of skills (Perfetti, 1983, 1985; Stanovich and Cunningham, 1991), and the case has been extended to reading in a second language (Polson, 1992; Segalowitz, 1986). If true, this would be a serious argument against further development of TM, especially a new generation of it designed to exploit the proliferation of machine-readable text. We believe the argument is false, but must dredge up a little history to frame the issue.

7.3.1. The Background to Interactive Reading: Reading as Writing

The interactive version of reading, with the reader contributing to the construction of text meaning in conjunction with the text itself, is often considered an attractive account of this ultimate human activity. In fact, this account rests on the less attractive fact that human working memory is far too limited for behaviorist theory to have much applicability to reading. The constant theme in cognitive studies from Miller (1956) onward is that the mind uses various tricks, like chunking and prediction, to compensate for processing limitations. Experiments have shown even simple acts of perception to be "knowledge-driven" to varying degrees, and more so complex information processing like reading. For example, on the level of word perception, Tulving and Gold (1963) found that deformed words were better perceived when primed by more context, in other words, by more prior expectation. On the level of discourse, Bransford and Johnson's (1972) "laundry story" showed that not only immediate comprehension but also subsequent memory for a story was determined by prior expectation. The studies are legion; the theme is that expectation, especially well-structured expectation (in the form of models, schemas, scripts, grammars, and other kinds of frameworks) is needed to cope with the otherwise overwhelming flow of incoming information. Such structures are also important in view of how much typically gets left out of texts and yet is required for their comprehension, to be supplied from the reader's store of "default", or schematic, knowledge (Minsky, 1975; Schank and Abelson, 1977).

To those interested in educational applications, the pedagogy of reading implied by this version of human information processing seemed straightforward. The application came mainly from Smith (1971) and Goodman (1967) under the heading "reading as a psycholinguistic guessing game". In their model, reading is barely perception-driven at all—at least, not after the first few sentences to set the scene. Having made predictions at various levels, from various contextual sources, and having activated the relevant schemas, the skilled reader "feedsforward" through the text, merely "sampling" from the words themselves and stopping for a closer look when there are mismatches with predictions. The role of text is thus changed from authoritative to merely suggestive. In the frameworks of both Smith and Goodman, the reader constructs the text almost as much as the writer, and the beginning reader should be encouraged to be as constructive as possible. The crucial point as concerns pedagogy is that readers should be discouraged from any major effort to pay close attention to the text itself, such as careful word decoding.

"Reading as writing" was very much the original basis of the text manipulation concept. The deformed on-screen text simulates, and at the same time exaggerates, the limited usefulness of any text surface as given. A "storyboard" with every word masked apart from the title is essentially Goodman's idea of what any text "really" looks like to the brain: a set of suggestive symbols encoding a message to be reconstructed through interaction with any prior and contextual information sources available. This notion is opposed to that of a text as a set of fixed signs whose single meaning is to be determined linearly from the combined independent meanings of the words.[2]

The applicability of psycholinguistic reading theory to second language reading seemed obvious (Clarke and Silberstein, 1977; Coady, 1979), and by the 1970's the theory had assumed the status of dogma in EFL/ESL practice (see Grabe, 1991, for more background). Clearly, if native speakers must bring a lot of their own information to the act of reading, then the second language learner brings even more. If reading is a guessing game even when most of the words and discourse conventions are familiar, how much more of a guessing game it must be when a large proportion of the words and discourse conventions are unknown or not well-understood.

This view of reading suggests providing second language readers with a practice environment in which to develop guessing and related strategies, especially one that feeds back to the guesses in shorter loops than are provided naturally in the reading process. Therefore, in the late 1970's the case seemed strong for developing TM, and the theory matched the technology becoming available.

7.3.2. Problems with Reading as Reconstruction

Given the enormous influence of the Smith-Goodman view of reading in both first language and second language instruction, its prescriptions and effects have been remarkably little researched. Perhaps this is because the theory, as a processing model, is actually quite short on specifics, as Perfetti (1985) maintains. Perhaps it seemed as if the copious psychological evidence for top-down processing made testing of the "obvious" instructional application unnecessary (an assumption that is almost never justified). Least researched of all, of course, have been the CALL applications of the model. And many involved in TM believe that to undertake such research now would be irrelevant, as the reading theory underpinning this predictive model of reading has already started to unravel.

It was probably inevitable that the Smith-Goodman theory of reading would come in for some criticism during the late 1970's and 1980's, since the pendulum has been swinging in first language reading all this century between expectation-driven and perception-driven reading theories, with the latter currently ascendant (Adams, 1990, provides good background to this theory). Fashion aside, however, some novel research paradigms and techniques emerged in these years that seemed to produce genuinely new information about the nature of skilled reading, resulting notably in the expert-novice comparison (Lesgold, 1984). Unexpectedly, in several studies seeking to identify the actual characteristics that divide skilled readers from unskilled, guessing and predicting often came in quite low on the list.

Sampling from a very large pool, Mitchell and Greene (1978) argued that Goodman's eye movement data could represent any number of underlying cognitive processes, and that when a less ambiguous measure was used, no evidence at all of the use of prediction in skilled reading would emerge. Their consistent experimental finding was that reading speed is not a function of the degree of predictability of a text. Balota, Pollatsek, and Rayner (1985) examined the visual mechanisms of reading directly and concluded it was simply not true that reading is driven mainly by "expectations and predictions about forthcoming information", with visual information providing only confirmatory evidence of predictions. Perfetti, Goldman, and Hogaboam (1979) discovered that while contextually predictable words are identified a little more quickly than unpredictable ones, even skilled readers' predictions are accurate at a rate of only 20-30% and therefore this cannot be the basis of their success. Graesser, Hoffman, and Clark (1980) found that for good readers, neither speed nor comprehension is significantly affected by the degree of syntactic predictability of additional words in a sentence, although weak readers are significantly aided by higher predictability. Possibly the most persuasive evidence is provided by Stanovich and West (1979, 1981), who uncovered an effect similar to that of Graesser, Hoffman, and Clark (1980), but for semantic predictability: Good readers are aided by semantic predictability, moderately and unconsciously, but weak readers rely on it strategically, to the extent that they are thrown off when their predictions are wrong.

The theme emerging from this research was that poor readers guess and predict a good deal, because they do not know enough words, do not know them well enough, or cannot quickly enough recognize visually those words which they know phonologically so as to beat the rate of information decay in working memory. A coherent sequence of studies on this subject is reviewed in Perfetti (1985). Study after study in the 1980's showed speed of context-free, expectation-free, word decoding to account for the main part of the variance in multiple regression analyses in which numerous reader attributes were pitted against general reading comprehension as the dependent measure. The instructional implication is that practice in rapid word recognition, not practice in guessing, is what can turn weak readers into strong.

The decoding issue was slow to arrive in second language reading theory, possibly because reading-as-predicting had become such a dominant view (as suggested by Grabe, 1991). However, a sign that the tide is turning can be found in a number of the contributions to Huckin, Haynes, and Coady (1993), which qualify severely the nature, role, importance, and conditions of guessing in reading in a second language. Coady, as noted above, was one of the original importers of psycholinguistic notions of reading into second language acquisition theory. The emergence of findings counter to guessing theory suggests that CALL reading software, rather than promoting the development of strategies in predicting and hypothesizing, would be better devoted to helping learners develop the ability to automatically decode the highest frequency words. In fact, some large-scale CALL projects now seem headed in that direction (for example, Coady, Magoto, Hubbard, Graney, and Mokhtari, 1993).

If second language theory and practice were to embrace the latest first language reading theory as quickly and thoroughly as it once did the so-called psycholinguistic theory, then we shall inevitably all be teaching word lists and rapid decoding via our various media. Selinker (1992) characterizes EFL/ESL as a field fond of throwing out the little it achieves in periodic swings to discover ever newer and more exciting theoretical underpinnings. Second language reading research is bound to follow the lead of first language research in significant ways, given the relative size and gravitational pull of the two enterprises. In any case, it is no doubt true that there is a greater role in reading in a second language for more specific vocabulary and word recognition training, particularly at the early stages, as argued by many of the contributors to the volume by Huckin, Haynes, and Coady (1993). However, an argument can be made for encouraging second language reading researchers to be more discriminating about what they borrow from first language research and how they interpret and adapt it (also the view of Grabe, 1991).

7.3.3. Reading in a First and a Second Language: Same or Different?

First language reading research does not map onto second language reading in any simple or obvious way. Even Perfetti (1985), an arch foe of guessing theory, suggests as much, noting that:

> Skilled reading is, by definition, a very fluent process. If a skilled reader fixates three or four words per second, around the normal rate, where is there time to guess? Moreover, if he is skilled at reading, why bother? Reading is much easier than guessing. The case may be different in, for example, reading in a foreign language that is incompletely mastered. There is plenty of time to guess in such cases and perhaps enough payoff for doing so. (p. 26)

Studies looking into subtle differences between first language and second language reading are somewhat sparse. However, a number have attempted to replicate some of the first language reading experiments mentioned above with second language readers and obtained rather different results. For example, the key Stanovich and West experiment mentioned above was replicated in Quebec by Favreau and Segalowitz

(1983) with skilled and less skilled bilingual readers, and patterns of context sensitivity were found that did not confirm the Stanovich and West results. What Stanovich and West characterized as less skilled readers' over-reliance on and yet poor use of contextual information was found precisely to characterize slow but otherwise highly skilled second language readers. In other words, both weak first language readers and skilled second language readers appear to be strategically reliant on context to recognize a large proportion of words, and yet not very successful in using the information context offers. Therefore, skilled, flexible, automated use of context apparently does not automatically transfer from the first to the second language, even when the foundations for such transfer appear to be in place.

Second language readers' apparent context-insensitivity even when otherwise highly skilled in reading is not an extensively documented phenomenon, yet it appears to exist. For example, it appears in a series of mainly unpublished studies described in McLaughlin (1987) and McLeod and McLaughlin (1986). The latter study compared the read-aloud errors of both more and less skilled second language readers against those produced by first language readers in terms of meaningfulness, or contextual goodness-of-fit. One sentence in the text the subjects read was, "She shook the piggy bank, and out came some money" (McLeod and McLaughlin, 1986, p. 115). Predictably, if young first language subjects did not know the word *money*, they might replace it with *dimes*, a semantically reasonable alternative. But if second language students did not know the word *money*, they tended to replace it with something orthographically similar but contextually violating, such as *many*. This tendency was even more interesting with the advanced ESL students in the study. Advanced students made far fewer errors than beginners, as one would expect, but of those that remained, just as large a proportion were context violating or non-meaningful. This phenomenon was confirmed by McLaughlin (1987) in a cloze test given to both advanced and beginning ESL readers as well as to native speakers. The advanced readers scored significantly higher than beginners, but once again the point of interest is in the character of the errors that remained: only 20% of beginners' errors were plausible within the context, and for advanced readers the figure was only 29%; for native speakers, the figure was 79%. In other words, if recognition was not automatic, there was no workable strategy for producing a reasonable guess. A few other experiments confirm the existence of this phenomenon in second language learners, including Arden-Close's (in press) work in Oman; and it has been noted as well in first language studies (e.g., Oakhill, 1993).

Thus, direct instruction or practice in reading-as-interaction or even reading-as-educated-guessing makes some sense in principle in the second language context, whatever other realities may exist in the case of reading in the first language. Therefore, the recent decoding movement has not made the idea of reading as interaction, or its applications such as TM, untenable. Psycholinguistic reading theory has not then been unraveled as much as it has been moderated, supplemented, and specified, in that it has been shown to have a special relevance in the second language case. In order to delimit the potential for TM to train the reading process in the second language case, a number of empirical questions need to be explored:

> (1) To what extent does work on text manipulation software produce context sensitivity for second language readers of various types and at various proficiency levels?
>
> (2) Does TM produce a more interactive reader, who habitually integrates text information with his/her own prior knowledge in such a way that non-grammatical sequences become impossible?
>
> 3) Who needs TM-based training, all or merely some readers, and how do we find out?
>
> (4) If training is required of both high-and low-level reading skills, what are the optimal proportions and sequencing of these skills?
>
> (5) What, if anything, do learners actually do with reading courseware of different kinds? What are the variables in their behavior and the outcomes of that behavior? What strategies (if any) seem to emerge in a CALL reading context?

This excursion into theoretical background, we would argue, builds a plausible case for text manipulation in line with what is currently known about the reading process, and suggests a number of hypotheses for empirical research and a rationale for doing that research. Where should one begin an empirical examination? We follow Long's (1980) argument that in second language acquisition research, the research cycle ideally moves from descriptive, to correlational, to experimental studies, and that no phase should be skipped. Chapelle (1990)—see also discussion by Chapelle, Jamieson, and Park, this volume—has proposed the applicability of this cycle to the CALL area, and, as mentioned before, notes that the descriptive phase has hardly begun.

Cloze is one template for reading and language skills development on which a substantial body of research has been carried out toward describing what reading skills it exercises, and it is also a template which lends itself well to text manipulation. Therefore, it seems reasonable when embarking on a course of inquiry into text manipulation to take as an example what has been done with computer-based implementations of cloze.

7.4. SECOND LANGUAGE READERS AND CLOZE

7.4.1. Some Problems with Cloze

Lee's (1990) survey of the previous decade of research on reading examines several genres of research instrument including cloze. The section on beginners draws heavily on Nunan (1985), who finds that:

> unlike more advanced learners, beginning language learners are less able to perceive (or perhaps utilize) intratextual relationships when carrying out written cloze tests ... . Beginning language learners are not able to take in the text as an integrated expression of ideas, when the text is violated by blanks. This finding may be a by-product of the fact that the text itself, as presented to readers, is not an integrated expression of ideas. (p. 5)

Similarly, Douglas (1981) finds that advanced second language readers, unlike native-speaking readers, are more reliant on local redundancy in a text than they are on longer range redundancy in their completion of cloze exercises.

If, as has already been noted, second language readers are not even able to perceive non-degraded text as an integrated expression of ideas, it is not surprising that a degraded text such as a cloze passage would be even more impenetrable. This partially explains Feldmann and Stemmer's (1987) finding that of twenty subjects in their study of C-tests (which are similar to cloze tests), only two attempted to skim the entire text as instructed, and they gave the task up as impossible because of the gaps. Cohen, Segal, and Weiss (1985) instructed students to skim cloze passages first, and reported a similar breakdown. Alderson (1980) gives further evidence of students not treating cloze passages as integrated readings, and concludes that "the nature of the cloze test, the filling in of gaps in connected text, forces subjects to concentrate on the immediate environment of the gap ... ." (p. 74). He further finds that varying the amount of context has no predictable bearing on the ability of either native speakers or non-native speakers to solve cloze tests: "Neither native nor nonnative speakers were aided in their ability to restore deleted words, or a semantic equivalent, or a grammatically correct word, by the addition even the doubling, of context around the deletion" (Alderson, 1980, p. 72).

If paper-based cloze poses such problems for language learners, then one advantage to computer-based cloze is enhancement of the reader-to-text interaction made possible when the gaps violating the text respond to the students' attempts at recovering them. In the first place, students receive feedback as they go, to whatever degree granted by the program designer. Secondly, as Feldmann and Stemmer note, it is possible that as the text is resolved, the learners have more and more redundancy at their disposal to elucidate unsolved blanks, and students working on computer-based cloze activities have the added advantage of knowing whether blanks solved have been filled in correctly or not (incorrect words left intact in paper-based cloze passages might further skew meaning). So, whereas a computer-based cloze passage may initially appear indecipherable to students, they are at least handed a set of tools to work with in attempting to tease the message out of the text as they render it gradually less degraded. That second language learners are in fact able to work effectively in interaction with computer-based cloze has been borne out in at least one study (Stevens, forthcoming). Before discussing that study, however, we will discuss a crucial choice to be made by researchers in collecting data in such studies.

7.4.2. Examining Text Manipulation Non-Intrusively

Because of the interest of cloze to researchers as a measure of language proficiency, learner strategies when working on cloze passages have been extensively examined, though not necessarily as computer-based exercises. One useful description occurs in the work of Feldman and Stemmer (1987), who found that in solving C-tests, solution of gaps was either "automatic" or "non-automatic", i.e., spontaneous or considered. In the latter case, recall strategies were used, leading to delay, to giving up, or to activation of another recall strategy. Once an item was recovered, evaluation strategies were employed to check appropriateness (also used for automatic recovery), leading to acceptance or rejection of the item for that blank. Since production problems (e.g., spelling) could still occur after recall of the item, application strategies might also have to be employed.

Since they felt that their use of student introspection as one means of generating data was a factor in their study, Feldmann and Stemmer comment on gathering data on cognitive processes intrusively. An "intrusive" protocol is one for which the act of gathering data interferes with the process under study; for example, where the presence of video equipment or the need to "think aloud" causes learners to monitor their behavior more closely than they might if left to their own devices. In solving cloze passages or C-tests, students are constrained in what they can process simultaneously. Signal data limits occur when the quality of the data is eroded, as with phone call interruptions, or in the case at hand, with the blanks in a cloze exercise. Memory data limits occur when language items are encountered which the learner does not know or has forgotten. Furthermore, there are resource limits, where the learner is given too much to process beyond his/her capabilities. Focus on multiple tasks can be maintained until one task starts drawing attention preponderantly from the others. Feldmann and Stemmer (1987) suggest that having to think aloud could interfere with the subjects' ability to focus properly on the task under study.

In order to get a clear picture of actual self-access use of TM, some researchers opt for non-intrusive research techniques. Unobtrusively tracking key presses of second language students performing computer-based cloze activities in unmonitored self-access situations has yielded evidence of engagement in interaction with the text of the type noted above—e.g., hypothesis formation, testing, and reformation. In a study of 100 cloze paragraphs completed by second language learners at university level, Stevens (forthcoming) found that students successfully used feedback from the program to substantively complete 36 of the passages (with 22 of those paragraphs entirely completed). However, there is also evidence in the same data of students giving up on passages which they had started: 49 of the interactions were essentially nil sessions, where students logged on, checked things out, and logged off again with little or no interaction; and a further 16 quit after working only within the first sentence. Although it is not clear if this minimal time spent on computer is because the students were unable to complete the passages or simply did not want to complete them, the latter possibility seems more likely, as use of the hint and help features built into the program practically guarantee solution of any problem by anyone who persists.[3]

We therefore find that many of the students in the Stevens study were simply "window shopping", just looking for something to do for a few minutes, but not in the mood for cognitive engagement. This appears to be fairly typical student behavior, and indeed, many computer users, not just students, enjoy browsing. There is probably nothing inherent in the medium that would elicit this outcome other than the fact that it was possible, given the circumstances of the investigation, to gather data unobtrusively, without students knowing that they were being monitored, and so these data were collected. Such data might not have emerged in an intrusive study. This is but one way that results from non-intrusive studies might contradict those from intrusive ones. As another example, Windeatt (1986), in a study where screens were videotaped as students thought-aloud about their reading processes while going through the text and were later interviewed about their experiences, found that while reading the students made little use of program help features (see also Hubbard et al., 1986). The unobtrusive studies of Stevens (1991a-c, forthcoming) suggest, however, that students working under self-access conditions tend to abuse help features rather than to apply more self-reliant cognitive strategies in solving the problems they encounter. If whether students know they are being monitored is a factor in their use of computer-based help, then whether a study is intrusive or not is itself an important consideration in assessing the results.

7.5. LEARNER CONTROL ISSUES

There is some evidence that students who rely excessively on program-supplied help are not learning as much as those who try to solve problems through their own self-generated trial-and-error feedback. Pederson (1986), for example, demonstrated differences in cognitive processing when comparing students who had access to help in the form of the option to review reading passages while answering comprehension questions as contrasted with those to whom such access was denied. In the author's words: "The results indicate that passage-unavailable treatment always resulted in a comparatively higher comprehension rate than occurred in counterpart passage-available treatments regardless of the level of question or level of verbal ability" (Pederson, 1986, p. 39). In other words, "greater benefit was derived from the subjects' being aware that they were required to do all of their processing of the text prior to viewing the question" (Pederson, 1986, p. 38). It follows then that in using text manipulation as a means of having students engage in "reading as guessing", help should not be allowed to such an extent that guessing is suppressed.

One strategy frequently noted when students use TM programs is a tendency to proceed linearly rather than holistically, as one might be expected to do if reading a passage and drawing inferences from outside the immediate context. Edmondson, Reck, and Schroder (1988) tracked nine secondary level students doing a combined jumbled sentence/paragraph exercise called *Shuffle* and noted a tendency for students to use "frontal-attack" strategies; that is, to take the first available sentence and try to place it, or to build from the first sentence to the next, and so on. Accordingly, Windeatt (1986) found that his subjects completed computer-based cloze blanks in a predominantly linear fashion, even though the system did not require it—perhaps because they did not like to scroll from screen to screen—and similar findings have consistently obtained in more recent work by the present authors (e.g., Stevens, forthcoming). If, as Windeatt suggests, this tendency to proceed linearly with computer-based exercises occurs at the expense of more holistic strategies, then it may be that a more effective implementation would encourage or even force students to jump around in the text instead.

The possibility (indeed, the likelihood) that students may not of their own free will choose a pathway through CALL materials leading to optimal learning suggests a re-examination of the magister-pedagogue dichotomy introduced by Higgins (1983, 1988) which has strongly influenced CALL software development over the past decade. Rather than the computer acting as a pliant slave which unquestioningly obeys all student commands (the role favored in the dichotomy), it may be that an entity which aids the learner on demand while exercising enlightened authority over the learning process is more conducive to learning. But how much authority can a program exert without depriving students of benefits of autonomous learning (thus tending to be a magister, in terms of the dichotomy)?

One problem with allowing learners control over their own learning is getting them to take advantage of available options. How, for example, can students be encouraged to select and learn to interpret unfamiliar forms of feedback? Bland, Noblitt, Armstrong, and Gray discovered in a SYSTÈME D implementation that although students had access to both dictionary and lexical help, they avoided lexical help for fear of getting lost in it. "We were initially surprised at the very few queries of this nature in the data" (Bland, Noblitt, Armstrong, and Gray, 1990, p. 445). Furthermore, in an attempt to reverse the outcome of the Stevens' (1991a) Hangman study, where it was found that 53% of the students were touring the material with unacceptably low levels of cognitive engagement, the program was reconfigured to present varying amounts of context surrounding the target word when demanded by the user. The demand feature comes at the cost of points, the idea being for students to request just as much context as they need to solve the problem. On examination of the first set of data after the revised program was implemented, it was found that cognitive engagement remained at about the same level and that the students were not using the context feature, probably because the program failed to make them aware of it. These are just two examples of the caveat that simply providing options to students by no means ensures that they will use them.

One of the present authors is finding much the same thing in his research into learners' use of on-line concordancing with keyword masked as the help in a systematic deletion exercise (*Textpert*). In this study, learners' use of concordance help in self-access was virtually non-existent, in spite of their previously having tried it in a practice session, and also (in the practice session) having doubled the success rate of either a no help or dictionary help option. In order for the experiment to continue, the system had to be reconfigured three times to make the concordance window unavoidable (*Petwords*). Admittedly, spontaneous use of the concordance increased with familiarity, but not entirely in proportion to the increasing advantages it produced, both on-line and later on in classroom paper-and-pencil cloze tests for the same vocabulary items.

7.6. CONCLUDING REMARKS TO CHAPTER 7

In this chapter, we have attempted to broaden the notion of reading courseware beyond a replication of what instructors might try to teach in a reading class to courseware that emulates the reading process. We submit that text manipulation, besides being easy to program and to implement in an educational context, is capable of promoting interactive reading. Most importantly, TM programs are able to take advantage of the increasingly widespread access to machine-readable text and are thus potentially able to supply learners with substantial amounts of input, which teachers—or the learners themselves—can filter to ensure that it is comprehensible input.

Designers of TM programs are often accused of succumbing to expediency at the expense of pedagogical merit in churning out text manipulation templates. In this chapter, an attempt has been made to explain how text manipulation programs enhance the reading process by promoting interactions with the text. In particular, TM can provide feedback that enables second language readers to perceive meaning when work with the same text might be too difficult for them if attempted via less interactive means.

It now seems that whatever processes are instigated by TM are beneath the learner's level of conscious perception or attention. This should come as no surprise, as the same applies to much of language learning. Although the "reading as guessing" model from which TM is derived has been challenged, it is shown in this chapter that reading in the native language differs enough from second language reading that much of this criticism applies only obliquely to the second language case. Hence, there remains a plausible scenario for pursuing the development of TM materials, particularly in second language reading, and in conjunction with other types of materials aimed at a lower or less holistic level.

However, this plausibility must be supported by more definite evidence that TM actually produces differences in skill acquisition over alternatives, on-line or off. In this chapter, the importance of making empirical inquiry into positions taken with regard to TM is stressed, and work on cloze is taken as an example of one such line of inquiry. Notes of caution are sounded in interpreting results without taking into account the degree of intrusion in the process afforded by the protocol, and also in assuming that features built into a program will as a matter of course be used as expected by students.

Developers at this point should take advantage of the descriptive data available and feed it back into the design process, particularly that part of the process relating to learner control. As pointed out by Chapelle and Mizuno (1989), the issue of optimal degree of learner control over CALL had not yet been investigated in the latter part of the 1980's. With investigation now tentatively under way, it is fair to say that the issue of learner control is still far from being resolved in CALL or TM, as is also true in the wider world of computer-assisted instruction (see Steinberg, 1989). We are finding that we may have to make our TM programs somewhat more magisterial if we wish to obtain significant research results from their use. The questions we must now address concern what we need to do so that our learners will use them most effectively as well.

NOTES TO CHAPTER 7

1. Ease of access would be an important variable determining the nature of the reading process based on corpora and databases.

2. Although a TM routine insists in the end on a single exact surface reconstruction, the focus on a set text can be de-emphasized to some extent by imaginative programming.

3. In this study no attempt was made to identify individual students; thus, there were no violations of privacy, and also no compunction on students to concentrate on the task unless self-motivated to do so.

8. Exploring the Virtual World: Computers in the Second Language Writing Classroom

Marianne Phinney

8.1. INTRODUCTION

If you ever doubt that a technology can change the way we teach, learn, and live, look at the microcomputer. Less than 20 years ago, the Apple was a gleam in Steve Jobs' eye and some writers still debated whether you could really write on an electric typewriter: it just did not have the same feel as those old Underwood manuals. Yet in 1992, for example, the ERIC database included over 100 papers and books published about word processing in composition, as it has for the past several years. Have computer-assisted composition studies come of age in such a short time?

8.1.1. Word Processors for Revision

The early studies of computer use in composition focused almost exclusively on word processing. Many of the publications dealt with case studies or anecdotes about the encounters of one teacher or writer with word processing. The promise of the computer as a writing tool seemed to match the newly strengthened emphasis on the writing process in English composition and rhetoric. Teaching methods that focused on multiple revisions seized on a tool that seemed to make those revisions easier and faster.

Those early studies (as noted in Phinney, 1989, p. 83) seem to be imbued with an almost "born again" euphoria. Computer enthusiasts, often isolated in non-technical English departments, appeared to be selling their readers on the benefits of this new technology (see, e.g., Bradley, 1982). In a comment that typifies this period, Helen Schwartz (1984) claimed "writing becomes a playground where revising is part of the fun instead of part of the punishment" (p. 240). Professional writers, themselves experienced revisers, were often the most enthusiastic adherents of the new technology.

Many of the early reports included descriptive case studies of writers using everything from mainframe line editors (Collier, 1982) to microcomputers (e.g., Benesch, 1987; Cross, 1990; Piper, 1987). These case studies ranged from anecdotal accounts of teaching or learning experiences to short-term observations of particular types of students. Early studies made many claims about the effects of word processing, often with conflicting results. On the positive side (as previously reviewed in Phinney, 1989), students who use word processors have been said to spend more time writing (Nichols, 1986; Womble, 1984); to alter revision behavior (Bradley, 1982; Hunter, 1984; Madigan, 1984; Monohan, 1982; Phinney and Khouri, 1993; Schwartz, 1982); to make more and different types of revisions (Bean, 1983; Bradley, 1982; Hunter, 1984; Monohan, 1982; Womble, 1984); to show less of a tendency towards writer's block (Daiute, 1983; Phinney, 1991a, 1991b); and to improve their attitudes toward writing (Daiute, 1985; Phinney, 1991a; Phinney and Mathis, 1989; Schwartz, 1984).

Pennington (1991a) uses an artifact analysis to illustrate the positive and negative claims that can be and have been made for word processing. For every positive claim, there is a negative counter-claim. For example, the word processor does make it easier to revise. However, the revision process is more complex, in that it involves more steps and more different types of manipulation. Cutting and pasting, or even drag-and-drop editing, is more complicated than drawing an arrow on a paper draft and recopying it, at least for some students. The complexities of the system may in fact reduce the amount of revision for some students or slow down the acquisition of effective writing processes.

Most researcher-teachers made the logical deduction that if word processors made revision easier, using word processing would lead to more revision. The implication, of course, especially for English departments and school districts on tight budgets, was that computers would help students become better writers. Thus, a good deal of the early research tried to support the hypotheses that computer-using students would write more, revise more, and produce better papers.

Studies that compared computer-assisted composition to composing with traditional methods often yielded mixed results (Hawisher, 1989). In general, researchers found that writers made different types of revisions and applied different revision strategies when computers were used (Owston, Murphy, and Wideman, 1992). However, the results on the question of writing quality were mixed. While some investigators found that papers written on computer were more highly rated (McAllister and Louth, 1988; Owston, Murphy, and Wide-man, 1992), others did not (Joram, Woodruff, Bryson, and Lindsay, 1992). Results often depended on a number of variables (Pennington, 1993b), including the students' ability or proficiency level (Cross, 1990; Piper, 1987), the system or the software used (Collier, 1983; Pufahl, 1984); and the length of experience with the computer (Phinney, 1993b; Phinney and Khouri, 1993).

The field of computer-assisted writing was stirred by "the interface controversy" in 1990, when Marcia Peeples Halio published a (now-infamous) paper (Halio, 1990) in which she claimed that students using Macintosh computers produced essays that were consistently evaluated as poorer than those produced by students using MS-DOS computers. While Halio's research was criticized as being seriously flawed (Kaplan and Moulthrop, 1990; Slatin, Batson, Boston, and Cohen, 1990; Youra, 1990), the article triggered a debate on the use of graphic user interfaces (GUIs) versus text interfaces. However, little controlled research on the effects of different interfaces ensued. In fact, with the advent of Windows on MS-DOS machines, the interface question has become largely moot, since most word processors on Windows look and feel much like word processors on the Macintosh.

8.1.2. An Enlarged View of Computer-Assisted Writing

In the past five years, the field of computer-assisted composition has reached a certain level of maturity—we might say that we are now in our adolescence. Because of the mixed results in studies that compare computer-assisted texts to traditionally produced texts, the focus in research has moved away from the question of whether using a computer helps students produce better texts. Computers are ubiquitous; we will write and teach writing with computers regardless of the final product. More interesting to researchers now is the nature of the human-machine interface. Similar to the shifting emphasis noted by Chapelle, Jamieson, and Park (this volume) for CALL research in general, the emphasis in computer-assisted composition research has shifted to the changing writing behaviors and pedagogies engendered by the electronic medium, and the ways that computer technology affects how we think about the writing process. Important research questions are now: first, the general question of how the computer has changed the way we approach the writing process, and second, the more specific question of how new computer software products have changed the way we as teachers approach the teaching of writing.

Although word processing in and of itself does not produce better writing or better writers, it does appear to change the way writers approach the writing process. Haas (1989), for example, observed experienced and student writers composing given the choice of word processing, pen and paper, or both word processing and pen/paper, by examining their planning behaviors. In the word processing condition, she found that there was less planning overall, less conceptual planning, and more local planning than in the pen and paper condition. Experience as a writer made no difference in results. The "both" condition elicited a variety of responses, from use of the computer alone to writing the paper out by hand and then typing it on computer.

This variety of strategies for computer use has been found in several studies. Some students carry over their paper-based habits to composing in the electronic medium, recopying drafts several times either by hand or on the computer. Cross (1990) describes a student who recopied his draft three times; only the last version was entered on the computer. Many studies (e.g., Cross, 1990; Hill, Wallace, and Haas, 1991; Phinney, 1993b; Phinney and Khouri, 1993) describe students who treat the word processor as an elaborate typewriter. Phinney and Khouri (1993) argue that this behavior is due at least in part to a lack of experience with the computer, but it may also be linked to the student's self-confidence in composing or ability to write by hand. The writers described by Cross (1990) are all basic writers who have difficulties dealing with the writing process on paper as well. In case studies of second language writers, Benesch (1987) and Piper (1987) both noted that their basic ESL writers continued some of their pen-and-paper strategies when writing on the computer.

Recent studies have begun to identify profiles of computer writers that may be different from those of pen-and-paper composers. Van Waes (1992), for example, found that some writers change their focus when writing on the computer. Some revised earlier in the process than they did when writing by hand; others revised and reviewed their text less on screen than they did on paper. Two studies with advanced non-native writers (Phinney, 1993b; Phinney and Khouri, 1993) identified three different profiles of computer writers based on the amount of computer experience and the level of English proficiency among ESL writers. They found that computer experience affected the amount and type of revision more than language proficiency did. The novice computer users wrote by hand and copied the text onto the computer, or drafted a text into the computer and then revised very little. Novice users did not take advantage of the spelling checker or the thesaurus available in the word processing package. Intermediate users made some revisions and used the spelling checker, but did not make many "macro"-level (as opposed to "micro"-level) revisions. They often attempted to revise the text on screen, but did so tentatively. Experienced users, those with two or more years of computer writing experience, revised and reviewed their texts extensively and made little distinction between first and final draft. The writing process was for them a continuous spiral through the activities of composing, revision, and editing.

8.2. A PARADIGM SHIFT?

As CALL researchers have become more interested in the nature of interaction in the computer environment (Chapelle, Jamieson, and Park, this volume), the computer-assisted composition community has moved from a focus on the word processor as a tool to an examination of the interactions among teachers, learners, and technology. Recent topics of interest have included the use of hypertext and hypermedia in writing, collaborative writing environments, electronic mail, synchronous and asynchronous conferencing, and the changing relationships between teachers and learners in the electronic classroom. As part of the changing culture of composition instruction, there is a new emphasis on decentering authority, coupled with a recognition of the importance of collaborative learning, and a realization of the need for new models of writing and rhetoric. These topics have a familiar ring to many ESL and second language teachers, for they are many of the same issues that have figured prominently in second language teaching. Computers, however, add a new dimension to matters of classroom communication and interaction, as Chapelle, Jamieson, and Park (this volume) have noted.

8.2.1. Shift in Emphasis from Word Processing to Collaborative Writing

Although the word processor is still the primary tool used in computer writing classrooms, the environment of these classrooms has changed, often radically. For example, the first writing lab, opened in 1985, at the University of Texas at El Paso (where I taught until 1994) consisted of fourteen stand-alone PC's with two dot-matrix printers. The second lab at that institution, installed in 1987, expanded to almost 50 PC's set up in six rows. Each row was attached to a PC server that controlled the software and the printing. Those of us who worked in that computer writing lab found it to be a very difficult teaching environment: the teacher had access to the end of the row only, and the room was so large that talking to more than one or two rows of students at a time was impossible.

The current lab at the University of Texas at El Paso, opened in 1992, has 85 MS-DOS stations and 50 Macintosh computers. All are connected to networks (Novell and AppleShare) and also to the university's mainframe system through Ethernet. The computers are arranged in pods of eight with a printer on each pod. Students can face each other or work together at a single computer.

How has this layout changed teaching? In the old lab, students came in, sat down, and wrote. To talk with the teacher or with another classmate about their papers, they had to get up or wait until the teacher threaded his/her way to them. To leave messages or drafts for another student, the teacher had to share disks or make a note of the computer the student was using and then later to retrieve the paper from the hard drive of that machine.

In the new lab, teachers and students have complete freedom of movement. Students often cluster around a single machine or a group of machines to work on collaborative projects. Teachers are free to move in order to speak with any student in the class, even to sit at the computer to work with that person. On the network, students can leave electronic mail messages for their teachers or for each other. Through the mainframe system, they can participate in a synchronous chat or join a bulletin board. Within the local network in the lab, they can leave drafts for their partners, have a class discussion, or write mail using the *Daedelus* system, collect a variety of comments on a paper, search the Internet for term paper resources, or use other computer systems on campus. As in the examples described by Hoffman (this volume), the networked computer lab has greatly expanded the opportunities to use and interact in the target language.

Such non-traditional spaces as this university computer writing lab force teachers to develop a variety of new strategies in a computer writing class (Rodrigues and Rodrigues, 1989). Instructors can model the writing process as it occurs, e.g., by using a projection system to show their word processing activity on a large screen, and can also help students adapt their individual writing strategies to a computer environment. They can communicate with their students verbally or on-line, with both teacher and student often developing on-line personas that are quite different from their classroom personas (Hoffman, this volume). In such a writing class, the textbook becomes much less important as a pedagogical focus than the writing which the students produce (Barnes, 1989). The result is often a classroom that "is noisy, seemingly chaotic, and demands new teaching strategies" (Rodrigues and Rodrigues, 1989, p. 21). Such computer lab classrooms seem to lend themselves naturally to collaborative writing activities.

8.2.2. Development of Software by Writing Teachers

In another aspect of the shifting paradigm of computer-assisted composition, writing teachers are having greater input into the software tools developed for writing classes. Indeed, writing teachers have often produced their own software tools, sometimes in desperation, when suitable materials could not be found. Many of the most popular teacher-designed programs share the same ideology: writing is both a social and a personal process. From this dual perspective, writers should be encouraged to interact with other writers about their texts as well as to discover their own authorial voice. This type of pedagogical orientation has led to the development of software sometimes called "groupware" (Kemp, 1992). Such software allows writers to use the computer as a tool for collaborative communication, to share drafts, to critique written work, and to revise texts electronically. In classes where groupware is employed, word processing and the development of word processing skills take a back seat to the purposes for communication in interactions mediated within a computer environment. Some teachers have reported that electronically mediated interactions lead to a sharper sense of audience and voice among their student writers (Marx, 1990).

A number of writing teachers have used authoring software to develop their own programs for classroom use. DiPardo and DiPardo (1990) describe such a program for essay development. Other packages such as *The Daedelus Integrated Writing System, Realtime Writer, Collaborative Writer, Writer's Helper, StorySpace, Aspects,* and *Prep Editor* began as teacher responses to a perceived need in their classrooms. Many of these packages share a social-personal ideology of the writing process that values interactions among student writers as well as the texts they produce (Eldred, 1989).

8.3. THE COMPUTER AS TOOL, DOORWAY, AND LINKAGE

Bernhardt (1993) notes that text itself is changing with technology, becoming situationally embedded, interactive, functionally mapped, modular, navigable, hierarchically embedded, spacious, graphically rich, and customizable. These changes in the nature of text may in turn affect the way writers perceive the texts which they produce. In many classes, the traditional essay is no longer the primary aim or the sole product. Students may produce a range of documents, from brief electronic

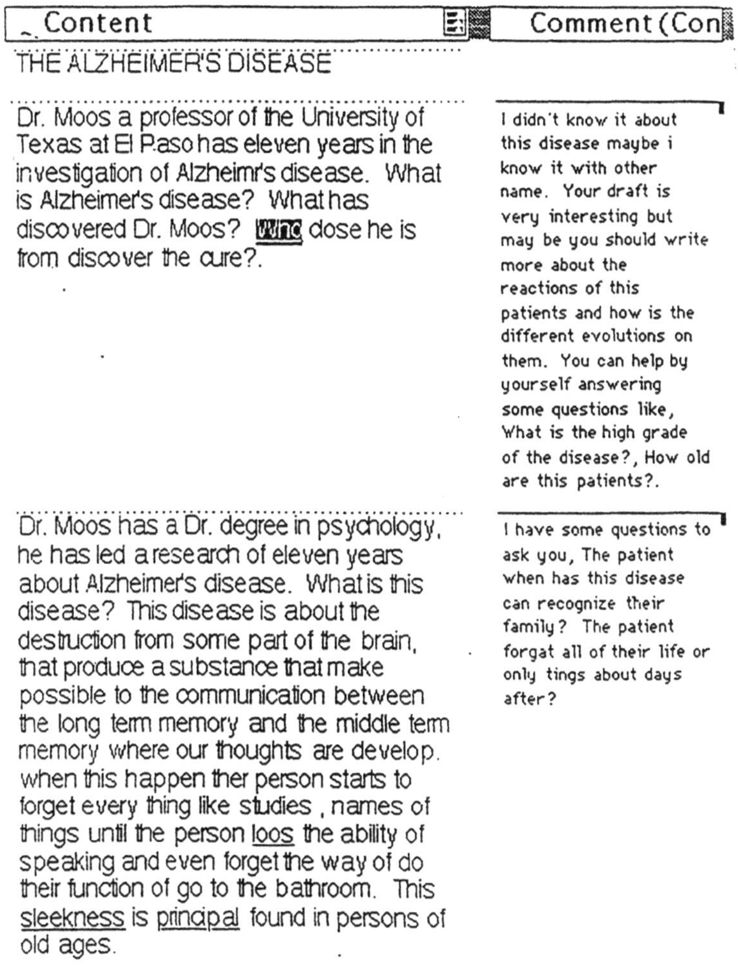

Content	Comment (Con
THE ALZHEIMER'S DISEASE	
Dr. Moos a professor of the University of Texas at El Paso has eleven years in the investigation of Alzheimr's disease. What is Alzheimer's disease? What has discovered Dr. Moos? **Why** close he is from discover the cure?.	I didn't know it about this disease maybe i know it with other name. Your draft is very interesting but may be you should write more about the reactions of this patients and how is the different evolutions on them. You can help by yourself answering some questions like, What is the high grade of the disease?, How old are this patients?.
Dr. Moos has a Dr. degree in psychology, he has led a research of eleven years about Alzheimer's disease. What is this disease? This disease is about the destruction from some part of the brain, that produce a substance that make possible to the communication between the long term memory and the middle term memory where our thoughts are develop. when this happen ther person starts to forget every thing like studies , names of things until the person loos the ability of speaking and even forget the way of do their function of go to the bathroom. This sleekness is principal found in persons of old ages.	I have some questions to ask you, The patient when has this disease can recognize their family? The patient forgat all of their life or only tings about days after?

Figure 8.1. Screen Shot of Prep Editor (Student comments on each paragraph)

mail notes to longer postings on a bulletin board, from hypertext documents with links and graphics to hypermedia packages including video and sound (Ashworth, this volume). The computer, more than a teaching method, is more properly viewed as a tool, a gateway for information, or a way to link teachers and learners, as discussed by Hoffman (this volume) and as explored further below.

8.3.1. Electronic Commenting

An important part of a process-oriented writing class involves getting a reader's comments on a text in progress. This aspect of process writing, known variously as peer feedback, peer response, or peer review, involves one or more students making comments on the content and organization of a draft. Comments are often generated using question heuristics (for examples, see Phinney, 1989, 1994; Schenk, 1988). The technique has been incorporated into some writing software (the *Daedelus* system is one example). Observations of students suggest that putting the heuristics on computer rather than on paper often elicits longer, more detailed comments.

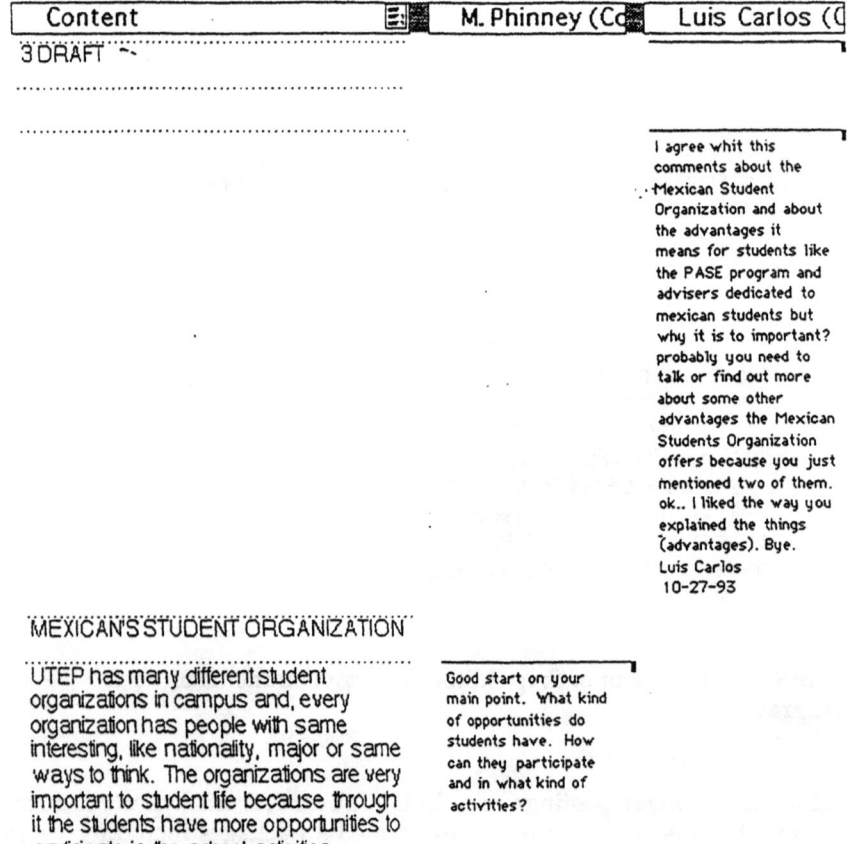

Figure 8.2. Screen Shot of Prep Editor (Student comments at beginning of paper)

I have also used *Prep Editor*, a package under development at Carnegie-Mellon University for collaborative writing, for commenting, and for reading logs. *Prep Editor* allows comments or revisions to be placed in a separate column linked to the main text (see Figure 8.1). While it was less successful for reading logs than I had hoped, I was surprised at the amount and quality of the comments students made on their partners' papers using the program. When they used heuristics written as questions on a piece of paper, they often made very general comments like "You need more detail". When using *Prep Editor*, they often made comments specific to a particular paragraph, as illustrated in Figure 8. 1, or an extended comment about the paper as a whole, as illustrated in Figure 8. 2. The comments made when prompted by *Prep Editor* seemed to be more specific, more detailed, and more on-task than those which students made when giving comments without the computer medium.

One of the advantages of the program is that the number of commenters is unlimited; each commenter can start a new linked comment column. Students can then look at all reviewers' comments together to plan revisions. Parts of the original text can be copied to the comment column to help the writer understand the reviewers' comments better. Students can also use the columns for alternative wordings, additional information, or revision notes. The program is well-suited for peer revision and for its original purpose of promoting collaboration among writers.

Many word processors now provide similar features. *WordPerfect*, for example, has always provided linked columns (parallel) in addition to the standard newspaper-style columns. Adding a new column in that program, however, is not as easy as in *Prep Editor*. Microsoft *Word* allows a variety of annotations to text, including voice in the Macintosh version. *Word for Windows* will compare two versions of a file and mark the differences (revisions) for review. These advanced features of word processors can help students and instructors enhance their processes of writing and the learning and teaching of writing.

8.3.2. Manipulation of Information

The use of electronic tools for writing and information gathering has also changed the tasks that students undertake in the classroom. The research paper, for example, is no longer simply a product of the resources available in the local library. With CD-ROM databases, knowledge bases, and the resources of the Internet, students can access information anywhere in the world (as also noted by Hoffman, this volume). Somehow, signing on to the Clinton White House is more intriguing than poring through the government documents section of the library.

Many of the commercially available knowledge bases have useful applications for the language classroom. Encyclopedias, simulations, timelines, or video and audio compilations can provide reading material, videos, audio clips, and photographs for writing prompts, research material, or supplementary listening practice. Search facilities such as *Gopher* or *Mosaic*, interfaces that help a user search different sites on the Internet, can make it easier for students to look through Internet databases for material. In addition, electronic mail allows students to connect with experts in their subject area to obtain first-hand knowledge.

When students who work with such applications are ready to put together the information they have gathered into their own unique synthesis, they are as likely to produce an electronic product as a paper product. Accessible authoring systems like *HyperCard*, *ToolBook*, and *HyperStudio* make it easier for both teachers and students to build their own software products, from information kiosks to electronic books. Recently, we experimented with electronic research products in place of the typical research paper in a second semester ESL writing class (Phinney and Khouri, 1992). Students had the option of producing a *ToolBook* application—which might include digitized sound, video, or still images—to present their argument instead of writing a traditional paper. The students who chose to do the electronic "paper" enjoyed it immensely. Although the mechanics were often more difficult, many spent more time on the project, appeared to be more involved in their product, and produced interesting, although relatively linear, hypertexts. With few exceptions, their documents were designed to be read from beginning to end, but almost all students included some links between sections and different types of information (text, pictures, graphics).

One of my technical writing classes produced an elaborate on-line information kiosk for international students, a project which has been updated by intermediate level writing students. The kiosk provides information about the campus, admissions, financial aid, and advising, with an elaborate map and directions to each building. The intermediate students added sections on student activities, organizations, and research activities, including video and photographs. Figure 8.3 shows a screen from the financial aid section of the kiosk.

Such projects can foster cooperative efforts, as students pool their energies and talents into a product or project that interests them (Susser, 1993). In the case of the information kiosk, students immediately saw the usefulness of the project. Perhaps more than any other task, the kiosk made them aware of audience needs (Phinney, 1993a). The students also discovered that they could contribute a real service to their fellow students and to the university. The group working on financial aid requirements found that they were the first to put all of the information on financial aid together in one package. They were justly proud of their efforts.

Products such as *HyperCard*, *ToolBook*, *StorySpace*, and *HyperStudio* make producing such applications relatively quick and easy for students. Students in groups will naturally divide up the tasks: one student often becomes the computer expert; another checks the language and grammar; a third takes care of pictures, video, or sound; and a fourth might conduct interviews to gather relevant first-hand accounts. Discussions about the project and the decision-making process are often conducted in the target language in a mixed language group; in groups

Exploring the Virtual World 147

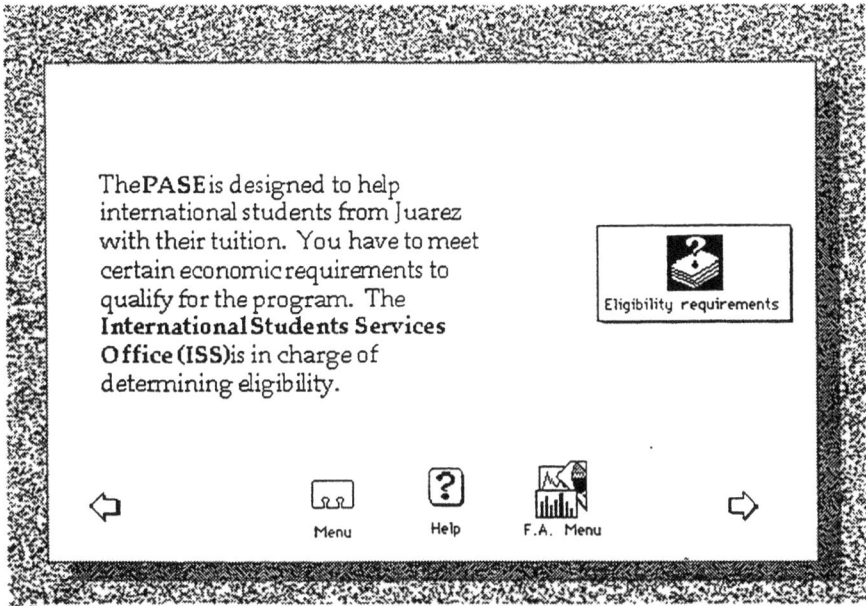

Figure 8.3. Screen Shot Of Collaborative Student-Produced Information Kiosk (HyperCard)

that share a native language, code-switching is common. The resulting combined effort is always greater than that which any single student could produce. These collaborative efforts help the students learn the skills they will need in the working world, where collaboration and team effort are the norm rather than the exception. They also allow individual students to develop a specific role or interest that they can contribute to the group.

8.3.3. Electronic Mail

Electronic mail has become the new "toy of choice" for many teachers who have discovered the Internet. Many teachers have tried to incorporate electronic mail into their writing classrooms in some way. In second language teaching, the most common use of electronic mail may be for pen pals (see discussion by Hoffman, this volume). Classes which share only the target language may be matched, or a second language class may be paired with a class of native speakers of the target language. In a basic pen pal activity, students write electronic messages to their pen pals much as they might write traditional letters. The difference, of course, is that mail is delivered almost immediately, so students can write many more letters than might be possible otherwise.

E-mail has a different rhetoric, including header information, emoticons (the special symbols used to indicate emotions, as illustrated

Handout: Using Music for Electronic Mail

On MemTel machines: Double-click "MUSIC" icon On Macintosh: Click "Documents" folder, then click "MUSIC" button.
At the UTEP screen:
   Press the TAB key twice and type d music
Press ENTER or RETURN twice.
When the cursor is on the login screen following /ID, type your MUSIC code (two letters and two numbers) and press ENTER. Then type your MUSIC password. You will not see it echoed on the screen.
If this is your first log-in, follow the directions to register your name and ID number. If you are an international student, type "4" instead of "D" in your number. MUSIC will not accept letters in IDs.
When you see *Go, type mail to enter the mail facility.
To read mail:
   Type 2 (Read and answer mail). When you see the list of your mail, type V to view each mail item.
To send mail:
   Type 1 (Create and send mail)
The first screen is an "envelope" screen. Type the e-mail address of the person you are writing to on the line marked "To". Make sure you type the address exactly!
   Press the TAB key to get to the "Subject" line. Type a phrase to indicate the topic of your mail.
   TAB to the "Copy To" line. Type your teacher's e-mail address if he or she requires you to send a copy of all your mail.
   Press ENTER to go to the editing screen. Write your letter. Use the TAB key instead of the ENTER key to go to the next line. When you finish your letter, make sure you sign it with your name and e-mail address. Press F5 and ENTER to send your mail.
Handy tips:
   When you are looking at your list of mail, V will let you view an item. D will delete it. C will copy it as a file to your directory in MUSIC. You will have to give it a file name.
   When you are viewing a mail item, F6 will delete it, F11 will skip it, F2 will let you answer it. You might want to delete your mail after you read it, especially if you have signed on to an electronic list.
   To get back from any screen, press F3.

Figure 8.4. Sample Instructional Handout For Electronic Mail

in Hoffman, this volume), and a style that lies somewhere between that of speech and writing (Hawisher and Moran, 1993). The mechanics of e-mail, including the sometimes arcane commands required by the mainframe installation, may prove to be a barrier for second language students at first. An instructional handout (Figure 8.4) may ease the transition, as may using the metaphor of paper mail such as "envelope" (the screen for the address), "address", and "letter". However, once they master the difficulties, students usually enjoy e-mail and wait eagerly for the responses.

More specific to writing courses, e-mail can make collaboration easier and may lead to more cross-disciplinary collaboration (Hawisher and Moran, 1993; Sirc and Reynolds, 1990). As Hoffman (this volume) has observed, students may find it easier to send messages to fellow students or their instructor rather than try to schedule a face-to-face interaction. Some instructors now hold an electronic "office space" in addition to or in lieu of traditional office hours.

Marx (1990) describes peer critiquing through a network and how it combines oral discourse and written communication. Such critiquing can be done synchronously or asynchronously (see Hoffman, this volume, for discussion of these types of communication) through a discussion program like *Daedelus* Interchange or Internet *Relay Chat* (IRC). Marx's students, working synchronously on a network, showed a growing sensitivity to audience; the distance ironically led to closer communication.

8.3.4. Synchronous "Chat" or Discussion

One of the major benefits of a networked writing class can be found in synchronous discussion. Sometimes called "chat" (as in Internet Relay Chat, IRC), synchronous discussion allows writers to conduct a discussion through the keyboard. Their comments can be read at almost real-time speed by other participants, who can then respond (for details, see Hoffman, this volume).

For second language students, synchronous discussion has several advantages. Students can take time to frame their responses, allowing those who are less fluent orally to catch up with the fast talkers. In such discussions, more students can and most likely will contribute to the discussion (Phinney, 1992; Wusnack and Strongman, 1993). Compare this with an oral discussion in class, which is likely to involve a smaller percentage of the group with a few individuals dominating the session (Hoffman, this volume). Batson (1993, p. 15) points out that more students will participate in an on-line classroom because several students can be writing their contributions at the same time. When working in a networked class, instructors may have to give up some of their accustomed authority as they become simply another voice on the net (Kremers, 1990).

Some second language students may view the electronic discussion as more "academic" than an oral discussion and thus may be more likely to stay on task or stick to the target language. Figure 8.5 shows a partial transcript of such a session with advanced ESL students. While there is

G.O. : I think that Meg Greenfield believes that the animals should be treated better, but she doesn't accept the methods the activist use.

F.L..: The only justification is use animals for medical progress.

R.G.: [J.C.]H: What I'm assuming? Because my assumptions are what we mostly think.

G.O. : Very funny "Poli"

M.P.: The writter is expressing his concern towards the right that these companies and laboratoreis have to do these types of experiments, since they are in his mind innevetable for the salvation of the human race. They are medical experiments, concerning various sicknesses such as for the heart, lungs, and viruses. He says that the "Animal Rights Movement" is more of a political non-sence than real concern for th animals, and that they do more bad then good.

J.C.H.: J[A.]. Ok Now I get your point, even though there are two issues involved.

L.O.: B[.M.]: But what about rats, they are ugly and usually they put the cat's and dog's eyes away. I once had a litte dog, his name was Kasan and he was a Pug, pug is the kind. Any way his eyes were like "canicas" because that is the way that pug's eyes look like. And one day a desgusting rat put his eye away. Isn't that sad. You should have seen it, he looked so ugly, but oh well.

P.B.: E[.S.]: According to this essay, you are in favor of the animals sacrifices, or just for medical experiments?, please explain more O.K.?

L.R.: The difference between animal experimentation for health reasons and experimentation for cosmetics is that animals are necessary to find some kind of cure for some diseases like cancer and for cosmetics reasons is not justified.

R.G.: [J.C.]H: Aren't they neccesary for our existence? Don't we eat meat and use leather shoes and jackets

E.V.: I think that animals can be tested to find a cure for disease, not for thinks like hairspray, wich are considered not to be a neccesity.

J.C.H.: L[.O.]: I think that your example is completely irrelevant. I agree with B.M. [who responded previously]

Figure 8.5. Partial Transcript Of Daedelus Interchange Discussion in an Advanced University ESL Class

some off-task discussion, the transcript shows a remarkably focused class, with little instructor intervention. The discussion remains in English, and at least one student (E.V.) participated who rarely spoke up in oral discussions. Two students, R.G. and J.C.H., were conducting a private argument on the topic.

A recent analysis of electronic transcripts (Wusnack and Strongman, 1993) indicated that students made a clear distinction between on-and off-task discourse, using the target language (English) for on-task discourse and reserving the home language (Spanish) for off-task discourse. This distinction was so strongly felt by the class that even non-Spanish speakers used Spanish for personal off-task comments, apparently getting help from their Spanish-speaking classmates. When compared with face-to-face discussion (Wusnack and Strongman, 1993), the electronic environment led to more on-task discourse in the target languages, whether the instructor was physically present or not. In a face-to-face environment, the absence of the instructor decreased the amount of talk and led to less on-task discussion and much less use of the target language.

8.4. THE IMPACT OF THE COMPUTER ON SECOND LANGUAGE WRITING

The electronic writing classroom has changed and will continue to change the perception and the practice of writing in both first and second languages. In an electronic classroom, students can interact with each other and with the instructor in both written and oral modes, both synchronously and asynchronously. For those students who are less dominant in the classroom, an electronic discussion may allow them to participate at their own pace without having to interrupt or to wait for another student to finish. While such an effect has not been documented, it is conceivable that the freedom of communication that they experience in an electronic discussion may help students to participate more fully in oral discussions off-line. Certainly, more students produce more language in an electronic discussion than in many classroom contexts, and that is all to the good.

In developing an effective pedagogy for using computers in the writing class, we not only must adjust our teaching focus, but also must recognize the variety of adaptations that individual students make to the technology and to their writing process in a computer environment (Kozma, 1991; Pennington, 1993b; Rodrigues and Rodrigues, 1989). Because of the time it takes for them to adapt their attitudes and behavior to the machine environment, students may need several weeks or months of exposure before they reach an adequate comfort level. Depending on their writing experience and language proficiency, students may need different types of software to make an effective use of the computer (Kozma, 1991). Novice writers may need software that explicitly models the writing process, while advanced students may be able to handle more free-form computer writing tools such as "plain" word processors. While the interface in most educational settings may not be a matter of choice, both the keyboard and the mouse can still be a formidable challenge or barrier to some users. In addition, menus in the second language may be more of a hindrance than a help for non-native writers; the advent of multilingual operating systems on Macintosh and Amiga computers may ease the transition to computers and to writing in a second language. On the other hand, modern word processors such as *WordPerfect* or Microsoft *Word* do so much that students may feel overwhelmed.

For students and instructors who have limited time for conferencing, electronic commenting and conferencing may lead to more and longer interactions. Tillyer (1993) has reported that her students make great strides in the quality and quantity of their messages to her when they write them by computer means and communicate them electronically. Like Hoffman (this volume), I have found that my students enjoy what they perceive to be more personal contact and will write me short notes on e-mail to address questions or problems they would not normally bring up in class. I also prefer journal submissions on disk or by e-mail: I find them easier to read, they do not weigh as much as paper notebooks, and I am more likely to respond at greater length to journal entries electronically.

If a class can set up a paper directory on the network, commenting and revising need not take up class time. Students can log in to the network whenever it is convenient for them in order to comment on their classmates' papers. This way of working may free up class time for discussion of the comments and for planning revision. In fact, an electronic writing classroom tends to be less structured than many traditional classrooms, with students in various stages of composing and revising, working on different personally determined schedules.

Most importantly, the variety of "documents" my students have made using the computer has engaged their interest, motivated them to use the second language (English) outside the classroom, and helped them to learn the cooperative skills they will need in the working world. Many of the ESL students I have worked with, who are mainly Spanish speakers, prefer working in groups. Together, they can develop a document or a product that is far superior to what one student can produce alone.

These students are able to develop negotiating skills to work within their group. They also must interact with native speakers on campus to collect the information they need for their projects. Finally, they are able to organize the information and present it in a way that is quite different from the standard essay. Through the process, they become more aware of audience needs and authorial voice.

8.5. CONCLUDING REMARKS TO CHAPTER 8

More than classroom publishing, "electronic publishing" can be developed for a real audience; it costs next to nothing to leave students' *HyperCard* stacks, *ToolBooks*, or electronic books on the system for other students to use. In the electronic sharing and co-production of multimedia products—more than any other aspect—computers have changed the way we teach writing and the way our students approach the writing process in their second language.

9. Computer-Assisted Development of Spoken Language Skills

Martha C. Pennington and John H. Esling

9.1. INTRODUCTION

Since its widespread appearance in educational contexts in the 1970's, the computer has been more associated with applications in the area of written language—comprising reading, writing, and the associated grammatical and lexical knowledge—than spoken language—comprising pronunciation and speaking skills. Nevertheless, since that time, many in applied linguistics and education have realized the potential of the computer medium for the spoken language curriculum in a range of applications of the available technology to achieve a variety of purposes in language learning. Among these applications are those which provide (1) speech analysis and training in phonology; (2) speech output, video, and hypermedia enhancements to reinforce language learning activities; and (3) activities which offer a focus for discussion by students working at the computer in pairs or small groups. While the technology is available for a range of useful applications in the spoken language curriculum and research has been conducted to test many of these, there is nevertheless a need for research and development to clarify the ways in which the computer medium is most usefully applied and its capabilities most effectively exploited in the acquisition of spoken language skills (Pennington and Stevens, 1992).

In this chapter, we begin by characterizing the nature of spoken language competence and the types of spoken language work that are possible as implicit or explicit pedagogical input. We then go on to describe the technological status quo for work on spoken language, the available systems, and some research conducted on these. Through this discussion, we are able to show the ways in which the computer most effectively supports the development of both mechanical and meaningful aspects of spoken language and, in the final section, to plot new directions for pedagogy, research, and development of computers in the spoken language curriculum.

9.2. SPOKEN LANGUAGE COMPETENCE

Spoken language competence, or what is generally referred to as "communicative competence", comprises many different aspects of linguistic performance, taken broadly to include both comprehension and production of speech. As described in Pennington (1989a), spoken language competence has both a "mechanical" aspect and a "meaningful" aspect. The mechanical aspect of speech involves learning to discriminate and produce the sounds of a language and to tie these together prosodically in fluent strings of sounds comprising syllables, words, phrases, and longer utterances. The meaningful aspect involves learning to build as well as to decompose grammatically coherent utterances and to tie these to communicative functions according to rules of pragmatic appropriateness in a given speech community.

The mechanical aspect of speech comprises the articulation and decoding of individual sounds (phonemes) as well as the production and comprehension of fluent stretches of speech. It therefore requires a knowledge of the ways in which sounds are linked in running speech and of the suprasegmental properties of stretches of speech involving such features as pitch, tone, rhythm, stress, and voice quality (Pennington, 1989b). A deep knowledge of phonology entails, moreover, an understanding of the links between these mechanical features and the meanings that are conveyed by a certain style of pronunciation, "accent", or voice quality. It furthermore means being able to link the decoding process in listening with the articulation process in speaking to form a cross-referenced system for interpreting and producing speech.

An important distinction of relevance to the development of spoken language proficiency is that between so-called "free conversation", termed "chat" or "interactional language" by Brown and Yule (1983) and classified as "pre-generic" discourse by Swales (1990), and "transactional language" (Brown and Yule, 1983) or "generic" discourse (Swales, 1990). While the former is essentially open-ended, loosely structured, and unpredictable in terms of topics, the latter is a structured form of language built on certain topical areas and linguistic conventions for the organization of text to achieve certain purposes. In learning a language, a speaker must acquire the competence for fluent production and the give and take that is conversation as well as mastering the topical lexis and grammatical and rhetorical structures of specific genres and types of transactions.

The essentially unstructured discourse of conversation, chat, or interactional language differs from the essentially structured discourse of generic or transactional language in being listener-oriented and in being highly situated and dependent for its interpretation on the extralinguistic context (e.g., prior knowledge of speakers, visual context). It is thus a type of "context-embedded" (Cummins, 1983) or "contexted" language in which interactants invoke different types and levels of shared context through a variety of signals or discourse markers

(Schiffrin, 1987). In contrast, generic or transactional language, which comprises the message-oriented discourse associated with a certain field, topical area, or task, is essentially "decontexted" or "context-reduced" (Cummins, 1983). In contrast to the implicitness of conversational discourse and the continuous signalling of shared knowledge of context in this highly interactional form of language, the more explicit form of transactional or generic discourse does not assume the availability of external context to interpret language. Rather, the latter type of discourse provides its own context within the discourse itself, following relatively predictable patterns of development and making use of specific lexis associated with a given topic.

While competence in both of these forms of language requires the development of skilled behavior to produce fluent and understandable stretches of speech, and while speaking often involves a combination of both types, one embedded within the other, they nevertheless also presuppose different types of knowledge and skills. Because much of the meaning of the discourse is not available in the speech signal itself but is rather a matter of interpreting the relationship of explicit signals to implicit information, competence in conversation requires a global and relatively abstract focus of attention coupled with strong inferencing and signalling skills of various types. Competence in the more explicit forms of discourse demands close attention to linguistic detail such as grammatical markers and exact meaning and places heavier demands in terms of speakers' knowledge of content, including the lexis, syntax, and rhetorical patterns associated with specific linguistic tasks and functions.

As we will see below, the computer in various applications may be especially useful for improving the fluency and accuracy of speech in the mechanical dimension of spoken language and for developing competence in discourse genres and topical areas in the meaningful dimension, while having less immediate utility for developing language through the negotiated interaction process of conversational discourse. At the same time, electronic mail and interactive networks may to some extent fill this gap in providing a simulated, or virtual, conversational environment which, though decontexted in terms of some normal situational features of conversation such as voice and visual contact of participants, provides new contextual features which stimulate and develop conversation-like written discourse and which might have a carryover to spoken language.

9.3. INPUT TYPES FOR LEARNING

As discussed in Pennington (in press, c, d), input which is of different types and which is provided at different stages in the learning process can be of value in helping learners to develop spoken language skills in mechanical and meaningful dimensions. The figure below shows the different types, each of which is relevant to spoken language applications on computer.

1. **Pre-Production**	2. **In-Production**	3. **Post-Production**
Stimulation	Stimulation	Review
Familiarization	Monitoring	Feedback
Rehearsal	Negotiation	Correction
Training	Feedback	
	Adjustment	

Figure 9.1. Input Types

Pre-production input is that which helps the learner prepare for a subsequent spoken language task by stimulating attention and/or learning, familiarizing the learner with relevant task characteristics or background information, or rehearsing or training performance in some way. Such input might be of a "receptive" type, i.e., for sharpening perception, developing vocabulary, previewing content, preparing structure, overviewing organization, modeling a task, or otherwise increasing the learner's receptivity to and preparation for what is to come. Or it might be of a "productive" type which prepares the learner to speak by relaxation exercises (as in drama training), mechanical exercises of the vocal organs (as in vocal training for singers), or rehearsal of lexis and syntax by mechanical practice (e.g., repetition or reading aloud of lexical items or sample constructions).

In-production input is a kind of in-progress stimulation or "formative" assessment that offers practice opportunities and ongoing feedback to adjust performance accordingly. In-production input may be of a type which stimulates the learner to perform or to perform in a certain way. When a learner monitors his/her own production while it is occurring, this is also a type of in-production input. Input which is negotiated with other speakers is another form of in-progress feedback which is of value for language learners, as is communicative feedback from an interactional partner indicating whether or not the message has been received as intended. Self-made or other-offered adjustments of performance during interaction are a final type of in-production information that assists learning.

Post-production input is for the purposes of review and post-hoc feedback, for reflection and contemplation on performance. Post-production feedback may involve explicit work to correct habitual errors or to bring these to the learner's attention for self-correction.

The computer technology related to spoken language development offers myriad opportunities for the pre-production, in-production, and post-production development and modification of spoken language skills. As yet, there are no commercially available applications, as far as we are aware, which offer all three types of input, making full use of the available technology and implementing a specific theoretical or pedagogical model of the development of speaking skills in a computer-assisted environment, for comprehensive training of spoken language in one system. However, several new initiatives (e.g., as described by Goh, 1993; Hiller, Rooney, Laver, and Jack, 1993; Jones, 1995; Price and Imbier, 1993; Rochet, 1992) lay the groundwork for such systems and point in promising directions for the future.

9.4. TECHNOLOGY AND PEDAGOGY

The computer is a promising medium for increasing the salience, the authenticity, and the variety of input to language learners. The computer makes possible presentation of speech coordinated with written text or with other visuals on a computer screen. The simplest system is one which synchronizes the recording and/or the playing of audiotaped speech with computer text. Such systems have been used in instructional contexts for training or testing purposes to coordinate spoken productions of lexical items, sentences, or discourses with their written transcriptions appearing on the computer screen. Common uses of this capability are for listening cloze and audio reinforcement of vocabulary or illustrations of grammatical structures.

In addition to these "low-tech" speech enhancements of computerized language instruction, software and hardware for converting English text to speech is available for the microcomputer.[1] However, the available software for voice output varies in quality. While some voice output is nearly indistinguishable from a recorded human voice, other speech output systems produce a voice with a mechanical quality that can be difficult for language learners to understand. Although such devices have novelty value and may stimulate play, chat, or discussion around the computer, they may not be of great value for training spoken language by computer means. Most of the systems which have paid relatively minimal attention to the quality of the "computer voice" are not in fact designed for the purposes of training spoken language or listening comprehension.

Because storage of the highest quality digitized speech takes a great deal of computer memory, it is not always possible to offer such high quality when the program is directed primarily at other purposes. For example, talking word processors, which provide speech output to match what is being typed on the keyboard and appears on the computer screen, do not make use of the most memory-intensive form of computer storage for their output of speech. Rather than storing speech which has been converted into digital form—an extremely memory-hungry form of storage—what is stored in these simpler systems is rules for synthesizing speech from text input at the keyboard. In some software, the computer can produce relatively natural speech from individual phonemes stored as digital codes which are then strung together by rule as the user types on the keyboard (Ciarcia, 1984). The amount of memory used depends on the complexity of the stored speech and the rules for text-to-speech conversion. In synthesis-by-rule, the conversion can be done reasonably well while still leaving plenty of memory to carry out other tasks, such as word processing. Synthesis-by-rule has the added advantage that it can convert any text to speech, whereas digitized speech allows for retrieval only of the speech that was originally input.

The method of "linear predictive coding" offers a compromise between the two alternatives of digitization and synthesis-by-rule. This process is memory-efficient yet produces a relatively natural-sounding voice and highly intelligible speech. It is a process whereby selected portions of recorded speech are stored and then analyzed by a computer-derived rule which generates the whole from the stored portion. Thus, only a portion of the original quantity of speech, along with the analysis rule, needs to be stored. However, as in the case of digitized speech, a linear predictive coding approach to speech storage and output does not allow for the open-ended, i.e., unpredictable, output of authentic linguistic production, as in the creative act of composing or—if the computer were to really have its own voice—of speaking.

Each of these methods of allying a speech component to the computer requires additional equipment, or hardware. Since naturally produced sound waves are of an analog type, whereas computer storage must be in digital code, both analog-to-digital and digital-to-analog converters are required for digitizing, storing, and then playing back digitized speech. For linear predictive coding, special analysis and compression software and hardware are required, and synthesized speech requires special software to make conversions as well.

Other than computer applications with speech output, there are on the market today a range of affordable systems for speech analysis on the microcomputer.[2] Several computerized systems are able to perform a phonological analysis of running speech for suprasegmental measures such as fundamental frequency (roughly equivalent to pitch) and intensity (roughly equivalent to stress) as well as for segmental features and to display these as a contour or other type of visual graphic. With a slight delay, additional analysis, e.g., in terms of a spectrographic display, is possible. As Goh (1993) notes, speech analysis is extremely memory-demanding, so that a math co-processor is recommended to speed analysis time. Advances in storage technology, and the increasing availability of this technology, are rapidly solving the memory problem surrounding speech output in a computer environment.

Some computerized speech analysis systems have been designed to remediate speech or hearing problems, while others are geared for application by linguists in phonetic analysis or training.[3] Since the 1970's, those working with second and foreign language learners have realized the utility of speech analysis software and the associated visual displays for training the production and perception of a second language, and some software has been designed explicitly for use with non-native speakers of English and other languages.

Software and hardware is currently available that allows a user to digitize any audio source, compress it, edit it, and add it to a HyperCard stack. Some systems allow control by the user of such features as volume, pitch, and tempo of the speaker whose voice is stored. Some computer hardware, as Ashworth (this volume) reports, allows verbal commands to be stored in place of menu commands. Where speech analysis software is based only on native speaker or standard accents, such a capability could be used, as Ashworth (this volume) suggests, to encourage non-native users to adjust their pronunciation toward the model which the computer "understands". Other uses of computer speech analysis for training pronunciation are explored below.

The possibility of storing speech and having it analyzed by the computer suggests other options for applications of electronic media in language teaching. As detailed by Ashworth (this volume), CD-ROM makes possible the storage of large and diverse forms of information in databases that can be accessed for speaking and listening practice, including the digitized speech samples of the phonetic databases developed at the University of Victoria (Esling, 1987b, 1987c, 1990, 1991b, 1992a, 1993, 1994b) and at Carnegie Mellon University (Jones, 1995). As explored more fully below, students may compare their own speech characteristics to that of a pre-recorded or stored, digitized speech sample for purposes of evaluation and feedback. They may also manipulate and analyze stored speech samples in various ways, e.g., as in the suggestions of Price (1992) and Price and Imbier (1993). In addition, speech output can be tied to other skill activities such as reading (Tuman, 1992) or writing (Daiute, 1992). Tying speech to other informational modalities may make communication of ideas easier and more effective for some learners, particularly weaker ones.

Besides the computer's capability of analyzing or reproducing speech, the various types of structured and motivating learning environments created within the electronic medium often serve as a catalyst for speaking that may promote language development. When two or more students work together at a computer terminal, the characteristics of the medium generally stimulate some sort of interaction. Though the particular attributes of individual programs and the type of speech they elicit vary considerably, it does appear that a computer environment makes input to learners more accessible (Pennington, 1986, 1991d), in the sense of being more salient and hence easier to notice, to understand, to remember, and to integrate into the learner's developing language system. In addition, the computer medium offers learners information in a very wide range of forms and formats to support and contextualize interaction.

9.5. COMPUTER APPLICATIONS IN THE SPEAKING CURRICULUM

The available computer-based systems of value for spoken language development include those which analyze and train suprasegmental and segmental phonology and those which marry speech output, videodisc, or hypermedia to some other type of CALL presentation. In fact, virtually any type of software when used by students in pairs or small groups can be employed to stimulate, focus, and structure their language as a goal-directed or problem-solving discussion. In what follows, each of these ways of applying computer technology to the development of language is discussed, with a focus on applications in the second language speaking (and by extension, listening) curriculum.

9.5.1. Phonology

The computer can provide various types of visual input to model or supplement audio input. Besides graphics to represent aspects of sound waves, it can also make use of any type of creative graphic or textual stimulus which encourages and/or provides feedback on accuracy of performance as the learner tries to match a pronunciation target.

Drawing on a classic article by Abberton and Fourcin (1975, pp. 158-159) about the requirements of computer-generated visual feedback on intonation, one can posit the following desirable features for systems offering a visual graphic display derived from a computer-generated analysis of speech input to the computer by a user live or via audiotape:

> (1) Clear and interpretable visual image without too much complexity or detail in display
>
> (2) Real-time feedback
>
> (3) An indication in the display of the user's input in relation to the baseline or the essential parameters for target performance
>
> (4) Inexpensive, reliable, and easy-to-operate equipment

Condition (1) is obviously an important one for the feedback to be of value to the (naive) learner. Complex spectrographic or oscilloscopic displays, which can only be read by trained phoneticians, provide too much information for the learner to attend to and interpret. Much of the phonetic software on the market today is based on simplified waveforms or models of articulatory space. At the same time, attention is starting to be paid to more creative ways of visualizing aspects of pronunciation and motivating performance. Thus, software available for use with the Kay Elemetrics Visi-Pitch machine (see next section) incorporates game-like and challenge features to make it motivating for a student to try to achieve a pronunciation target—e.g., controlling an animal to run a race, to reach fruit on a tree, or to avoid obstacles in its path by varying vocal pitch, intensity, or amount of voicing (e.g., if the student has difficulty producing a distinction between the voiced and voiceless stop consonants, /b,p/, /d,t/, /g,k/).

The second feature, that of immediate or real-time feedback, may not be as essential as was once thought, as long as feedback is not delayed for long. Weltens and de Bot (1984) have shown that the feedback need not be real-time to be effective but may be delayed slightly—a quarter of a second or even until just after the utterance has been completed—giving ample time for speech equipment to perform an analysis.

In relation to point (3), in fact, the display of performance, to be useful, need not be based on the learner's own speech—just as a concordance of someone else's text can provide valuable information to a language learner (Flowerdew, this volume). Any two visual representations of speech input shown together in the same display—e.g., displays of the same utterance as spoken by native speakers of two different varieties of the target language—will have contrastive value, especially if the computer user can also hear the two stretches of speech which are the basis of the screen display. Or, rather than a representation of a baseline generated by a native speaker, as is commonly employed in the training of the prosodic features of speech, the display may represent the user's own variable output in two different utterances. The learner may then decide which of the utterances is better—or which one he/she prefers—on the basis of its sound or appearance on the screen (i.e., in comparison to the auditory or visual target which the learner has previously internalized).

Through digitized speech samples, videodiscs, or CD-ROM speech databases, learners can be provided with a range of models of English phonology which they can analyze themselves using speech analysis equipment. In this way, users can gain exposure to a diversity and quantity of input on the basis of which they can develop their own targets for English sounds, gradually, through a variety of models, on the principle of "collection", not "correction", of sounds (Esling, 1987a, p. 469). As Esling (1987a) maintains, "attempting to teach students to sound exactly like one particular group as opposed to another is counterproductive, and not consistent with the need to provide as much input as possible in order for cognitive processes [of the learner] to select modes of performance that are appropriate for the individual learner" (pp. 468-469).

With respect to point (4), the price of computer speech analysis equipment is definitely going down, but much of it is still beyond the means of the ordinary student or "casual" computer user. As to reliability, speech analysis technology is relatively reliable for some kinds of voices (e.g., those which are reasonably loud and fully voiced; it is less reliable for soft, or weak voices, or for those of speakers who devoice to a considerable degree. Regarding ease of operation, the newest technology is very easy to use; the basic usage can be mastered in 15-30 minutes.

Suprasegmental Phonology

Systems for training suprasegmental phonology (Chun, 1989; Hiller, Rooney, Laver, Jack, 1993; Lefèvre, Hiller, Rooney, Laver, and Di Benedetto, 1992; Pennington, 1989a, 1991b) offer the user visual displays of simplified waveforms, fundamental frequency (pitch), intensity, duration, and location of pauses. One well-known system, the Kay Elemetrics Visi-Pitch, can analyze prerecorded or running speech spoken "live" into a microphone. The user can view the pitch or intensity of the voice as a continuous display or "freeze" an analyzed segment of speech for review and reflection. The pitch and intensity displays can be viewed separately or together on one screen, and in whole-screen or split-screen mode. In split-screen mode, it is possible to store and to analyze one utterance on one channel and to display its pitch or intensity contour on one half of the screen, then store and analyze another utterance and display its pitch and/or intensity contour on the other half of the screen.

A learner may compare his/her utterance with that of a previously stored one, which may be, for example, that of a teacher or other native speaker, the utterance of another learner, or an earlier performance by the same learner. In this way, learners can gain access to a model which they attempt to match in their own performance, pairs of learners can compare their performance as a basis for metacognitive learning, or individual learners can assess their own improvement or variation in performance. Figure 9.2 illustrates the Visi-Pitch split-screen mode for pitch alone, and Figure 9.3 shows the split-screen mode for pitch and intensity displayed together on one screen.

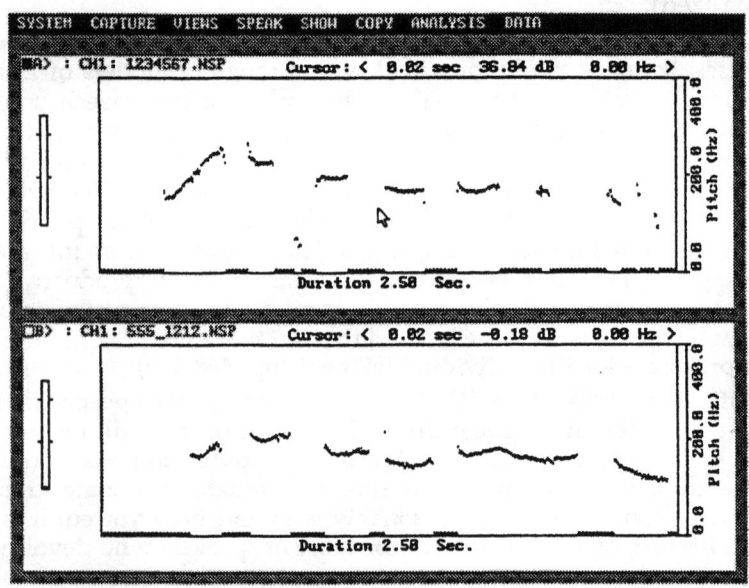

Figure 9.2. Double-screen Visi-Pitch Display after Real-time Input of Two Number Sequences

The analysis also provides for measurements of duration in the portion of an utterance which is displayed on the screen or of any part of that utterance. Such measurements help the user, for example, to note the rhythm of an utterance as made up of longer and shorter segments surrounded by pauses of varying lengths. The Visi-Pitch machine also allows measurements of pitch and intensity to be taken of the contour overall as well as of its individual segments. Thus, the user may compare the average pitch or intensity in one utterance with another or compare two points in the pitch or intensity contours within one utterance or across two different utterances—e.g., in split-screen mode. In addition, the software calculates the percentage of the utterance or any part of it that is voiced (i.e., with vibrating vocal cords), voiceless (i.e., without vocal cord vibration), or silent.

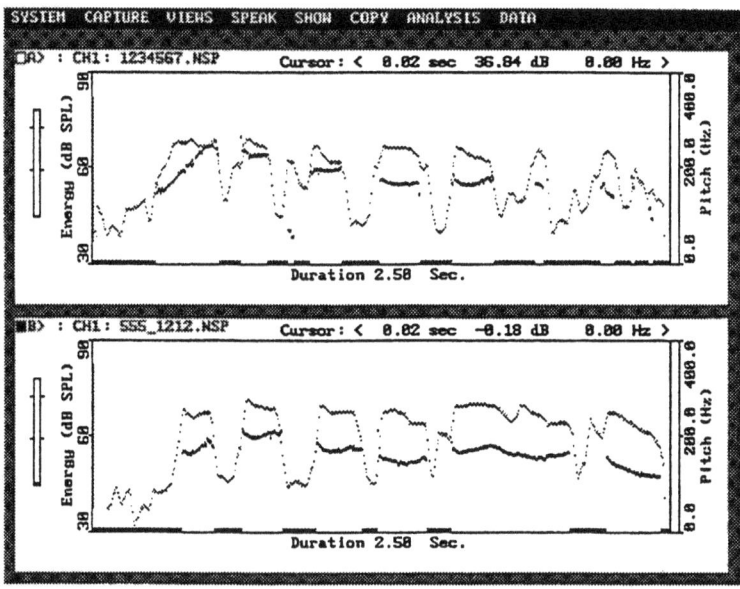

Figure 9.3. Double-screen Visi-Pitch Displays of the Number Sequences Showing Both Pitch (Dark Line) and Intensity (Light Line)

While such comparisons have obvious value for research (see below and Pennington, 1991b, for discussion), they also have pedagogical value in helping learners to pinpoint and to develop an understanding of the characteristics of their own language and the ways in which their speech differs from that of others. Such intellectualization and conscious comparison may be especially valuable for older learners, who often feel more secure and in fact make greater progress when they can reflect metacognitively on their language learning.

It may be useful, for example, to illustrate the rhythmic and intonational properties of English with the combined intensity and pitch display in Figure 9.3. The top view is a counting sequence from one to seven. The bottom view is a telephone number. In the counting sequence, loudness remains about the same while pitch (the dark line) declines over the whole utterance until the last two syllables (the tonic of the phrase), which show the phrase-final drop in pitch down to creaky voice that is characteristic of English. In the telephone number, the breaks in the rhythmic pattern come not after the '555' or the '12' but rather in sets of two-syllable rhythmic feet, with the last number (the tonic) showing the phrase-final lengthening and falling pitch which is characteristic of English. These rhythmic and intonational relationships within spoken English have been pointed out by Brown (1990).

Software is also available for use with the Visi-Pitch machine which does not display pitch, intensity, or voicing directly but which rather analyzes the user's utterance as input to a program which responds to pitch or intensity level to produce a different kind of visual display related to a goal. For example, as the user's pitch rises or falls, a giraffe's neck grows longer or shorter in order to reach apples hanging on trees which are located in different areas of the screen. Or, increased voicing makes one turtle move ahead of another in a race, while decreased voicing makes the other racing turtle forge ahead.

The Visi-Pitch is just one example with which the authors are familiar of computerized systems for analyzing and displaying characteristics of speech waves. Other well-known systems are MacSpeech Lab (GW Instruments) and Signalize (Infosignal). As reviewed in Read, Buder, and Kent (1992), these systems differ mainly in processing speed, memory size, and type of spectrographic analysis performed.

De Cheveigne, Abe, and Doshita (1985) describe a speech work station which functions in "flow" (real-time input and display) and "freeze" (data manipulation) mode. In "freeze" mode, the user can "browse through the frozen speech data" (p. 24). Like other speech analysis systems such as some of those described by Read, Buder, and Kent (1990, 1992) in their review, a cursor can be used to define a fixed point, bring it to the center of the display, then expand or shrink the part of the waveform surrounding that point to develop a visual focus.

Such technology provides a milieu for displaying, training, and testing the prosodic or suprasegmental aspects of speech in a visually appealing and useful manner. However, this type of system has the limitation of not offering information about whether the user's imperfect attempts at imitation are "true misses", "near misses", or non-significant variation. The basic problem is the lack of a theory of intonational variation which includes non-native performance and which can therefore be applied to a machine-generated analysis to supply feedback to non-native users.

At the very least, information can be supplied that makes an overall analysis of one contour in comparison to another. While the various systems available calculate the difference between two contours in terms of such measures as average pitch, intensity, voicing, and silent periods, they give no indication of what the average amount or type of variability is. Analysis of the prosodic characteristics of speech in databases that include samples from native and non-native speakers would provide much-needed baseline information towards the development of realistic learning programs for mastering the prosodic aspects of speech.

A new system in development, SPELL (Hiller, Rooney, and Jack, 1993), aims to remedy many of these problems. In particular, it is designed to compare a user's pronunciation with that of a stored target based on linguistic analyses derived from theoretical linguistics and from a database of native speaker productions. The prototype system includes modules for intonation and rhythm, as well as for vowels (see below) in English, French, and Italian. Using the SPELL system, a user receives simplified, user-friendly visual and textual feedback on performance, which can also be matched to a target contour displayed in a "teacher window".

The intonation program has been field-tested
> as a complete teaching module, which included courseware for teaching a single intonation contour ... [in] four phases: *Demonstrate*, in which audible demonstrations with various utterances are used to highlight the pronunciation features of interest; *Evaluate Listening*, where small tests are completed by the student to evaluate his/her ability to perceive those features reliably; *Teach*, in which students practice the pronunciation features of interest, with quantitative feedback for the student and directions for modifying inadequate performance; and *Assess*, in which a formal evaluation of the student's ability to pronounce and generalise the features is made. (Hiller, Rooney, and Jack, 1993, p. 471)

Although the evaluation of the intonation module indicated that "the demonstrator as it stands is not ready to be used as an autonomous teaching system" (Hiller, Rooney, and Jack, 1993, p. 472), the developers envision that SPELL will eventually be practicable as a self-teaching system.

Segmental Phonology

Not only the suprasegmental but also the segmental aspects of speech can be analyzed, trained, and tested by computer means. For example, the Kay Elemetrics Sona-Match is a device which can analyze the user's vowel productions and display them in a vowel chart, as in Figure 9.4. It can also show a vowel's spectral properties (its intensity at various frequencies), match this to stored vowel targets, and indicate the nearest vowel, as in Figure 9.5. The reference targets can be changed or retrained at any time—e.g., by the teacher, another native speaker, or a learner—for purposes of comparison, to note degree of difference, variation, or changes over time for training, testing, or "consciousness raising" purposes.

Beyond the possibility of such analysis and comparison of vowel productions, Rochet (1992) describes a system which uses Hypercard on the Macintosh to train a particular vowel distinction—that between French /ü/ and /u/ for English speakers. His system is designed to train

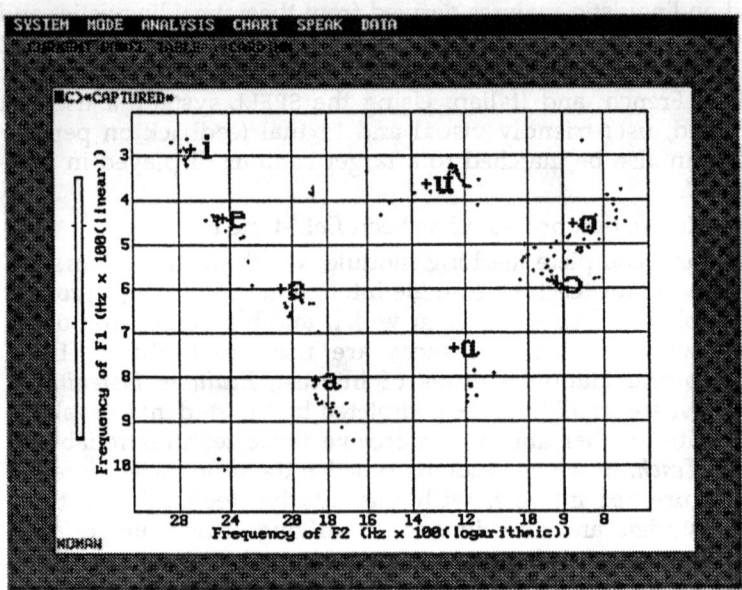

Figure 9.4. Sona-Match Display of Vowel Targets as Drawn in Real Time on a Prespecified Back

first the most central representatives, or "exemplars", of the /ü/ phoneme, then the more peripheral targets, only later adding "distractors" representing typical errors made by English speakers learning French. In the system, learners can access programs to (1) familiarize them with the target sounds and help them to discriminate /ü/ and /u/, (2) distinguish the target sounds from errors and to recognize errors as deviations from the target, and (3) differentiate between sounds representing the typical errors of their own native language (English) group and the correct second language (French) sounds. These programs may be accessed in tutorial, browsing, and text modes.

The SPELL system for analyzing vowels (Hiller, Rooney, and Jack, 1993) is similar but perhaps more user-friendly in its use of windows, mouse "buttons", and graphics. An especially interesting feature is the placement of a graphic target in a side-view of a head with a small dart showing whether or not the target was hit. Like the other SPELL modules, the vowel program is based on a database of native speaker samples. The system, like that described by Rochet (1992), is as yet quite limited, in that it only handles selected monophthongs in the carrier frame h_d, and coarticulation (i.e., the natural overlapping of neighboring speech sounds) is ignored. Nevertheless, like the intonation

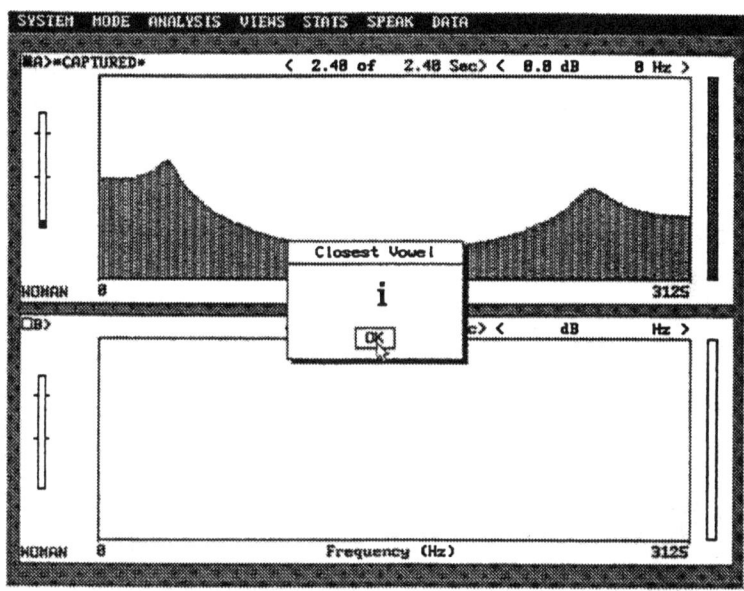

Figure 9.5. Sona-Match View of the Spectral Energy of a Vowel Spoken in Real Time into the Microphone and Compared to the Pre specified Models

and duration modules, and like the software developed by Rochet (1992) for working on a problematic French vowel, the SPELL vowel module shows careful attention to features of authenticity and pedagogical design.

Individual phonemes can be visualized and compared via on-line spectrographic analysis such as is available in the Kay Elemetrics CSL (Computerized Speech Lab) equipment or using the intensity display of Visi-Pitch. Either mode shows clearly the difference between, for example, the English alveolar and pre-palatal sibilants (as in the initial consonants of *sip* and *ship*) or between initial voiced and voiceless stops (as in *den* vs. *ten*). While such displays are generally too complex to be of great pedagogical value, for limited purposes (e.g., as described by Molholt, 1988), they can be useful for training such difficult aspects of articulation as aspiration, as in the initial sound of *ten* (vs. *den*) and frication, such as the difference between *ship*, *sip*, and *zip*.

In addition, the University of Victoria Phonetic Database (Esling, 1991b; 1994b), which has stored samples of digitized speech from over 40 languages on CD-ROM, can be run with the CSL 4300 hardware to illustrate the sounds and phonetic symbols associated with these for the stored languages. The database material is organized so that it is possible to illustrate different series of places and manners of articulation, as well as the prosodic characteristics of intonation, tone (i.e., lexical pitch in tone languages such as Chinese and Thai), and voice quality. Two other programs which have been designed around the CSL environment are the *IPA* (International Phonetic Alphabet) *Tutorials* (Dickson, 1992; Esling 1987b, 1987c, 1990, 1992a) and *IPA Labels* programs (Esling, 1991a).

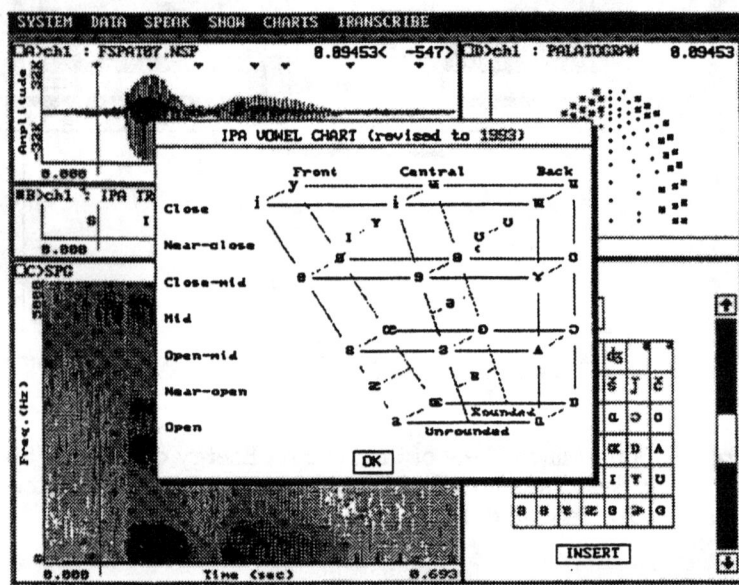

Figure 9.6. IPA Tutorials Screen Showing the Speech Waveform, Transcription Line, Palatogram, Spectrogram, with the Phonetic Vowel Chart Superimposed

In the *IPA Tutorials* program, the user selects a speech sample, and the screen displays a spectrogram (which shows the characteristics of the speech wave) and a palatogram (which shows the tongue contact on the roof of the mouth) of the speech sample. The program also provides training for the user to enter a line of phonetic transcription to represent the selected utterance. Tutorials also allow students to compare the features of the IPA vowels and consonants (see Figure 9.6 and 9.7). Thus, for example, the user can click the mouse button on any vowel or consonant in the charts of Figures 9.6 and 9.7 and hear that sound pronounced by two phoneticians. By clicking on a second mouse button, the spectrograms of the two productions of the vowel or consonant are displayed side by side for the user's comparison. The *IPA Labels* program is similar but somewhat more dynamic, in that the symbols and their labels can be moved around on the screen and rearranged in various orders while the sounds are listed to, according to mixing and matching tasks set by the instructor (Esling, 1993).

Going beyond individual phonemes, Goh (1993) describes an interactive self-access learning system based on automatic speech recognition algorithms for teaching the pronunciation of individual lexical items of English. In the words of the developer: "The speech recognition algorithms are used in providing the student with a score based on the similarity or dissimilarity between his/her pronunciation of a word and a stored sample" (Goh, 1993, p. 349). A linear predictive algorithm is used to extract numerical data on the waveform of a word and these figures are then compared with those for the target words. A score representing how closely the two match is shown as a graphic of a thermometer with the mercury rising towards the top as the match becomes closer. As Goh (1993) notes, the software can be used, in language lab fashion, for individual students to record their performance and then hear it replayed, but "with the added benefits of being able to evaluate a student's performance" (p. 352) against a stored model.

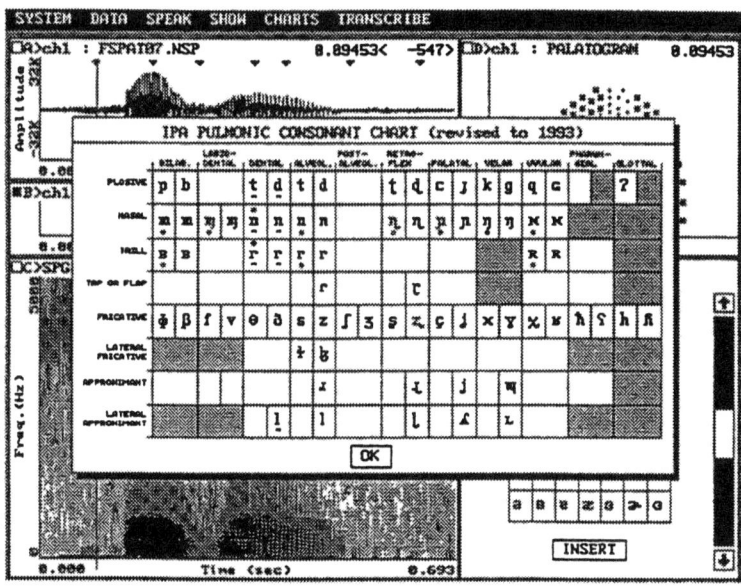

Figure 9.7. IPA Tutorials Screen with the Phonetic Consonant Chart Superimposed

Goh (1993) notes that the feedback on his system has generally been favorable, though some have noted inaccuracies in the speech teaching algorithms: This is mainly due to the fact that, in word teaching, the algorithm is sensitive to adjacent phonemes and does not only check on the phoneme being taught" (p. 357). Of course, this is a problem only if the purpose of the speech teaching algorithms is seen as the training of individual phonemes rather than the larger units of connected speech occurring in whole words and longer utterances.

Potentials and Drawbacks

The visual displays of pronunciation offered on these computer systems can be used for pre-production training—e.g., to help students prepare for speaking activities—as well as in-production monitoring, feedback, and adjustment of performance. The input from the machine to the user may even be "negotiated" or interactive, if, like Rochet's (1992) system, it evaluates successive tries as closer or farther from the target. In most systems, post-production review of performance is possible via storage of speech samples and statistical calculations. As an extension of this latter capacity, students could be offered specific or holistic feedback on their performance by the teacher and then try to match this with the computer analysis and to correct performance accordingly. With stored speech samples, these devices can also be used for whole-class review of performance. Another possibility is to videotape the user's session at the machine as the basis for additional post-production input by the teacher or other students who view the videotaped session.[4]

The possibility of comparing performance with a model avoids what Goh (1993) refers to as the "vicious circle" problem of language laboratory work: If students do not perceive the difference between their performance and that of the model on tape, they will simply produce the same output in response to the tape stimulus on every repetition. Thus, although they might practice for hours on end, they never improve because they fail to perceive the gap between their production and that of the native speaker voice on tape. Even learners who are able to perceive the gap may not be able to close it. For these learners as well, a visual modality displaying some attributes of their performance in relation to the target and motivating improvement towards that target might be effective in a way that repeated focused listening may not be. At the least, it can be hypothesized that such additional input of a different kind, juxtaposing two different communicational modalities or symbol systems (Dickson, 1985; Salomon, 1979), may help the learner to translate between them and so to learn something new by pattern matching, analogy, and reconceptualization.

One study (Molholt, 1988) has claimed positive effects in second language acquisition for training of segmental phonology by use of computer-generated displays of information in the speech signal, and several researchers have addressed the question of the effectiveness of training intonation by computer means (see, e.g., Abberton and Fourcin, 1975; de Bot, 1983; de Bot and Mailfert, 1982; James, 1986; Kalikow and Swets, 1972; Leather, 1990). This group of studies shows definite positive effects in as short a period as 12 minutes for training of intonation using computer-generated visual displays of pitch contours.

De Bot (1983) and de Bot and Mailfert (1982) report on training efforts geared to French and Dutch learners of English using a pre-production tutorial mode to instruct the learners on the elements of intonation and an in-production feedback mode to supply them with visual displays of their pitch contours in comparison to target contours. De Bot (1983) found that Dutch learners of English as a second language would spend more time trying to attain an intonational target when they were given a combination of auditory and computer-generated visual feedback on their performance than when provided with only auditory feedback. As noted elsewhere (Pennington, 1989a), "the visual image of the contour not only represents auditory information in a different modality, thereby making it easier to comprehend or remember, but also provides affective feedback or reinforcement, thereby making it easier or more interesting to attain the target production" (p. 114).

Leather (1990) studied the acquisition by Dutch-speaking adults of Chinese tone in a computer-mediated environment, making comparisons to similar research on English speakers. Leather separately examined the effects of training in perception and production on two different groups of subjects, considering the effect on perception of training production as well as the effect on production of training perception. He reports that in the perception training group, about half of those learners who attained a high level of perceptual competence for tone recognition based on the computer-mediated lessons were also able to achieve accurate production of the tones. In the group which received production training to master the Chinese tones, the level of perceptual competence achieved was comparatively more modest at an equivalent level of tone production. These results confirm the value of computer-based training of tone and intonation and suggest that perceptual training may be more strongly related to, and have more carryover for, production of intonation than productive practice does for perception of intonation.

One of the features of systems offering visual representations of characteristics of the speech signal is that, in providing the learner an alternate symbolization of sound, they increase the accessibility of input (Pennington, 1986, 1991d). As illustrated by the research on training phonology in an electronic environment, the computer modality affords the learner new avenues for acquiring knowledge and additional channels for interacting with input which may enhance attention and the learnability of information, promoting new insights and understanding of a phenomenon that might result in more immediate gains in performance, more rapid improvement, or more sustained or substantial improvement over the long run.[5]

Another feature of speech analysis technology is that it is highly motivating, so that even learners who had formerly shown no inclination to work on their pronunciation will often willingly spend time working alone or with a trainer using this computer-based form of input and practice. A computerized training system also offers a private environment for working on pronunciation without fear of embarrassment at phonetic inaccuracies or the number of repetitions needed for full comprehension or accuracy of production. For all these reasons, learners may practice more and with greater attention and effectiveness in a computer environment offering feedback or other types of input on pronunciation than they would in other kinds of pedagogical environments.

In spite of the attributes which make speech analysis systems attractive for educational purposes, they suffer from some drawbacks that make them less than perfect instructional tools for second language learning. One problem with this software is that some utterances are not very useful for illustrating the pitch of an utterance, as Cranen, Weltens, de Bot, and Van Rossum (1984, p. 28) note, because they contain many voiceless sounds, which show up as breaks in a pitch contour. On the other hand, voiceless sounds may be very clearly visible and easy to differentiate in an intensity contour, where, for example, a voiceless alveolar sibilant (as in *sip*) shows up as an energy spike, while an initial voiceless palatal sibilant (as in *ship*) shows up as a rounded ("normally distributed") energy curve. It is also easy to see on an intensity contour of an English initial voiceless stop (as in *ten*) the aspirated burst period, which is absent from the intensity contour of an English initial voiced stop (as in *den*). As this example demonstrates, not only developers but also teachers must help to ensure that the technological capabilities are appropriately and usefully exploited (Pennington, 1991d; Pennington and Stevens, 1992), e.g., by selecting for illustration and training those contrasts which are clearly visible in the computer displays, as in the language teaching suggestions provided by Molholt (1988).

A further drawback to computerized systems for training pronunciation is that there is little in the way of ready-made lessons or training modalities for these computer tools—though what does exist (e.g., as available for the Visi-Pitch or Sona-Match systems through the Kay Elemetrics Corp) is of high quality. Because of the small amount of prestructured training available, these systems are generally used for working on students' expressed areas of need, or those areas which are best addressed by the equipment. In addition, users may learn better in an intensive interaction in which their teacher, or another expert, is involved, thus making this type of system not very practical for use in a normal teaching situation, i.e., with a class of thirty students or more. However, as more and more pronunciation software is designed for self-access and as more and more different types of networking become available in educational environments as well as to the average home user, this problem may become less important in the future.

Another limitation of computerized speech analysis is that the machine must be adjusted by an operator or must be able to self-adjust to suit an individual user's voice. For example, Suzuki, Kiritani, and Imagawa (1989) note that in their system to train English intonation according to a model utterance:

> The learner's overall pitch is usually different from that of the speaker of the model, and the speech tempo may also be different. In order to make it easier to compare the learner's patterns with those of the model, the system has a normalizing function in terms of pitch and tempo. The pitch normalization is based on the average

frequency of the utterance. (Suzuki, Kiritani, and Imagawa, 1989, p. 59)

Probably the biggest problem with this software as a pedagogical tool is that there is no definite quantifiable standard as to how far a learner's pronunciation might deviate from the model and still be acceptable. As Suzuki, Kiritani, and Imagawa (1989) point out, this is an important area of indeterminacy in computer-assisted pronunciation work:

> We found that the most important problem ... is to determine the acceptable range of curve deviation. The students tried repeatedly to make their curves identical with that of the model. Although there were still some discrepancies between theirs and the model, their speech sounded quite satisfactory in most cases. Research into acceptability level and its visual representation [is] needed to make this system really feasible. (p. 61)

Rochet's (1992) and Hiller, Rooney, and Jack's (1993) approaches to training, which seek to define targets and common deviations from these, represent an important step forward.

9.5.2. Speech Output, Video, and Hypermedia

Speech output married to other forms of computer software and hardware is becoming increasingly common in the elementary language arts classroom:

> It is no longer unusual for beginning readers and writers to use talking word processors when writing, reading, and sharing their stories. In a classroom equipped with computer technology, students can practice their spelling words and even take their weekly tests with the aid of computerized speech. For a class project, students might write and produce an electronic play in which different characters have distinctly different voices. And down the hall, students with special needs might use drill and practice programs in which instructions and feedback are given spokenly. (Anderson-Inman et al., 1991, p. 53)

Anderson-Inman et al. (1991) review research demonstrating the value of software with these speech enhancements in the reading and writing processes of young or unskilled readers and writers. Yet, interestingly, these devices are hardly known or applied within the adult language learning curriculum, where more attention has been trained on speech analysis—specifically, pronunciation, as discussed above— rather than speech synthesis or output.

There is also a growing quantity of software designed to make use of speech output to work on the micro reading processes of phonetic decoding and the matching of phonological and semantic representations of lexical items as background for reading. These applications can be classified as falling mainly into the category of pre-production training. The training involves presenting word pairs and sets—both real words and non-words—synchronized with synthesized speech and having the learner perform a task such as classifying words as same or different or identifying the odd word in a group. In these training systems, speech output is added as feedback on performance. Most of the applications of this type of software, which have been shown to be effective in helping learners to develop "preliteracy" skills, have been used with children who are native speakers of English (Barron et al., 1992; Olofsson, 1988; Olson, Foltz, and Wise, 1986; Olson and Wise, 1987; Wise et al., 1989; Wise, Olson, and Treiman, 1990), though this type of software has obvious value for non-native speakers as well.

Within the ESL curriculum, speech output has mainly been used as listening material for cloze passages and to complement the presentation of lexical items or a grammatical point on the screen. At the present time, however, some of the reading software described above is beginning to find its way into the second language curriculum, as are talking word processors. It is hoped that the current applications of the available speech output technology in the second language curriculum will point the way to improvements and adaptations to better meet the needs of a non-native speaker audience. At the present time, however, it can be said that speech output has been underutilized in second language teaching.

One ESL application is a module to test the knowledge of spoken vocabulary and listening comprehension included as part of Goh's (1993) system. The computer, in spoken output, directs the student to point to a certain item in a certain location. If the student does it correctly, then the computer display zooms in to that location. One can imagine extensions of this capability by Hypertext as a training medium in which buttons lead into other information about the lexical items. In addition, speech output can be married to problem-solving software to not only stimulate but also model the desired response.

Another type of resource for the spoken language curriculum is an *Oral Language Archive* now in development at Carnegie Mellon University in the United States (Jones, 1995). This archive will make available to foreign language learners and their teachers a database of digitized conversations at different levels of complexity in a range of foreign languages such as Japanese, French, Spanish, German, and Russian. In addition to the digitized speech samples, the Carnegie Mellon system includes a variety of tools for managing the database and developing teaching materials. The uniqueness of the Carnegie Mellon system resides in its ease of operation, comprehensiveness, and accessibility. In the view of the developers:

> This combination of information, and the tools to interactively access that information, make the [*Oral Language Archive*] unique in its attempt to provide a universal structure to describe, categorize and listen to all major languages via a single access system, ... using a single application without swapping CD-ROMs, access tools or authoring environments. The intention of the [*Oral*

Language Archive] is to make oral language, with an emphasis on authentic dialogues, available directly to any network-based computer desktop, moving toward national access through the Internet. A software 'browser' will allow instructors and researchers to search the Archive and to either listen directly to the language discovered or establish links from other software authoring environments for insertion into interactive language learning materials. (Jones, 1995, pp. 1-2)

For students, material from the database, accessed across a network, can be used "to enrich all basic language instruction, including self-paced, maintenance and intensive language study" (Jones, 1995, p. 2).

In addition to this kind of audio database, video archives hold particular promise for exposing students to natural speech and offer content that can be developed into pedagogical exercises. The potential for allying this kind of video information with the audio information of the Carnegie Mellon and other databases (e.g., that of the University of Victoria as described above and any other type of database as described by Ashworth, this volume), combined with various kinds of authoring tools and database management software, suggests an obvious direction for CALL development in the immediate future.

Programs like *Where in the World is Carmen Santiago* and *The Animals!* (Cobb and Stevens, this volume) mix hypertools and video media with stimulating activities to produce models and prompts for communication. A program designed at Harvard University specifically for ESL students, *Who Should Do the Housework?* (Price and Imbier, 1993), makes use of Level III interactive laserdisc technology to give users access to print, aural, and visual information as a range of people speak their opinions about to who should do household chores. The system incorporates a number of other electronic resources, including:

- A "Language Tools" resource for analyzing the speakers' language;
- A "Video Concordance" allowing the user to search for specific idioms and grammatical items in the speech of different speakers shown in the video scenes;
- A "Salesman" game based on the range of speaker opinions;
- The capability of storing different users' opinions and then doing comparisons.

The Harvard program not only allows second language students to freely browse natural speech with a stimulating informational focus, but also offers them an interesting game to help them internalize and creatively extend the information. The program makes it possible, moreover, for non-native speakers to analyze authentic speech systematically in a "maximal" context that includes the visual aspect as well as a variety of speakers' voices and accents. The program is highly flexible in the ways it can be used and in the range of activities it makes possible for language learners at elementary or advanced levels of proficiency.

Another system in development at Harvard is designed "to automate much of the tedious work involved in coding and analyzing classroom discourse" (Price, 1992, p. 73). Using *MIDI (Musical Instrument Digital Interface)* and original software, the system allows the user to locate and compile specific features of the spoken language of a videotaped class session, such as who speaks when and for how long. The system can analyze certain features of a speaker's utterances, such as volume (loudness), length of turns, wait time between speakers, and amount of turn overlap. In addition to its obvious research applications regarding amount and type of teacher talk and student talk in various types of classroom activities, the system has pedagogical utility when used by the students themselves:

> Using a computer-assisted system for discourse analysis may help students and teachers become more aware of patterns of discourse in the classroom. The data the system provides may help guide students in developing better oral skills, and instructors in developing better instructional strategies. (Price, 1992, p. 79)

9.5.3. Interactive Discourse

Computers can model spoken discourse and can simulate or stimulate spoken interaction by two or more users in contact on-line or off. In this category are included structured discussions around the computer that involve tasks as diverse as convergent or divergent problem-solving, peer or group composing, and solving a computer-based exercise. Based on Brown and Yule's (1983) task types, Esling (1991c, pp. 116-121) gives examples of the tasks and techniques available on computer and how these relate to various kinds of tasks for generating spoken discourse. In what follows, the tasks are ordered from less to more challenging according to Brown and Yule's (1983) categories.

Static Relationships

(1) *Describing an object or photograph to someone.* For this basic descriptive task type, computer-based options include describing images in a database or using hypermedia or videodisc. *HyperCard* also makes it possible for students to organize images in any way they wish, linking different parts of the database as desired.

(2) *Instructing someone how to draw a diagram.* Students can work in pairs or groups to instruct each other to draw diagrams or pictures with computer software or with a graphics pad. The computer environment is a good one for working on commands and directional language, as the output is immediately visible and can be adjusted according to instructions.

(3) *Instructing someone how to assemble a piece of equipment.* For this type of task, students might work together to set up a computer program by connecting various components to assemble something, reading and verbalizing instructions, and practicing on the program once installed.

(4) *Describing to someone how a number of objects are to be arranged.* In a computer environment, this type of task might involve students in decisions and actions to reorganize words or paragraphs on the screen, as in ordinary word processing. Or, students could discuss different options for formatting a document. Some specific programs also involve moving objects on the screen, as in the game described by Dickson (1985).

(5) *Giving route directions to someone.* Route directions such as those explaining how to get to a place using a map or how to move from one part of an on-screen house (castle, etc.) are a part of some CALL programs. This is a fairly challenging activity, as it requires translating between a visual map and a "discourse map" so that the listener can intuit a "cognitive map" which represents his/her understanding of the directions.

Dynamic Relationships

(6) *Telling someone a story.* Telling a story is a cognitively demanding yet highly motivating task and so is of particular benefit for language learners. Computer applications include storyboard programs, reading cloze passages, and other types of text reconstruction activities. They might also involve making up a story to go with a series of pictures digitized and input with *HyperCard* or created with a graphics program.

(7) *Giving an eye-witness account to someone.* Hypertext reading programs and the various types of search or exploratory programs making use of a database can function as the basis for developing information that can then be reported to a partner working at the same terminal or to another group of students working at a different terminal. Another types of eye-witness account suggested by Esling (1991c) is for students to recount computer experiences when working through a simulation or solving a problem.

Abstract Relationships

(8) *Expressing an opinion to someone.* Students can evaluate software or use programs to design surveys or questionnaires and then discuss the differences in opinions that result.

(9) *Justifying a course of action to someone.* Computer simulations, mysteries, and other kinds of problem-solving activites (e.g., as described by Jones and Fortescue, 1987) performed in a group around the computer will lead to discussion of the reasons one course of action rather than another was chosen.

As noted in Dever and Pennington (1989), computers do not actually communicate because they can neither understand nor produce spontaneous language. A computer can be said to "understand" and "generate" language only in a limited domain of discourse. A series of studies have investigated the type of language produced when students work around a computer. This group of studies includes work with second language students using adventure programs such as *Mystery House* (Baltra, 1984) and several studies making use of the program, *ELIZA* (Weizenbaum, 1976). The latter program elicits (typed) responses by simulating a doctor-patient psychotherapy session approximating a highly structured form of "conversation", in which the doctor asks questions which generally reflect what the patient has just said.

These studies as a group suggest that "normal" conversation, i.e., that produced when a computer program is not operating and does not form the focus of users' visual attention, is more extensive and sometimes also more complex than that generated by working on a computer in pairs or groups. At the same time, this research clearly indicates that different types of computer programs stimulate different types of language. Specific findings are that problem-solving, adventure, and simulation programs seem to elicit the most language from students (see, e.g., Dickson, 1985), and that more task-related verbal interaction is produced with cooperative tasks than with competitive or individualistic tasks (Johnson, Johnson, and Stanne, 1986).

Of particular interest is a group of studies carried out by Abraham and Liou (1991), Esling (1992b), Mohan (1992), Piper (1986), and Young (1988), in which the discourse of ESL students generated by different types of computer programs was investigated. Piper (1986) compared the language generated by adult ESL learners when working with a sentence reordering program (*Copywrite*), a cloze program (*Clozemaster*), and a vocabulary program (*Vocabulary*). Piper (1986) found that the adult students did not produce very elaborated discourse nor much input that was modified or negotiated in the course of the interaction when using any of these programs. Instead, they produced a narrow range of syntax and lexis and a great deal of repetition. As compared to the conversation produced by ESL learners in another study, Piper's (1986) subjects generated far less language, as they tended to use short conversational moves to express their opinions, such as "yes", "no", or "OK". The main type of negotiated input-output, and the most complex language, was generated while the students were preparing to use the programs.

Young (1988) compared spoken interaction in four different types of CALL, two drill-and-practice programs (*Gapkit* and *Word Sequencing*) and two simulation-type programs (*London Adventure* and *FastFood*) which involve problem-solving and negotiation of meaning. The output generated by the first two programs was more restricted and tied to program content, while that generated by the other two was more open-ended and conversational. In a similar vein, Abraham and Liou (1991) compared the speech generated with adult non-native speakers of English by three different types of programs, ELIZA, a business simulation (*Lemonade Stand*), and a grammar program (*Articles*); and Mohan (1992) compared the speech generated in four male-male and female-female pairs of adult ESL students using a business simulation (*Market*), a grammar program on past tense, and a word processing program, as compared with "free conversation".

In the research of Abraham and Liou (1991):

> Comparisons of the talk elicited by the three programs studied revealed fewer differences than expected. There were relatively small differences among the programs in words per minute, turns per minute, words per turn, and words per act. However, in types of acts, differences were apparent in several categories: 'repeating,' 'managing mechanical aspects of tasks,' 'responding,' and 'showing concern for language form.' These differences point up contrasting characteristics of the three programs. (p. 99)

As compared to Piper's (1986) study, Abraham and Liou's (1991) study generated more elaborate discourse and much longer turns, possibly because in the former study, talk was generated as a by-product of completing the computer task, whereas in the latter study, the subjects had been instructed not only to complete the computer task but also to discuss the content of the programs and any questions or problems they were having with them.

In the Abraham and Liou (1991) investigation, *Lemonade Stand* generated more novel utterances than *Articles* or *ELIZA*, which generated comparatively more repetitions. Moreover,

> ... the discussion in **Articles** was limited almost exclusively to analyzing and trying out permutations of the sentences provided. **Lemonade Stand**, in posing the problem of running a small business profitably, generated a variety of cause/effect and evaluative comments, albeit all on the same general topic. **Eliza** elicited talk on a number of subjects ranging from loneliness (as suggested in the instruction sheet) to the weather, to subjects' ability to use English. Yet despite this variety, no topic was every fully developed because of the

mechanical nature of the computer's response. The most coherent discussion occurred when subjects finally realized that the computer was "fooling" them. If one considers these characteristics along with the relative amount of repetition in the three programs, one might conclude that **Lemonade Stand** provided the best practice. (p. 101)

Mohan's (1992) investigation uncovered greater quantity and quality of input—via clarifications and other kinds of negotiated language—in free conversation than in tasks centered on the computer. However, more cognitively demanding—"high-inference", "high cognitive load"—communication activity occurred in the computer environment, which also produced less of a focus on self and personal topics and more of a focus on other kinds of topics and academically relevant content and process of communication, particularly abstract reasoning and problem-solving discourse.

In a follow-up to Mohan's (1992) study, Esling (1992b) analyzed videotaped data from dyads of native speakers and non-native speakers using a text-completion program (*Rhubarb*) and a problem-solving program (*InVENNtion*), as compared to free conversation. A comparison of his results to those of Mohan are given in Tables 9.1 through 9.4. For the eight pairs of non-native speakers who were at a low-intermediate level of proficiency, output was significantly lower during the CALL tasks than in free conversation for all three quantitative measures taken. This implies that the learners exercised a higher quality of negotiation of meaning when conversing with each other in an open-ended format. Although the lower level of output in the CALL environment seems clearly inadequate for developing conversational fluency, it is less clear as to whether this level of output is adequate for reinforcing acquisition of task-specific skills.

Variable	Grammar Mean	Simulat. Mean	Wordproc Mean	Convers. Mean
Utterances per Minute	3.1	2.9	2.2	6.6
Words per Minute	11.7	9.7	9.2	39.2
Words per Utterance	3.5	3.1	3.6	5.9
Repetitions (Self)*	.26	.19	.19	.58
Repetitions (Other)*	.14	.10	.06	.19
Clarification Requests*	.01	.04	.04	.22
Confirmation Checks*	.05	.07	.06	.39

* per Minute, based on 10 minutes of dyadic interaction.

Table 9.1 Nonnative-Speaker Pairs (8 dyads) – Low Intermediate (Adapted from Mohan, 1992)

Variable	Rhubarb Mean	InVENN Mean	Convers. Mean
Utterances per Minute	10.6	25.4	19.1
Words per Minute	23.8**	101.0	115.3**
Words per Utterance	2.26**	4.04**	6.30**
Repetitions (Self) *	1.2**	3.0**	1.6**
Repetitions (Other) *	.6**	6.4**	1.6**
Clarification Requests *	.2	.2	.3
Confirmation Checks *	.2	0	.5

* per Minute, based on 5 minutes of dyadic interaction.
** Categories significant to p<.05 compared across tables 2, 3 and 4 are double starred.

Table 9.2 Nonnative-Speaker Pair – Low Advanced – Males

Tables 9.2 and 9.3 compare the output of male and female non-native speaker dyads in the two CALL tasks and in free conversation. In general, the numbers are far higher than for the subjects in Mohan's (1992) study, and higher for the female than for the male subjects. The high level of interactive speaking can probably be attributed to the higher proficiency level of subjects in the Esling (1992b) study. Secondly, free conversation does not produce more output than the particular CALL activities examined by Esling (1992b); in fact, the reverse seems to be true for some measures. Thirdly, the two CALL activities differ substantially from each other. The amount of output generated, for students at a low-advanced level of proficiency, appears to depend on the nature of the task far more than for the low-intermediate subjects in Mohan's study.

Quantitatively, the number of words used by both male and female non-native dyads in Esling's study was greater in free conversation than in the CALL tasks, but the number of utterances was not. In other words, utterances were longer when speakers were conversing freely. Qualitatively, the number of repetitions, on average, was greater in the CALL activities than in free conversation, with the highest number of repetitions occurring in the *InVENNtion* task. A comparison with a female native speaker dyad shows a higher number of words used than by the non-native pairs. On the other hand, as can be seen in Table 9.4, the qualitative variables, on the whole, have a lower incidence for native speakers than for the non-native pairs.

Variable	Rhubarb Mean	InVENN Mean	Convers. Mean
Utterances per Minute	19.8	23.8	19.8
Words per Minute	51.4**	105.6	133.7**
Words per Utterance	2.59**	4.47**	6.95**
Repetitions (Self) *	2.4**	4.0**	2.8**
Repetitions (Other) *	3.0**	4.6**	.3**
Clarification Requests *	.6	.2	.1
Confirmation Checks *	.2	.4	.1

* per Minute, based on 5 minutes of dyadic interaction.

Table 9.3 Nonnative-Speaker Pair – Low Advanced – Females

VARIABLE	Rhubarb Mean	InVENNtion Mean
Utterances per Minute	23.5	24.8
Words per Minute	70.5	120.8
Words per Utterance	3.19**	4.97**
Repetitions (Self) *	3.8**	1.6**
Repetitions (Other) *	4.0	1.2**
Clarification Requests *	0	.2
Confirmation Checks *	.8	0

* per Minute, based on 5 minutes of dyadic interaction.

Table 9.4 Native-Speaker Pair – Females

Overall, these results suggest that proficiency level is a significant factor in the ability of language learners to perform verbally in a CALL activity, with advanced level students demonstrating better performance according to quantitative and qualitative measures than intermediate students. They also confirm the results of other studies demonstrating that the type of task is a crucial factor influencing the type of language generated in a CALL environment. Generally, free conversation exceeds CALL activities in the amount of language produced but not necessarily in the types of language which are associated with increased negotiation of meaning. In addition, the type of task interacts with the proficiency of the speaker. Thus, in Esling's (1992b) study, the native speaker dyad had more negotiated input using *Rhubarb*, while in the case of the non-native speakers, more negotiation occurred with the *InVENNtion* program. These results suggest that certain kinds of CALL programs, such as those in a game format, can generate as much spoken interaction and negotiation of meaning in one-on-one discourse as in free conversation, depending on the proficiency level of the participants.

Piper (1986) noted that much of the negotiation in which her students were engaged while working at the computer seemed to be taking place not verbally but mentally, through "inner speech". Dickson (1985) showed how computers can usefully bring these inner negotiations to a conscious level by modeling the reasoning process a learner goes through when manipulating objects on the computer display screen. Thus, the computer may help to provide the direction and the language for non-native learners to describe and to negotiate their problem-solving process aloud. In addition, programs may be specifically designed to model and/or elicit certain types of language, such as the referential communication game which Dickson (1985) described, where "the visual display is deliberately designed to evoke specific linguistic forms and patterns of social interaction" (p. 32).

Craven (1990) believes that the characteristics of certain types of programs, even though highly artificial such as *ELIZA*, can be instructive for students. She divided a class of university ESL students into two groups, one of which was to work with *ELIZA* on a simulated problem and the other of which was to make up a doctor-patient dialogue in which the patient was a student. According to Craven (1990): "The students then had a rich data-base with which to discover a number of sociolinguistic conventions" (p. 251). Students compared human-human and machine communication and

> ... wrote papers analyzing *ELIZA*'s lack of intelligence. At the end of a six-week period, the students had learned about the importance of context in understanding, and about the limitations of computer-human communication (Craven, 1990, p. 251).

Other approaches to conversation which make use of the computer include Ashworth's (this volume) description of *The Observer* program as used for transcribing natural speech. In addition, students might benefit by working with peers to caption computer-managed video. Under this section heading, we might also include the "pseudo-conversations" carried out on computer networks (Daiute, 1986b; Esling, 1991c; Hoffman, this volume; Kreeft Peyton, 1986). Although these do not usually involve actual speaking (unless, for example, messages are composed and sent by student pairs or groups working together at one terminal), they do have some of the characteristics of spoken language, as messages display an interactive and informal type of conversational grammar, humorous elements, and creative and spontaneous use of language. It seems likely that this modality may have some transfer to actual spoken language.

There may also be transfer from simulated interactive environments like *Habitat* (Ashworth, this volume) to other "real-life" or school-based communicational environments.

9.6. NEW VISTAS FOR INSTRUCTION, RESEARCH, AND DEVELOPMENT

In spite of the interesting new directions for working on the spoken aspect of language on computer, many of the potentials outlined in an earlier work (Pennington, 1989a) are still awaiting development. There is at present considerable room for innovation to implement new ideas as well as design concepts and approaches which have already been articulated for use of computers in the spoken language area. There is also still room for creative elaboration and new applications of existing systems to make them easier or more attractive for students to use. In this final section, we attempt to plot a course for the future of computers in the spoken language curriculum by offering up ideas for additional directions based on what is available as well as on what might be made available, given suitable attention and allocation of resources. We hope that in so doing we may stimulate others to explore this rich but still relatively underdeveloped aspect of CALL.

9.6.1. Speech Analysis

Drawing on the findings and recommendations of De Bot (1983) and Leather (1990), together with the discussions of Chun (1989, p. 40), Pennington (1989a, pp. 116-120,) and Esling (1987b), the following goals can be generated for computer-based spoken language training:

> (1) Both perception and production should be trained, possibly with a period of working on "comprehensible input" before "comprehensible output".
>
> (2) Visual and auditory training should be coordinated.
>
> (3) A range of targets should be (a) provided in a database and (b) accepted by the machine, covering different social and geographical accents, native and non-native speakers, affect, and situational features.
>
> (4) Motivating features such as high quality audio and visual feedback, attractive visuals, and creative uses of media should be a central part of the system.
>
> (5) Feedback should be direct, specific, and with minimal time lag.
>
> (6) Simplified or limited material used to focus on the mechanics of pronunciation targets should be complemented by meaningful and if possible authentic material.

(7) The system should be flexible in its capabilities, allowing for self-access, one-on-one tutorial instruction, and peer work modes.

(8) The training and analysis system should have a record-keeping capability for research, training, and assessment purposes.

A project recently begun by Pennington and Ellis (1995) aims to explore the learnability of prosody in a combined auditory and visual mode, with visuals and analysis provided by the computer. The project examines the nature and learning of English phonology by native Cantonese speakers, with the ultimate goal of developing computer-managed, self-access training in English pronunciation for non-native speakers. The project centers on prosody as a foundation for a comprehensible and native-like accent. The type of presentation will be varied in order to investigate the effect on phonological production and perception of:

- **Visual reinforcement** – graphic of prosodic contour
- **Productive reinforcement** – verbal repetition of the input
- **High salience presentation** – contrasting prosodic patterns
- **Alternate language medium** – written presentation of the input

The subjects' tape-recorded productions will be analyzed in comparison to baseline measures of Cantonese speakers and British and North American English speakers and by means of the same analysis techniques used for establishing the baseline measures.

In addition to this sort of training of phonology, it is hoped that in the future there will be more emphasis on the use of speech analysis equipment for "exploratory CALL", e.g., for comparison of the pronunciation of individual phonemes or of individual voices or regional accents—including one's own—in terms of the features analyzed by the software and hardware. For example, more emphasis could be placed on having students develop a tape recording library themselves, or they could analyze speech already or soon-to-be accessible in CD-ROM or in on-line digitized audio and video databases, using any type of available compatible analysis software. Making such databases available to users—students or their teachers—would begin to solve the problem of lack of information on prosodic variability.

It is hoped that more efforts—such as that of Jones and colleagues at Carnegie Mellon University, and Price and colleagues at Harvard University—will be made to develop maximally simple, accessible, and comprehensive interactive systems making authentic samples of spoken language accessible to language learners via analysis and teaching software of various types. With increasing learner autonomy can come a focus on self-access pronunciation and more generally spoken language learning, a modality which is becoming increasingly popular in other areas of language learning.

An interesting direction for development of speech analysis for independent learning would be programs which allow the user to set parameters for such features as the number of strong and weak beats in a list of like-stressed words or phrases, or in heavily rhythmic material such as Mother Goose rhymes, and then to try to meet the specified parameters for production. Feedback on performance can be both visual and evaluative, indicating how close the user has come to meeting the desired parameters. Using such a system, the user could gradually work from an "easy" mode of slow speech to a more challenging mode of rapid speech.

One can hope to see in the future more attention to speech analysis with a focus on aspects other than intonation or segmental phonology, such as rate of speech and pausing. In addition to different kinds of analysis, it is important for developers to pay at least as much attention to pedagogy as to technology. Thus, we would like to see more attempts by developers, such as that of Hiller, Rooney, and Jack (1993), to make feedback on speech as user-friendly and useful as possible, working not only from the direction of what is technically feasible, but also from the direction of what is pedagogically desirable. It also seems important to base feedback on an analysis of authentic speech samples from a diverse group of target language speakers.

As in the video system described by Price (1992), the computer can easily be programmed to analyze all pauses of more than one second in terms of the length of the pauses and the amount of speech between each one, giving such measures as mean and standard deviation, with the possibility also of comparing these in different parts of a discourse to find out the consistency or variability. The computer might also analyze such features as voice quality (long-term average spectra), utterance length in terms of syllables and/or beats or average/maximum number of words between pauses (Pennington, 1992b), amount of sibilance, retroflexion, or whatever feature may be particularly distinctive for one language. Through such analysis, Esling (1983), for example, found that native speakers of Cantonese from Hong Kong had a rather different voice quality, as measured by long-term average spectrum analysis, when speaking their native language than they did when speaking their second language, English. French speakers in Canada, in contrast, appeared to have a similar voice quality in speaking both languages. Although the interpretation of this finding is not entirely clear, the type of analysis is useful for building a general understanding of differences between languages to undergird instruction (Esling, 1994a).

Variation in timing, regional accents, and voice qualities can be studied to establish a baseline for training and to compile digitized databases to supplement the University of Victoria Phonetic Database, Carnegie Mellon University's Oral Language Archive, Harvard University's video archives, and computerized dictionaries such as those discussed by Ashworth (this volume) for instructional purposes. These databases, archives, and dictionaries will make it possible to perform a computerized contrastive analysis between two (or more) languages, such as a learner's native language and the target language. This type of analysis—which could be based on stored samples of both languages, such as translation pairs of lexical items, phrases, or common utterances—could help the language learner to plot a target and a trajectory for change in performance.

Phonological analysis and the other related forms of analysis described here give learners another modality besides the auditory mode for understanding both the overall phonological system of the target language and the individual items of greatest difficulty. Such analysis also makes it possible to quantify the learner's accent and problems he/she might be having in communication, as a rough evaluation of phonological proficiency or spoken fluency. It also offers useful feedback on the difference between the native and the second language that may help to conceptualize the distance between them which the language learner must traverse.

9.6.2. Other Applications

More creative uses of interactive video can be envisioned as a motivating and high-context form of input to language learners which offer models for performance and also stimulate learners' negotiated and comprehensible output. Taking a cue from Ashworth (this volume), interactive video might be used to indicate a participant's reaction when different levels of politeness or familiarity are chosen, as shown by voice and/or lexis and grammar. As in the research described above, interactive video could form the basis of interactions and discussions among students in pairs or small groups working at one computer terminal while also training certain aspects of language.

A need exists within the speaking area for more systematic elicitation and analysis of types of language generated by computer under different circumstances with different types of learners (Chapelle and Jamieson, 1989; Chapelle, Jamieson, and Park, this volume). There is also a need for more exploration of the ways in which the computer environment can be exploited to model and scaffold real speech for language learning, e.g., by facilitating a transfer or development of skills practiced in a computer-mediated simulation or problem-solving activity. One would also like to explore the potential for engineering the transfer and development of e-mail fluency and creativity to forms of language use off the computer, especially, conversation or other types of interactive discourse.

An urgent need in the spoken language area of CALL is for discourse analysis of different kinds of computer-stimulated or -mediated language and for comparison of the types of language, both written and spoken, generated for individual speakers and groups of speakers (e.g., of different language backgrounds) on e-mail or networks, using word processing, and in discussion within and outside of a computer environment. Such comparative research will clarify the special attributes of the computer communication environment, allowing educators to develop language instruction within the parameters of the medium.

9.7. CONCLUDING REMARKS TO CHAPTER 9

Although there is much of interest in the speaking area of the language curriculum, more attention needs to be trained on this aspect of CALL, with greater expertise from applied linguists and language educators directed to developing speaking skills in a computer-assisted environment. Considering the potential of the medium, we believe that language educators have only scratched the surface of what is possible in the marriage of the electronic medium to the development of oral language. One of the reasons seems to be that there are very few people with the requisite expertise in language learning, language teaching, and CALL. An equally important reason, however, seems to be the lack of initiative on the part of all but a very small number of individuals or teams to develop truly innovative, user-friendly, and useful applications of computers to spoken language. Thus, there is at the present time tremendous latitude for development, and we hope that our overview of this area may have helped to spark the interest of some educators and software developers to take the plunge into this neglected area of CALL.

NOTES TO CHAPTER 9

1. For specific products, see Klatt (1987) and Anderson-Inman, Adler, Cron, Hillinger, Olson, and Prohaska et al. (1991). Anderson-Inman et al. (1991) have assembled a comprehensive listing—including addresses of companies—of speech peripherals, speech output systems, and language software allowing speech input and output to accompany various language learning tasks.

2. As reviewed by Chun (1989) from a primarily pedagogical perspective and by Read, Buder, and Kent (1990, 1992) from a more technical perspective—all with listings of products and addresses of companies.

3. For an overview of phonetics software, see Parkinson and Bladon (1987).

4. Note that the video camera must be aimed directly at the computer screen (e.g., from above and behind the user's head) or at an angle (e.g., from beside and slightly behind the user, facing the display) to record what is happening on the screen as the user speaks. In the angle view, the user's motions and expressions may also be viewed for additional post-production feedback.

5. However, no one has yet, as far as we are aware, investigated the carryover of the effect of training on performance outside the controlled conditions of the computerized system.

REFERENCES

Abberton, E., and Fourcin, A. (1975). Visual feedback and the acquisition of intonation. In E. H. Lenneberg and E. Lenneberg (eds.), *Foundations of language development* (pp. 157-165). New York: Academic Press.

Abraham, R. G. (1985). Field independence-dependence and the teaching of grammar. *TESOL Quarterly, 19,* 689-702.

Abraham, R. G., and Liou, H.-C. (1991). Interaction generated by three computer programs: Analysis of functions of spoken language. In P. Dunkel (ed.), *Computer-assisted language learning and testing: Research issues and practice* (pp. 133-154). New York: Newbury House/HarperCollins.

Adams, M.J. (1990). *Beginning to read: Thinking and learning about print.* Cambridge, MA: MIT Press.

Ahmad, K., Corbett, G., Rogers, M., and Sussex, R. (1985). *Computers, language learning and language teaching.* Cambridge: Cambridge University Press.

Alderman, D. (1978). Evaluation of the TICCIT computer-assisted instructional system in the community college. Research Report. ERIC ED 167 606.

Alderson, J. C. (1980). Native and nonnative speaker performance on cloze tests. *Language Learning, 30,* 59-76.

Allen, E., Bernhardt, E., Berry, M., and Demel, M. (1988). Comprehension and text genre: An analysis of secondary school foreign language readers. *Modern Language Journal, 72,* 163-172.

Allwright, D. (1988). *Observation in the language classroom.* London: Longman.

Anandam, K., Kotler, L., Eisel, E., and Roche, R. (1979). RSVP: Feedback program for individualized analysis of writing. Research Report. ERIC ED 191 511.

Anderson-Inman, L., Adler, W., Cron, M., Hillinger, M., Olson, R., and Prohaska, B. (1991). Speech: The third dimension. In R. Boone (ed.), *Teaching process writing with computers* (pp. 53-58). Revised Edition. Eugene, OR: ISTE.

Anthony, E. (1963). Approach, method, technique. *English Language Teaching 17,* 63-67.

Arden-Close, C. (in press). NNS readers' strategies for inferring the meanings of unknown words. *Reading in a Foreign Language, 9,* (2).

Aspects. Group Technologies, Arlington, VA.

Bachman, L. F. (1982). The trait structure of cloze text scores. *TESOL Quarterly, 16,* 61-70.

Bachman, L. F. (1985). Performance on cloze tests with fixed-ratio and rational deletions. *TESOL Quarterly, 19,* 535-556.

Bachman, L. F. (1990). *Fundamental considerations in language testing.* Oxford: Oxford University Press.

Bacon, S., and Finnemann, M. (1990). A study of the attitudes, motives, and strategies of university foreign language students and their disposition to authentic oral and written input. *The Modern Language Journal, 74,* 459-473.

Bailey, K. (1980). An introspective analysis of an individual's language learning experience. In R. Scarcella and S. D. Krashen (eds.), *Research in second language acquisition* (pp. 58-65). Rowley, MA: Newbury House.

Bailey, K. M. (1983). Competitiveness and anxiety in adult second language learning: Looking at and thought the diary studies. In H. W. Seliger and M. H. Long (eds.), *Classroom oriented research in second language acquisition* (pp. 67-103). Rowley, MA: Newbury House.

Balota, D. A., Pollatsek, A., and Rayner, K. (1985). The interaction of contextual constraints and parafoveal visual information in reading. *Cognitive Psychology, 17,* 364-390.

Baltra, A. (1984). An EFL classroom in a mystery house. *TESOL Newsletter, 18*(6), 15.

Barnes, L. L. (1989). Why is there a text in this class: Classroom teachers' (re)views of computer-assisted composition textbooks. *Computers and Composition, 7*(1), 27-36.

Barron, R. W., Golden, J. O., Seldon, D. M., Tait, C. F., Marmurek, H. H. C., and Haines, L. P. (1992). Teaching prereading skills with a talking computer. *Reading and Writing: An Interdisciplinary Journal, 4,* 179-204.

Batson, T. (1993). ENFI Research. *Computers and Composition, 10*(3), 93-101.

Bean, J. C. (1983). Computerized word processing as an aid to revision. *College Composition and Communication, 34,* 146-148.

Beazley, M. R. (1989). Reading for a real reason: Computer pals across the world. *Journal of Reading, 32*(7), 598-805.

Benesch, S. (1987). Word processing in English as a second language: A case study of three non-native college students. Paper presented at Conference on College Composition and Communication. Atlanta, April 1987. ERIC ED 281383.

Bernhardt, S. A. (1993). The shape of text to come: The texture of print on screens. *College Composition and Communication, 44,* 151-175.

Bernhardt, E., and Berkemeyer, V. (1988). Authentic texts and the high school German learner. *Unterrichtspraxis, 21,* 6-28. Cited in Bacon and Finnemann (1990).

Biber, D. (1988). *Variation across speech and writing.* Cambridge: Cambridge University Press.

Bland, S. K., Noblitt, J. S., Armstrong, S., and Gray, G. (1990). The naive lexical hypothesis: Evidence from computer-assisted language learning. *The Modern Language Journal, 74,* 440-450.

Bradley, V. N. (1982). Improving students' writing with microcomputers. *Language Arts, 59,* 732-743.

Brown, G. (1990). *Listening to spoken English.* Second Edition. London: Longman.

Brown, G., and Yule, G. (1983). *Teaching the spoken language.* Cambridge: Cambridge University Press.

Beard, M., Bar, A., Fletcher, D., and Atkinson, R. C. (1975). The improvement and individualization of computer assisted instruction. Final report. ERIC ED 112 951.

Bialystok, E. (1981). The role of conscious strategies in second language proficiency. *Modern Language Journal, 65,* 24-35.

Blake, R. (1992). Second language reading on the computer. *ADFL Bulletin, 24,* 17-22.

Bland, S. K., Noblitt, J. S., Armington, S., and Gay, G. (1990). The naive lexical hypothesis: Evidence from computer-assisted language learning. *Modern Language Journal, 74,* 440-450.

Bransford, J. D., and Johnson, M. K. (1972). Contextual prerequisites for understanding: Some investigations of comprehension and recall. *Journal of Verbal Learning and Verbal Behavior, 11,* 717-726.

Brebner, A., Johnson, K., and Mydlarski, D. (1984). CAI and second language learning: An evaluation of program for drill and practice in written French. *Computers and Education, 8,* 471-474.

Breen, M. P. (1985). The social context for language learning—A neglected situation? *Studies in Second Language Acquisition, 7,* 135-158.

Brown, H. D. (1987). *Principles of language learning and teaching.* Englewood Cliffs, NJ: Prentice Hall.

Bruce, B. C., and Rubin, A. (1993). *Electronic quills: A situated evaluation of using computers for writing in classrooms.* Hillsdale, NJ: Lawrence Erlbaum.

Buckley, E., and Rauch, D. (1979). Pilot project in computer-assisted instruction for adult education students. Great Neck, NY: Adult learning centers, Great Neck Public Schools. Final three-year report. ERIC ED 197 202.

Bueno, K., and Nelson, W. A. (1993). Collaborative second language learning with a contextualized computer environment. *Journal of Educational Multimedia and Hypermedia,* 4(2), 177-208.

Butler, J. (1991). Cloze procedures and concordances: the advantages of discourse level authenticity in testing expectancy grammar. *System,* 19(1-2), 29-38.

CALICO Journal (1991). CALICO '92 OUTREACH Symposium: Overview of presentations. *CALICO Journal,* 9(2), 76-94.

Campbell, R., and Hanlon, P. (1988). Grapevine. In S. Ambron and K. Hooper (eds.), *Interactive multimedia: Visions of multimedia for developers, educators and information providers* (pp. 157-178). Redmond, WA: Microsoft Press.

Cazden, C. B. (1985). Classroom discourse. In M. C. Wittrock (ed.), *Handbook of research on teaching* (pp. 432-463). New York: Macmillan.

Cazden, C. Michaels, S., and Watson-Gegeo, K. (1987). Microcomputers and literacy project. Final Report. Grant no. G-83-0051. Washington, DC: National Institute of Education.

Chapelle, C. (1990). The discourse of computer-assisted language learning: Toward a context for descriptive research. *TESOL Quarterly, 24* (2), 199-225.

Chapelle, C., and Jamieson, J. (1986). Computer-assisted language learning as a predictor of success in acquiring English as a second language. *TESOL Quarterly, 20,* 27-46.

Chapelle, C., and Jamieson, J. (1989). Research trends in computer-assisted language learning. In M. C. Pennington (ed.), *Teaching languages with computers: The state of the art* (pp. 47-59). La Jolla, CA: Athelstan.

Chapelle, C., and Jamieson, J. (1991). Internal and external validity issues in research on CALL effectiveness. In P. Dunkel (ed.), *Computer-assisted language learning and testing: Research issues and practice* (pp. 37-59). New York: Newbury House.

Chapelle, C., and Mizuno, S. (1989). Students' strategies with learner-controlled CALL. *CALICO Journal, 7*(2), 25-47.

Chaudron, C. (1988). *Second language classrooms: Research on teaching and learning.* Cambridge: Cambridge University Press.

Chinews. Hypermedia CALL program for listening comprehension in Chinese. Designed by Y. C. Li and S. H. Ho. University of Hawaii at Manoa.

Christie, N., and Sabers, D. (1989). Using microcomputers to implement mastery learning with high-risk and minority adolescents. ERIC ED 326 178.

Chun, D. M. (1989). Teaching tone and intonation with microcomputers. *CALICO Journal,* September, 21-46.

Ciarcia, S. (1984). Build a third-generation phonetic speech synthesizer. *Byte, 9*(3), 28-42.

Clark, R. E. (1985). Counfounding in educational computing research. *Journal Educational Computing Research, 1*(2), 137-148.

Clarke, M., and Silberstein, S. (1977). Toward a realization of psycholinguistic principles for the ESL reading class. *Language Learning, 27,* 135-154.

Clifford, T., and Warren, C. (1993). The planet project. In Davies, G., and Samways, B. (eds.) *Teleteaching* (pp. 147-144). Proceedings of a conference held at the University of Trondheim, August 1993. International

Federation for Information Processing (IFIP), the University of Trondheim, and the Norwegian Computer Society.

Coady, J. (1979). A psycholinguistic model of the ESL reader. In R. Mackay, B. Barkman, and R. R. Jordan (eds.), *Reading in a second language* (pp. 5-12). Rowley, MA: Newbury House.

Coady, J., Magoto, J., Hubbard, P., Graney, J., and Mokhtari, K. (1993). High frequency vocabulary and reading proficiency in ESL readers. In T. Huckin, M. Haynes, and J. Coady (eds.) *Second language reading and vocabulary learning* (pp. 217-228). Norwood, NJ: Ablex.

Cobuild. (1990). *Collins Cobuild English grammar*. London: Collins.

Cohen, A., and Hosenfeld, C. (1981). Some uses of mentalistic data in second language research. *Language Learning, 31*, 285-313.

Cohen, M., Levin, J. A., and Souviney, R. (1986). Exemplary educational computer use: Coping with rapid changes in technology. Interactive Technology Laboratory Report No. 12. San Diego: University of California. ERIC ED 311 875.

Cohen, A., Segal, M., and Weiss, R. (1985). The C-test in Hebrew. *Fremdsprachen und Hochschulen*. AKS-Rundbrief 13/14, 21-127.

Coleman, D. W. (1985). TERRI: A CALL lesson simulating conversational interaction. *System, 13*, 247-252.

Collaborative Writer. Designed by Ann Duin. RDA/Mindbuilders, Greenlawn, NY.

Collier, R. M. (1983). The word processor and revision strategies. *College Composition and Communication, 34*, 149-155.

Cranen, B., Weltens, B., de Bot, K., and Van Rossum, N. (1984). An aid in language teaching: The visualisation of pitch. *System, 12*, 25-29.

Craven, M-L. (1988). Evaluating CUES: Some problems and issues in experimental CALL research. *CALICO Journal, 5*, 51-64.

Craven, M.-L. (1990). Choosing communicatively-oriented software: Focus on content-based curriculum. In M.-L. Craven, R. Sinyor, and D. Paramskas (eds.), *CALL: Papers and reports* (pp. 249-253). La Jolla, CA: Athelstan.

Crookall, D. (1991). *Project IDEALS* (informational brochure). University of Mississippi at Biloxi.

Crookall, D., Coleman, D. W., and Oxford, R. L. (1992). Computer-mediated language learning environments: Prolegomenon to a research framework. *Computer-Assisted Language Learning*, 5(1-2), 93-120.

Cross, G. (1990). Left to their own devices: Three basic writers using word processing. *Computers and Composition*, 7(2), 47-58.

Cullen, R. (1988). Computer-assisted composition: A case study of six developmental writers. *Collegiate Microcomputer*, 6(3), 202-212.

Cummins, J. (1983). Language proficiency and academic achivement. In J. W. Oller, Jr. (ed.), *Issues in language testing research* (pp. 108-129). Rowley, MA: Newbury House, Inc.

Curtin, C., Avner, A., and Provenzano, N. (1981). Computer-based analysis of individual learning characteristics. *Studies in Language Learning, 3,* 201-213.

Curtin, C., and Shinall, S. (1987). An example of the use of microcomputers in fordign language learning and teaching from a high school for the academically talented. ERIC ED 345 523.

CUSeeMe. Cornell University, Ithaca, NY.

Daedelus Integrated Writing Environment. Includes Invent, Re-spond, Mail, Interchange, and NetManager. The Daedelus Group, Austin, TX.

Daiute, C. (1983). The computer as stylus and audience. *College Composition and Communication, 34,* 134-145.

Daiute, C. (1985). *Writing and computers.* Reading, MA: Addison-Wesley.

Daiute, C. (1986a). Do 1 and 1 make 2? Patterns of influence by collaborative authors. *Written Communication, 3,* 382-408.

Daiute, C. (1986b). Physical and cognitive factors in revising: Insights from studies with computers. *Research in the Teaching of English, 20,* 141-159.

Daiute, C. (1992). Multimedia composing: Extending the resources of kindergarten to writers across the grades. *Language Arts, 69,* 250-260.

de Bot, K. (1983). Visual feedback of intonation I: Effectiveness and induced practice behavior. *Language and Speech, 26,* 331-50.

de Bot, K., and Mailfert, K. (1982). The teaching of intonation: Fundamental research and classroom applications. *TESOL Quarterly, 16,* 71-7.

de Cheveigne, A., Abe, M., and Doshita, S. (1985). The human interface of a speech work-station. *Studia Phonologica, 19,* 18-26.

Dever, S. Y., and Pennington, M. C. (1989). Computer capabilities underlying computer-learner interaction. In M. C. Pennington (ed.), *Teaching languages with computers: The state of the art* (pp. 9-28). La Jolla, CA: Athelstan.

Dick, W. (1991). An instructional designer's view of constructivism. *Educational Technology,* May, 41-44.

Dickson, B. C. (1992). User's manual and application notes to the IPA Tutorials program. Vitoria, BC: Speech Technology Research, Ltd.

Dickson, W. P. (1985). Thought-provoking software: Juxtaposing symbol systems. *Educational Researcher,* May, 30-38.

DiPardo, A. and DiPardo, M. (1990). Towards the metapersonal essay: Exploring the potential of hypertext in the composition class. *Computers and Composition, 7*(3), 7-22.

Divine, K., and Whanger, R. (1990). Use of a computer learning laboratory with at-risk high school students. *Educational Technology, 30,* 46-48.

Dixon, R. (1981). PLATO reaches international students with English lessons. *Studies in Language Learning,3,* 98-112.

Doughty, C. (1986). A response to Robinson. In J. Fought and C. Doughty (eds.), *Second language teaching and educational technology: A state of the art symposium* (pp. 47-55). Washington, DC: Defense Intelligence Agency.

Doughty, C. (1987). Relating second-language acquisition theory to CALL research and application. In W. F. Smith (ed.), *Modern media in foreign language education: Theory and implementation* (pp. 133-167). Lincolnwood, IL: National Textbook Company.

Doughty, C. (1992). Computer applications in second language acquisition research: Design, description, and discovery. In M. C. Pennington and V. Stevens (eds.), *Computers in applied linguistics: An international perspective* (pp. 127-154). Clevedon, UK: Multilingual Matters.

Doughty, C., and Fought, C. (1984). On investigating variable learner response: Toward achieving better CALL courseware design. Report from the language analysis project. Philadelphia: University of Pennsylvania. Cited in Doughty (1987).

Douglas, D. (1981). An exploratory study of bilingual reading proficiency. In S. Hudelson (ed.), *Learning to read in different languages* (pp. 93-102). Washington, DC: Center for Applied Linguistics.

Drave, N. (1993). Stimulating simulations. *Focus on OUP*, 16, 14-15. Hong Kong: Oxford University Press.

Dunkel, P. (1987). The effectiveness literature on CAI/CALL and computing: Implications of the research for limited English proficiency learners. *TESOL Quarterly*, 21, 367-372.

Dunkel, P. (1990). Implications of the CAI effectiveness research for limited English proficient learners. *Computers in the Schools*, 7, 31-52.

Dunkel, P. (1991). The effectiveness research on computer-assisted instruction and computer-assisted language learning. In P. Dunkel (ed.), *Computer-assisted language learning and testing: Research issues and practice* (pp. 5-36). New York: Newbury House.

Eckhouse, J. (1993). Wider world plugs in to cruise the information super highway. *South China Morning Post*. Technology 4. June 8, 1993,

Edmondson, W., Reck, S. and Schroder, N. (1988). Strategic approaches used in a text-manipulation exercise. In U. O. H. Jung (ed.). *Computers in applied linguistics and language teaching* (pp.193-211). Frankfurt: Peter Lang.

Eichel, B. (1989). Computer-assisted cloze exercises in the adult ESL classroom: Enhancing retention. ERIC ED 345 493.

Eldred, J. M. (1989). Computers, composition pedagogy, and the social view. In G. E. Hawisher and C. L. Selfe (eds.), *Critical perspectives on computers and composition instruction* (pp. 201-218). New York: Teachers College Press.

Encarta. Microsoft, Inc.

Ericsson, K., and Simon, H. (1984). *Protocol analysis—Verbal reports as data*. Cambridge, MA: The MIT Press.

Erickson, F. (1981). Some approaches to inquiry in school-community ethnography. In H. Trueba, G. P. Guthrie, and K. H.-P. Au (eds.), *Culture and the bilingual classroom: Studies in classroom ethnography* (pp. 17-35). Rowley: Newbury House.

Esling, J. H. (1983). Quantitative analysis of acoustic correlates of supralaryngeal voice quality features in the long-time spectrum. In A. Cohen and M. Van den Brooke (eds.), *Abstracts of the Tenth International Congress of Phonetic Sciences* (p. 363). Dordrecht: Foris.

Esling. J. H. (1987a). Methodology for voice setting awareness in language classes. *Revue de Phonétique Appliquée, 85,* 449-473.

Esling, J. H. (1987b). Microcomputer-based phonetics instruction using the Phonetic Data Base. *Revue de Phonétique Appliquée, 85,* 425-448.

Esling, J. H. (1987c). Teaching phonetics using the Phonetic Data Base on microcomputer. *Proceedings of the XIth International Congress of Phonetic Sciences,* vol. 5, pp. 208-301. Tallinn: Academy of Sciences of the Estonian SSR.

Esling, J. H. (1990). La parole sur ordinateur dans l'enseignement de la phonétique et de la langue seconde: Matière académique au niveau avancé. *Revue de Phonétique Appliquée, 95/96/97,* 145-151.

Esling, J. H. (1991a). IPALabels: Learning phonetic sounds and symbols with HyperCard. *CAELL Journal, 2*(4), 27-29.

Esling, J. H. (1991b). *Phonetic Database* (Instruction Manual). Joint project of Kay Elemetrics Corp, Pine Brook, NJ; and Speech Technology Research, Ltd., and University of Victoria, Victoria, BC.

Esling, J. H. (1991c). Researching the effects of networking: Evaluating the spoken and written discourse generated by working with CALL. In P. Dunkel (ed.), *Computer-assisted language learning and testing: Research issues and practice* (pp. 111-131). New York: Newbury House/HarperCollins.

Esling, J. H. (1992a). Speech technology systems in applied linguistics instruction. In M. C. Pennington and V. Stevens (eds.), *Computers in applied linguistics: An international perspective* (pp. 244-272). Clevedon, UK: Multilingual Matters.

Esling, J. H. (1992b). *ESL-learner discourse in computer-assisted language learning.* Final report, December 17, 1992. University of Victoria Faculty Research Grant no. 1-41995.

Esling, J. H. (1993). Phonetics of less-known languages. In P. G. Liddell (ed.), *CALL: Theory and practice. Proceedings of the Second Canadian CALL Conference* (pp. 299-305). Victoria, BC: Fotoprint Ltd.

Esling, J. H. (1994a). Some perspectives on accent: Range of voice quality variation, the periphery, and focusing. In J. Morley (ed.), *Pronunciation pedagogy and theory: New views, new directions* (pp. 49-63). Alexandria, VA: TESOL.

Esling, J. H. (1994b). *University of Victoria Phonetic Database,* Version 3. Victoria, BC: Speech Technology Research, Ltd.

Faerch, C., and Kasper, G. (1983). Plans and strategies in foreign language communication. In C. Faerch and G. Kasper (eds.), *Strategies in interlanguage communication* (pp. 20-60). London: Longman.

Favreau, M., and Segalowitz, N. S. (1983). Automatic and controlled processes in the first- and second-language reading of fluent bilinguals. *Memory and Cognition*, 11 (6), 565-574.

Feldmann, U., and Stemmer, B. (1987). Thin- aloud a- retrospective da- in C- Te- taking: Diffe- languages diff- learners - sa- approaches? In Faerch, C. and G. Kasper (eds.), *Introspection in second language research* (pp. 251-267). Clevedon, UK: Multilingual Matters.

Flowerdew, J. (1993a). Concordancing as a tool in course design. *System*, 21(2).

Flowerdew, J. (1993b). Content based language instruction in a tertiary setting. *English for Specific Purposes*, 21(2), 231-244.

Frederiksen, J. R. (1986). Final report on the development of computer-based instructional systems for training essential components of reading. Report No. 6465. Cambridge, MA: BBN Laboratories.

Freed, M. (1971). Foreign student evaluation of a computer-assisted instruction punctuation course. Technical Memo 6. ERIC ED 072 626.

Freeman, D. (1992). Collaboration: Constructing shared understandings in a second language classroom. In D. Nunan (ed.), *Collaborative language learning and teaching* (pp. 56-80). Cambridge: Cambridge University Press.

Goh, I. S. H. (1993). A low-cost speech teaching aid for teaching English to speakers of other languages. *System*, 23, 349-357.

Goodman, K. S. (1967). Reading: A psycholinguistic guessing game. *Journal of the Reading Specialist*, 6 (May), 126-135.

Grabe, W. (1991) Current developments in second language reading research. *TESOL Quarterly*, 25, 375-406.

Graesser, A. C., Hoffman, N. L., Clark, L. F. (1980). Structural components of reading time. *Journal of Verbal Learning and Verbal Behavior*, 19, 135-51.

Haas, C. (1989). How the writing medium shapes the writing process: Effects of word processing on planning. *Research in the Teaching of English*, 23, 181-207.

Habitat. Fujitsu, Ltd., Tokyo.

Halio, M. P. (1990). Student writing: Can the machine maim the message? *Academic Computing*, 4(1), 16-19, 45.

Hall, E. (1976). *Beyond culture.* Garden City, NY: Anchor Doubleday Books.

Halliday, M. A. K., and Hasan, R. (1989). *Language, context, and text: Aspects of language in a social-semiotic perspective.* Oxford: Oxford University Press.

Hangul Express. Hypermedia CALL program for Korean. Designed by D. Ashworth, J. Kim, and J. Stelovsky. University of Hawaii at Manoa.

Hawisher, G. E. (1989). Research and recommendations for computers and composition. In G. E. Hawisher and C. L. Selfe (eds.), *Critical perspectives on computers and composition instruction* (pp. 44-69). New York: Teachers College Press.

Hawisher, G. E., and Moran, C. (1993). Electronic mail and the writing instructor. *College English, 55,* 627-643.

Heath, S. B. (1982). Ethnography in education: Defining the essentials. In P. Gilmore and A. A. Glatthorn (eds.), *Children in and out of school* (pp. 33-35). Washington, DC: Center for Applied Linguistics.

Heppner, F., Anderson, J., Farstrup, A., and Weiderman, N. (1985). Reading performance on a standardized test is better from print than from computer display. *Journal of Reading,* January, 321-325.

Hermann, F. (1991). Instrumental and agentive CALL in learning French as a foreign language. ERIC ED 332 545.

Herrmann, A. W. (1987). An ethnographic study of a high school writing class using computers: Marginal, technically proficient, and productive learners. In L. Gerrard (ed.), *Writing at century's end: Essays on computer-assisted composition* (pp. 79-91). New York: Random House.

Higgins, J. (1983). Can computers teach? *CALICO Journal, 1*(2), 4-6.

Higgins, J. (1988). *Language, learners and computers.* London: Longman.

Higgins, J. (1991a). Fuel for learning: The neglected element of textbooks and CALL. *CAELL Journal,* 2 (2), 3-7.

Higgins, J. (1991b). Which concordances: A comparative review of MSDOS software. *System, 19*(1-2), 91-100.

Higgins, J., and Johns, T. (1984). *Computers in language learning.* Reading, MA: Addison-Wesley.

Hill, C. A., Wallace, D. L., and Haas, C. (1991). Revising on-line: Computer technologies and the revising process. *Computers and Composition, 9*(1), 83-109.

Hiller, S., Rooney, E., and Jack, M. (1993). SPELL: An automated system for computer-aided pronunciation teaching. *Speech Communication, 13,* 463-473.

Hoffman, R. (1991). Working hard, working smart, or avoiding work? Reflections on electronic editing as a learning environment. In J. C. Milton and S. T. Tong (eds.), *Text analysis in computer assisted language learning: Applications, qualifications and developments* (pp. 57-70). Working papers from a seminar held at City Polytechnic of Hong Kong, March 13-15. City Polytechnic of Hong Kong and the Hong Kong University of Science and Technology.

Hoffman, R. (1993). The distance brings us closer: Electronic mail, ESL learner writers and teachers. In G. Davies and B. Samways (eds.), *Teleteaching* (pp. 391-399). Proceedings of a conference held at the University of Trondheim, August 1993. International Federation for Information Processing (IFIP), the University of Trondheim, and the Norwegian Computer Society.

Hoffman, R. (1994). The warm network, electronic mail, ESL learners, and the personal touch. *On-CALL: The Australian Journal of Computers and Education*, 8(2), 10-13.

Honeyfield, J. (1989). A typology of exercises based on computer generated concordance material. *Guidelines*, 11(1), 42-50.

Hopalong. MS-DOS software. Desigend by J. Higgins. Shareware available from author, or via TESOL/CALL-IS: MS-DOS/Window User Group.

Howard, T. (1992). WANS, connectivity, and computer literacy: An introduction and glossary. *Computers and Composition*, 9(3), 41-57.

Hubbard, P. (1987). Language teaching approaches, the evaluation of CALL software, and design implications. In W. F. Smith (ed.), *Modern media in foreign language education: Theory and implementation* (pp. 227-254). Lincolnwood, IL: National Textbook.

Hubbard, P. (1988a). An interated framework for CALL courseware evaluation. *CALICO Journal*, 6(2), 51-72.

Hubbard, P. (1988b). The teacher in the machine. *CATESOL Newsletter*, 19(6), 5-6.

Hubbard, P. (1992). A methodological framework for CALL courseware development. In M. C. Pennington and V. Stevens (eds.) *Computers in applied linguistics* (pp. 39-45). Clevedon, UK: Multilingual Matters.

Hubbard, P., Coady, J., Graney,, J., Mokhtari, K., and Magoto, J. (1986). Report on a pilot study of the relationship of high frequency vocabulary knowledge and reading proficiency in ESL readers. *Ohio University Working Papers in Linguistics and Language Teaching*, 8, 48-57.

Huckin, T., Haynes, M., and Coady, J. (eds.) (1993). *Second language reading and vocabulary learning*. Norwood, NJ: Ablex.

Hulstijn, J. (1993). When do foreign-language readers look up the meaning of unfamiliar words? The influence of task and learner variables. *Modern Language Journal*, 77(2), 139-147.

Hunter, L. (1984). Student responses to using computer text editing. *Journal of Developmental Education*, 8, 13-14, 29.

Hsu, J., Chapelle, C., and Thompson, A. (1993). Exploratory environments: What are they and do students explore? *Journal of Educational Computing Research*, 9(1), 1-15.

Hymes, D. (1974). *Foundations in sociolinguistics: An ethnographic approach*. Philadelphia: University of Pennsylvania Press.

Hymes, D. (1981). Ethnographic monitoring. In H. Trueba, G. P. Guthrie, and K. H.-P. Au (eds.), *Culture and the bilingual classroom: Studies in classroom ethnography* (pp. 56-68). Rowley, MA: Newbury House.

HyperCard. Apple Computer, Cupertino, CA. (Formerly published by Claris).

HyperStudio. Roger Wagner Publishing, Inc., El Cajon, CA.

James, C., and Garrett, P. (1991). *Language awareness in the classroom*. London: Longman.

James, E. (1976). The acquisition of prosodic features of speech using a speech visualiser. *International Review of Applied Linguistics, 14*, 227-243.

Jamieson, J., and Chapelle, C. (1987). Working styles on computers as evidence of second language learning strategies. *Language Learning, 37*, 523-544.

Jamieson, J., and Chapelle, C. (1988) Using CALL effectively: What do we need to know about students? *System, 16*, 151-162.

Jamieson, J., Norfleet, L., and Berbisada, N. (1993). Successes, failures, and dropouts in computer-assisted language lessons. *CAELL Journal, 4*, 12-20.

Johns, T. (1986). Micro-concord: A language-learner's research tool. *System, 14*(2), 151-162.

Johns, T. (1988). Whence and whither classroom concordancing? In T. Bongaerts, P. de Haan, S. Lobbe, and H. Wekker (eds.) *Computer applications in language learning* (pp. 9-33). Dordrecht: Foris.

Johns, T. (1991a). Should you be persuaded: Two examples of data-driven learning. *ELR Journal (New Series), 4*, 1-16.

Johns, T. (1991b). From printout to handout: Grammar and vocabulary teaching in the context of data-driven learning *ELR Journal (New Series), 4*, 27-46.

Johnson, D. M. (1991). Second language and content learning with computers: Research in the role of social factors. In P. Dunkel (ed.), *Computer-assisted language learning and testing: Research issues and practice* (pp. 61-83). New York: Newbury House.

Johnson, K. (1992). Learning to teach: Instructional actions and decisions of preservice ESL teachers. *TESOL Quarterly, 26*, 507-535.

Johnson, R. T., Johnson, D. W., and Stanne, M. B. (1986). Comparison of computer-assisted cooperative, competitive, and individualistic learning. *American Educational Research Journal, 23*, 382-392.

Jonassen, D. H. (1985). Learning strategies: A new educational technology. *Programmed Learning and Educational Technology, 22*, 26-34.

Jones, C. (1995, September). The oral language archive: An introduction. Paper presented at the CALL and the Learning Environment Conference. University of Exeter, Exeter, UK, September 1995.

Jones, C., and Fortescue, S. (1987). *Using computers in the language classroom.* London: Longman.

Jonz, J. (1990). Another turn in the conversation: What does cloze measure? *TESOL Quarterly, 24* (1), 61-83.

Joram, E., Woodruff, E., Bryson, M., and Lindsay, P. H. (1992). The effects of revision with a word processor on written composition. *Research in the Teaching of English, 26*, 167-193.

Jorden, E., and Noda, M. (1986). *Japanese: The spoken language.* New Haven, CT: Yale University Press.

Kalaja, P., and Leppänen, S. (1991). "Hello, it's me again" —Process writing and computer conferencing in EFL. In H. Savolainen and J.

Telenius (eds.), *EuroCALL 1991* (pp. 341-348). Proceedings of a conference held at the Helsinki School of Economics, August 21-23. Helsinki School of Economics and the Helsinki University of Technology.

Kalikow, D. W., and Swets, J. A. (1972). Experiments with computer-controlled displays in second-language learning. *IEEE Transactions in Audio and Electroacoustics, 20*, 23-28.

Kanji City. Hypermedia program for Japanese. Designed by D. Ashworth and J. Stelovsky. University of Hawaii at Manoa.

Kaplan, N., and Moulthroup, S. (1990). Other ways of seeing. *Computers and Composition, 7*(3), 89-102.

Karrer, U. (1991). Impacts of courseware and student characteristics on learning achievement: Results of an empirical study. *Journal of Computer Assisted Learning, 7*, 18-33.

Keith, C., and Lafford, P. (1989). Designing software for vocational language programs: an overview of the development process. In M. C. Pennington (ed.), *Teaching languages with computers: The state of the art* (pp. 125-143. La Jolla CA: Athelstan.

Kemmis, S., Atkin, R., and Wright, E. (1977). How do students learn? *Working Papers on Computer Assisted Learning*, UNCAL Evaluation Studies, No. 5. Norwich, UK: Centre for Applied Research in Education.

Kemp, F. (1992). Who programmed this? Examining the instructional attitudes of writing-support software. *Computers and Composition, 10*(1), 9-24.

Kienbaum, B., Russel, A. J., and Welty, S. (1986). Communicative competence in foreign language learning with authentic materials. Final project report, ERIC 275200. Klatt, D. H. (1987). Review of text-to-speech conversion for English. *Journal of the Acoustical Society of America, 82*, 737-793.

King, A. (1991). Effects of training in strategic questioning on children's problem-solving performance. *Journal of Educational Psychology, 83*, 307-317.

King, P. (1989). The uncommon core: Some discourse features of student writing. *System, 17*, 113-20.

Kleinmann, H. (1987). The effect of computer-assisted instruction on ESL reading achievement. *The Modern Language Journal, 71* (3), 267-276.

Kozma, R. (1991). Computer-based tools and the cognitive needs of novice writers. *Computers and Composition, 8*(2), 31-45.

Krashen, S. (1982). *Principles and practice in second language acquisition*. Oxford: Pergamon.

Kreeft Peyton, J. (1986). Computer networking: Making connections between speech and writing. *ERIC/CLL News Bulletin, 10*(1), 5-7.

Kremers, M. (1990). Sharing authority on a synchronous network: The case for riding the beast. *Computers and Composition, 7*(2), 33-44.

Kruglanski, A. W. (1989). *Lay epistemics and human knowledge: Cognitive and motivational bases*. New York: Plenum.

Kulik, C-L., and Kulik, J. (1986). Effectiveness of computer-based education in colleges. *AEDS Journal, 19*, 81-108.

Kulik, C-L., and Kulik, J. (1991). Effectiveness of computer-based instruction: An updated analysis. *Computers in Human Behavior, 7*, 75-94.

Kulik, C-L., Kulik, J., and Shwalb, B. (1986). The effectiveness of computer-based adult education: A meta-analysis. *Journal of Educational Computing Research, 2*, 235-252.

Kulik, J., Kulik, C-L., and Bangert-Drowns, R. (1985). Effectiveness of computer-based education in elementary schools. *Computers in Human Behavior, 1*, 59-74.

Lambert, S., and Ropiequet, S. (1986). *CD ROM: The new papyrus.* Redmond, WA: Microsoft Press.

Larsen-Freeman, D., and Long, M. (1991). *An introduction to second language acquisition research.* London: Longman.

Laurel, B. (1991). *Computers as theater.* New York: Addison-Wesley.

Lea, M. (1992). Introduction: Recontextualizing computer-mediated communication. In M. Lea (Ed.), *Contexts of computer-mediated communication* (pp. 1-6). Hempstead, UK: Harvester Wheatsheaf.

Leather, J. (1990). Perceptual and productive learning of Chinese lexical tone by Dutch and English speakers. In J. Leather and A. James (eds.), *New Sounds 90* (pp. 72-89). Amsterdam: University of Amsterdam.

Lee, J. (1990). A review of empirical comparisons of non-native reading behaviors across stages of language development. Paper presented at the Second Language Research Forum, University of Oregon, Eugene, Oregon.

Lefèvre, J.-P., Hiller, S. M., Rooney, E., Laver, J., and Di Benedetto, M.-G. (1992). Macro and micro features for automated pronunciation improvement in the SPELL system. *Speech Communication, 11*, 31-44.

Lesgold, A. M. (1984). Acquiring expertise. In J. R. Anderson and S. M. Kosslyn (eds.), *Tutorials in learning and memory* (pp. 31-60). New York: W. H. Freeman and Company.

Lesgold, A. M., and Perfetti, C.A. (1981). *Interactive processes in reading.* Hillsdale, NJ: Lawrence Erlbaum.

Levine, H. G. (1990). Models of qualitative data use in the assessment of classroom-based microcomputer education programs. *Journal of Educational Computing Research, 6*, 461-477.

Levy, M. (1990). Concordances and their integration into a word-processing environment for language learners. *System, 18*(2), 177-188.

Levy, M. (1993). *An inquiry into the conceptual frameworks and working methods of CALL authors.* Unpublished doctoral dissertation. Bond University (Australia).

Liou, H-C. (1986). Language use by pairs of ESL students working on interactive computer language programs. Unpublished master's thesis. Iowa State University.

Liou, H-C. (1993). Integrating text analysis programs into classroom writing revision. *CAELL Journal, 4*, 21-27.

Long, M. H. (1980). Inside the "black box": Methodological issues in classroom research on language learning. *Language Learning, 30,* 1-42.

Long, M. H. (1985). Input and second language acquisition theory. In S. M. Gass and C. G. Madden (eds.), *Input in second language acquisition* (pp. 377-393). Rowley, MA: Newbury House.

Longman Interactive Dictionary. CD-ROM software. Longman, London.

Lozano, A. (1985). Educational technology and language training. International Research and Studies Program. Final Report. ERIC ED 263 786.

Lysiak, F., Wallace, S., and Evans, C. (1976). Computer-assisted instruction 1975-75 evaluation report. A Title 1 Program. ERIC ED 140 495.

Ma, K. C. (1993a). Classroom concordancing: How and what students learn. Unpublished M.A. dissertation, City Polytechnic of Hong Kong.

Ma, K. C. (1993b). Text analysis of direct mail sales letters. In T. Boswood, R. Hoffman, and P. Tung (eds.), *Perspectives on English for professional communication* (pp. 271-288). Department of English. City Polytechnic of Hong Kong.

Madigan, C. (1984). The tools that shape us: Composing by hand vs. composing by machine. *English Education, 16,* 143-150.

Marcoulides, G. (1991). An examination of cross-cultural differences toward computers. *Computers in Human Behavior, 7,* 281-289.

Marx, M. S. (1990). Distant writers, distant critics, and close readings: Linking composition classes through a peer-critiquing network. *Computers and Composition, 8*(1), 23-39.

Mavis Beacon Teaches Typing. Version 2.02. The Software Toolworks, Berkeley, CA.

McAllister, C., and Louth, R. (1988). The effect of word processing on the quality of basic writers' revisions. *Research in the Teaching of English, 22,* 417-427.

McLaughlin, B. (1987). Reading in a second language: Studies with adult and child learners. In S. Goldman and H. T. Trueba, *Becoming literate in ESL* (pp. 57-70). Norwood, NJ: Ablex.

McLeod, B., and McLaughlin, B. (1986). Restructuring or automaticity? Reading in a second language. *Lanuage Learning, 36* (2), 109-123.

Mehan, H. (1979). *Learning lessons: Social organization in the classroom.* Cambridge: Harvard University Press.

Meredith, R. (1978). Improved oral test scores through delayed response. *Modern Language Journal, 62,* 321-327.

MicroConcord. Oxford University Press, Oxford.

Mikulecky, L., Clark, E., and Adams, S. (1989). Teaching concept mapping and university level study strategies using computers. *Journal of Reading, 32,* 694-702.

Miller, G. A. (1956). The magical number seven, plus-or-minus two: some limitations on our capacity for information processing. *Psychological Review, 63*, 81-97.

Milton, J. (undated). The Hong Kong University of Science and Technology learners' corpus. Hong Kong: The Hong Kong University of Science and Technology.

Mini Concordancer. Longman, London.

Minsky, M. (1975). A framework for representing knowledge. In P. H. Winston (ed.), *The psychology of computer vision.* New York: McGraw-Hill.

Mitchell, D. C., and Green, D. W. (1978). The effects of context and content on immediate processing in reading. *Quarterly Journal of Experimental Psychology, 30*, 609-636.

Mohan, B. (1992). Models of the role of the computer in second language development. In M. C. Pennington and V. Stevens (eds.), *Computers in applied linguistics: An international perspective* (pp. 110-126). Clevedon, UK: Multilingual Matters.

Molholt, G. (1988). Computer-assisted instruction in pronunciation for Chinese speakers of American English. *TESOL Quarterly, 22*, 91-111.

Monohan, B. D. (1982). Computing and revising. *English Journal, 7*, 93-94.

Mparutsa, C., Love, A., and Morrison, A. (1991). Bringing concord to the ESP classroom. *ELR Journal (New Series), 4*, 115-134.

Murison-Bowie, S. (1993). *MicroConcord manual.* Oxford: Oxford University Press.

Murphy, R., and Appel, L. (1977). Evaluation of the PLATO IV computer-based education system in the community college. Final Report. ERIC ED 146 235.

Naiman, N., Fröhlich, M., Stern, H., and Todesco, A. (1978). The good language learner. *Research in Education Series,* Report No. 7. Toronto: Ontario Institute for Studies in Education.

Nichols, R.G. (1986). Word processing and basic writers. *Journal of Basic Writing, 5*, 81-97.

Nunan, D. (1985). Content familiarity and the perception of textual relationships in second language reading. *RELC Journal, 16*, 43-50.

Nunan, D. (1991). Methods in second language classroom-oriented research: A critical review. *Studies in Second Language Acquisition, 13*, 249-274.

Oakhill, J. (1993). Children's difficulties in reading comprehension. Educational *Psychology Review, 5* (3), 223-237.

Oates, W. (1981). An evaluation of computer-assisted instruction for English grammar review. *Studies in Language Learning, 3*, 193-200.

Oller, J. W. (1979). *Language tests at school.* London: Longman.

Olofsson, A. (1988). Phonemic awareness and the use of computer speech in reading remediation: Theoretical background. *Fonetiks, 1*, 15-27. Cited in Barron et al., 1992.

Olson, R. K., Foltz, G., and Wise, B. (1986). Reading instruction and remediation with the aid of computer speech. *Behavior Research Methods, Instruments, and Computers, 18,* 93-99.

O'Malley, J., Chamot, A., Stewner-Manzanares, G., Kupper, L., and Russo, R. (1985). Learning strategies used by beginning and intermediate ESL students. *Language Learning, 35,* 21-46.

Owston, R. D., Murphy, S., and Wideman, H. H.. (1992). The effects of word processing on students' writing quality and revision strategies. *Research in the Teaching of English, 26,* 249-276.

Oxford, R. (1990). *Language learning strategies—What every teacher should know.* Rowley, MA: Newbury House.

Papert, S. (1987). Computer criticism vs. technocentric thinking. *Educational Researcher,* Jan-Feb, 22-30.

Park, Y. (1994). *Incorporating an interactive multimedia in an ESL classroom environment: ESL learners' interactions and learning strategies.* Unpublished doctoral dissertation. Department of Curriculum and Instruction, Iowa State University, Ames, Iowa.

Parkinson, S., and Bladon, A. (1987). Microcomputer-assisted phonetics teaching and phonetics word-processing: A survey. *Journal of the International Phonetic Association, 17*(2), 83-93.

Pederson, K. M. (1986). An experiment in computer-assisted second language reading. *Modern Language Journal, 70* (1), 36-41.

Pederson, K. M. (1987). Research on CALL. In W. F. Smith (ed.), *Modern media in foreign language education: Theory and implementation* (pp. 99-131). Lincolnwood IL: National Textbook Company.

Pennington, M. C. (1986). A discussion of Robinson. In C. Doughty and J. Fought (eds.), *Second language teaching and educational technology: A state of the art symposium* (pp. 56-59). Proceedings of a conference held at the Defense Language Institute. Monterey, CA, February 1986. University of Pennsylvania and Defense Intelligence Agency.

Pennington, M. C. (1989a). Applications of computers in the development of speaking and listening proficiency. In M. C. Pennington (ed.), *Teaching languages with computers: The state of the art* (pp. 97-121). La Jolla, CA: Athelstan.

Pennington, M. C. (1989b). Teaching pronunciation from the top down. *RELC Journal, 20*(1), 20-38.

Pennington, M. C. (1991a). A qualitative artifact analysis of the attributes of word processing for student writers. *Computer Assisted Language Learning, 4,* 93-105.

Pennington, M. C. (1991b). Computer-assisted analysis of prosody: Applications to research in English dialects and interlanguage. In P. Dunkel (ed.), *Computer-assisted language learning and testing: Research issues and practice* (pp. 133-154). New York: Newbury House/HarperCollins.

Pennington, M. C. (1991c). Positive and negative potentials of word processing for ESL writers. *System, 19*(3), 267-275.

Pennington, M. C. (1991d). The road ahead: A forward-looking view of computers in applied linguistics. *Computer-Assisted Language Learning*, 4(1), 3-19.

Pennington, M. C. (1992a). Beyond off-the-shelf computer remedies for student writers: Alternatives to canned feedback. *System*, 20(4), 423-437.

Pennington, M. C. (1992b). Discourse factors related to L2 phonological proficiency: An exploratory study. In J. Leather and A. James (eds.), *New Sounds 92*, Proceedings of the 1992 Amsterdam Symposium on the Acquisition of Second-language Speech (pp. 137-155). University of Amsterdam, April 13-16, 1992.

Pennington, M. C. (1993a). Computer-assisted writing on a principled basis: The case against computer-assisted text analysis for non-proficient writers. *Language and Education*, 7(1), 43-59.

Pennington, M. C. (1993b). A critical examination of word processing effects in relation to L2 writers. *Journal of Second Language Writing*, 2, 227-255.

Pennington, M. C. (in press, a). *The computer and the non-native writer: A natural partnership*. Cresskill, NJ: Hampton Press.

Pennington, M. C. (in press, b). *Language learning: An introduction*. London: Edward Arnold.

Pennington, M. C. (in press, c). *Phonology in English language teaching: An international approach*. London: Longman.

Pennington, M. C. (in press, d). Phonology in language teaching: Essentials of theory and practice. In K. Bardovi-Harlig and B. S. Hartford (eds.), *Beyond methods: Companion components in language teacher education*. New York: McGraw-Hill.

Pennington, M. C., and Brock, M. N. (1992). Process and product approaches to computer-assisted composition. In M. C. Pennington and V. V. Stevens (eds.), *Computers in applied linguistics: An international perspective* (pp. 79-109). Clevedon, UK: Multilingual Matters.

Pennington, M. C., and Ellis, N. C. (1995). Learnability of English prosody. Earmarked Research Grant, Hong Kong Research Grants Council.

Pennington, M. C., and Singer, S. (forthcoming). Into the future: Expanding frontiers of the computer in society. Unpublished ms.

Pennington, M. C., and Stevens, V. (1992). Introduction: Toward appropriate uses of computers in applied linguistics. In M. C. Pennington and V. Stevens (eds.), *Computers in applied linguistics: An international perspective* (pp. 1-8). Clevedon, UK: Multilingual Matters.

Perfetti, C. A. (1983). Reading, vocabulary, and writing: Implications for computer-based instruction. In A. C. Wilkinson, *Classroom computers and cognitive science* (pp. 145-163). New York: Academic Press.

Perfetti, C. A. (1985). *Reading ability*. New York: Oxford University Press.

Perfetti, C. A., Goldman, S. R., and Hogaboam, T. W. (1979). Reading skill and the identification of words in discourse context. *Memory and Cognition, 7* (4), 273-282.

Perkins, D. (1985). The fingertip effect: How information-processing technology shapes thinking. *Educational Researcher, 14*(7), 11-17.

Peterson, M. (1990). *An evaluation of VOXBOX: A computer-based voice-interactive language learning system for teaching English as a second language.* Unpublished doctoral dissertation. United States International University.

Petwords. Unpublished courseware for Macintosh. Designed by T. Cobb. College of Commerce and Economics, Sultan Qaboos University, Oman.

Phillips, M. (1985). Logical possibilities and classroom scenarios for the development of CALL. In C. Brumfit, M. Phillips, and P. Skehan, *Computers in English language teaching.* New York: Pergamon.

Phinney, M. (1989). Computers, composition, and second language teaching. In M. C. Pennington (ed.), *Teaching languages with computers: The state of the art* (pp. 81-96). La Jolla, CA: Athelstan.

Phinney, M. (1991a). Computer assisted writing and writing apprehension in ESL students. In P. Dunkel (ed.), *Research issues and studies on computer assisted language learning and testing* (pp. 189-204). New York: Newbury House/HarperCollins.

Phinney, M. (1991b). Word processing and writing apprehension in native and non-native writers. *Computers and Composition, 10*(1), 65-82.

Phinney, M. (1992). Using electronic mail: Exploring our virtual world. Paper presented at the Mexico-Caribbean-Latin America Joint TESOL conference. Acapulco, Mexico, October 1992.

Phinney, M. (1993a). Building a HyperCard information kiosk: An ESL technical writing project. Paper presented at the 9th annual Computers and Writing Conferenc. Ann Arbor, MI May 1993.

Phinney, M. (1993b). Studying the computer writing process. Paper presented at CALL Academic session, Computers and Writing: From Process to Product, 27th International TESOL meeting, Atlanta, Georgia, April 14-17, 1993.

Phinney, M. (1994). *Process your thoughts.* Boston, MA: Heinle and Heinle.

Phinney, M., and Khouri, S. (1992). The hypertext research "paper": Students writing for students. Paper presented at the 9th annual Computers and Writing Conference. Indianapolis, May 1992.

Phinney, M., and Khouri, S. (1993). Computers, revision, and ESL writers: The role of experience. *Journal of Second Language Writing, 2*, 257-277.

Phinney, M., and Mathis, C. (1990). ESL student responses to writing with computers. *TESOL Newsletter, 24*(2), 30-31.

Pickard, V. (1993). Empowering novice writers: Can concordancers contribute? Paper presented at the 17th Annual Meeting of the Teachers of English to Speakers of Other Languages. Atlanta, April 1993.

Piper, A. (1986). Conversation and the computer: A study of the conversational spin-off generated among learners of English as a foreign language working in groups. *System, 14,* 187-198.

Piper, A. (1987). Helping learners to write: A role for the word processor. *ELT Journal, 41,* 119-125.

Polson, C. (1992). Component processes of second language reading. Concordia University, Montreal. Unpublished Master's thesis.

Prep Editor. Designed by a research team at Carnegie Mellon University. Available through e-mail at: prepproject@andrew.cmu.edu.

Price, K. (1992). Look who's talking: A computer-assisted system for discourse analysis. *Cross Currents: An International Journal of Language Teaching and Intercultural Communication, 19*(1), 73-79.

Price, K., and Imbier, E. (1993). A videodisc project for ESL: "Who should do the housework?" In J. V. Boettcher (ed.), *101 success stories of information technology in higher education: The Joe Wyatt challenge* (pp. 214-219). New York: McGraw-Hill.

Pufahl, J. (1984). Response to R. M. Collier, The word processor and revision strategies. *College Composition and Communication, 35,* 91-93.

Reid, J. (1986). Using the writer's workbench in composition teaching and testing. In C. Stansfield (ed.), *Technology and language testing* (pp. 167-188). Washington, DC: TESOL.

Reid, J., Lindstrom, P., McCaffrey, M., and Larson, D. (1983). Computer-assisted text analysis for ESL students. *CALICO Journal, 1*(3), 40-42.

Read, C., Buder, E. H., and Kent, R. D. (1990). Speech analysis systems: A survey. *Journal of Speech and Hearing Research, 33,* 363-374.

Read, C., Buder, E. H., and Kent, R. D. (1992). Speech analysis systems: An evaluation. *Journal of Speech and Hearing Research, 35,* 314-332.

Realtime Writer. ENFI software. Realtime Learning Systems, Washington, D.C.

Rhubarb. Designed by J. Higgins and M. Higgins. Research Design Associates, Stony Brook, NY.

Richards, J., and Rodgers, T. (1982). Method: Approach, design, and procedure. *TESOL Quarterly, 16*(2), 153-68.

Rieber, R. W., and Carton, A.S. (1987). *The collected works of L. S. Vygotsky, vol. 1, Problems of general psychology.* N. Minick, trans. New York: Plenum Press.

Robinson, G. (1986). Focus on the learner. *University of Hawaii Working Papers in ESL, 5,* 61-86.

Roblyer, M., Castine, W., and King, F. (1988). *Assessing the impact of computer-based instruction: A review of recent research.* Binghampton, NY: Haworth Press.

Rochet, B. (1990). Training non-native speech contrasts on the Macintosh. In M.-L. Craven, R. Sinyor, and D. Paramskas (eds.), *CALL: Papers and reports* (pp. 119-126). La Jolla, CA: Athelstan.

Rodrigues, D., and Rodrigues, R. (1989). How word processing is changing our teaching: New approaches, new challenges. *Computers and Composition,* 7(1), 13-25.

Rubin, A., and Bruce, B. C. (1990). Alternate realizations of purpose in computer-supported writing. *Theory Into Practice,* 29 (4), 256-263.

Salomon, G. (1979). *Interaction of media, cognition, and learning.* San Francisco: Jossey-Bass.

Sarracho, O. (1982). The effects of a computer-assisted instruction program on basic skills achievement and attitudes toward instruction of Spanish-speaking migrant children. *American Education Research Journal,* 19, 201-219.

Schaeffer, R. H. (1981). Meaningful practice on the computer: Is it possible? *Foreign Language Annals,* 14, 133-137.

Schank, R. C., and Abelson, R. P. (1977). *Scripts, plans, goals and understanding: An inquiry into human knowledge structures.* Hillsdale NJ: Erlbaum.

Schenck, M. J. (1988). *Read, write, revise: A guide to academic writing.* New York: St. Martin's Press.

Schiffrin, D. (1987). *Discourse markers.* Cambridge: Cambridge University Press.

Schrupp, D., Busch, M. D., and Mueller, G. A. (1983). Klavier imhaus—An interactive experiment in foreign language instruction. *CALICO Journal,* 1(2), 17-21.

Schumann, F. (1980). Diary of a language learner: A further analysis. In R. Scarcella and S. D. Krashen (eds.), *Research in second language acquisition* (pp. 51-57). Rowley, MA: Newbury House.

Schumann, F. M., and Schumann, J. H. (1977). Diary of a language learner: An introspective study of second language learning. In H. D. Brown, C. A. Yorio, and R. H. Crymes (eds.), *On TESOL '77. Teaching and learning English as a second language: Trends in research and practice* (pp. 241-249). Washington, DC: TESOL.

Schwartz, H. J. (1982). Computers and the teaching of writing. *Educational Technology,* 22, 27-29.

Schwartz, H. J. (1984). Teaching writing with computer aids. *College English,* 46, 239-247.

Schwerin, J. (1993). Market monitor. *CD ROM World,* July, p. 15.

Segalowitz, N. (1986). Skilled reading in a second language. In J. Vaid (ed.), *Language processing in bilinguals: Psycholonguistic and neuropsychological perspectives* (pp. 3-19) . Hillsdale, NJ: Erlbaum.

Selinker, L. (1992). *Rediscovering interlanguage.* London: Longman.

Sequitur. MS-DOS software. Designed by J. Higgins. Research Design Associates, Stonybrook, NY

Sheingold, K., Kane, J. H., and Endreweit, M. E. (1983). Microcomputer use in schools: Developing a research agenda. *Harvard Educational Review,* 53(4), 412-432.

Sinclair, J. McH. (1991). *Corpus, concordance collocation*. Oxford: Oxford Uiversity Press.

Sinclair, J. McH., and Renouf, A. (1988). A lexical syllabus for language learning. In R. Carter and M. McCarthy (eds.) *Vocabulary and language teaching* (pp. 140-160). London: Longman.

Sirc, G., and Reynolds, T. (1990). The face of collaboration in the networked writing classroom. *Computers and Composition*, 7(2), 53-70.

Skehan, P. (1989). *Individual differences in second-language learning*. London: Edward Arnold.

Slatin, J., Batson, T., Boston, R., and Cohen, M. E. (1990). Computer teachers respond to Halio. *Computers and Composition*, 7(3), 73-79.

Spears, R., and Lea, M. (1992). Social influence and the influence of the 'social' in computer-mediated communication. In M. Lea (ed.), *Contexts of computer-mediated communication* (pp. 30-65). London: Harvester Wheatsheaf

Spindler, G., and Spindler, L. (1987). *Interactive ethnography of education: At home and abroad*. London: Lawrence Erlbaum.

Smith, F. (1971). *Understanding reading: A psycholinguistic analysis of reading and learning to read*, Third edition. New York: Holt, Rinehart, and Winston.

SonaMatch. Kay Elemetrics, Pine Brook, NJ.

Stanovich, K. E., and Cunningham, A. E. (1991). Reading as constrained reasoning. In R. J. Sternberg and P. A. Frensch (eds.), *Complex problem solving: Principles and mechanisms* (pp. 3-60). Hillsdale, NJ: Erlbaum.

Stanovich, K. E., and West, R. F. (1979). Mechanisms of sentence context effects in reading: Automatic activation and conscious attention. *Memory and Cognition*, 7 (2), 77-85.

Stanovich, K. E., and West, R. F. (1981). The effect of sentence context on ongoing word recognition: Tests of a two-process theory. *Journal of Experimental Psychology: Human Perception and Performance*, 7(3), 658-672.

Steinberg, E. R. (1989). Cognition and learner control: A literature review, 1977-1988. *Journal of Computer Based Instruction*. 16 (4).

Stevens, V. (1984). Implications of research and theory concerning the influence of control on the effectiveness of CALL. *CALICO Journal* 2(1), 28-33, 48.

Stevens, V. (1989). A direction for CALL: From behavioristic to humanistic courseware. In M. C. Pennington (ed.), *Teaching languages with computers: The state of the art* (pp. 31-43). La Jolla, CA: Athelstan.

Stevens, V. (1991a). Computer Hangman: Pedagogically sound or a waste of time? Revised version of a paper presented at the 24th Annual Meeting of the Teachers of English to Speakers of Other Languages. San Francisco, March 1990. ERIC Document Reproduction Service No. ED 332 524.

Stevens, V. (1991b). Strategies in solving computer-based cloze: Is it reading? Paper presented at the 25th Annual Meeting of the Teachers of English to Speakers of Other Languages. New York, March 1991. ERIC Document Reproduction Service No. ED 335 952.

Stevens, V. (1991c). Reading and computers: Hangman and cloze. *CAELL Journal*, 2 (3), 12-16.

Stevens, V. (1992). Humanism and CALL: A coming of age. In M. C. Pennington and V. Stevens (eds.), *Computers in applied linguistics: An international perspective* (pp. 11-38). Clevedon, UK: Multilingual Matters.

Stevens, V. (forthcoming). Promoting productive language learning strategies in an implementation of computer-based cloze through an investigation of on-line ESL learner interaction. Ph.D. dissertation. School of English Language Teaching, Thames Valley University.

StorySpace. Designed by Jay David Bolter, Michael Joyce, and John B. Smith. Eastgate Systems, Civilized Software, Cambridge, MA.

Stubbs, M. (1983). *Discourse analysis: The sociolinguistic analysis of natural language*. Oxford: Basil Blackwell.

Susser, B. (1993). Networks and project work: Alternative pedagogies for writing with computers. *Computers and Composition*, 10(3), 63-89.

Suzuki, H., Kiritani, S., and Imagawa, H. (1986). For improvement of English intonation learning system. *Annual Bulletin RILP*, 23, 59-63.

Swain, M. (1985). Communicative competence: Some roles of comprehensible input and comprehensible output in its development. In S. M. Gass and C. G. Madden (eds.), *Input in second language acquisition* (pp. 235-253). Rowley, MA: Newbury House.

Swales, J. (1990). *Genre analysis: English in academic and research settings*. Cambridge: Cambridge University Press.

Tammelin, M. (1991). Project ICONS: Using a multinational computer-assisted simulation in a language class. In H. Savolainen and J. Telenius (eds.), *EuroCALL 1991* (pp. 312-319). Proceedings of a conference held at the Helsinki School of Economics, August 21-23. Helsinki School of Economics and the Helsinki University of Technology.

Textpert. Unpublished courseware for Macintosh. Designed by T. Cobb. Educational Technology, Concordia University, Montreal.

The Animals!. CD-ROM software. The Software Toolworks, Inc., Novato, CA.

The Observer. A tool for logging and playing back user interactions with hypermedia. Designed by D. Ashworth, S. Sakamoto, and J. Stelovsky. University of Hawaii at Manoa.

Tillyer, A. (1993). Discourse analysis of student e-mail writing. Paper presented at CALL Academic session, Computers and Writing: From Process to Product, 27th International Meeting of the Teachers of English to Speakers of Other Languages, Atlanta, GA, April 1993.

Todman, J., and Lawrensen, H. (1992). Computer anxiety in primary schoolchildren and university students. *British Educational Research Journal, 18,* 63-72.

ToolBook. Software Construction Set for Windows. Asymetrix Corporation, Bellevue, WA.

Tribble, C. (1990). Concordancing and an EAP writing programme. *CAELL Journal, 1*(2), 10-15.

Tribble, C. (1991). Some uses of electronic text in English for academic purposes. In J. C. Milton and K. Tong (eds.) *Text analysis in computer assisted language learning* (pp. 4-14). Hong Kong: The Hong Kong University of Science and Technology and the City Polytechnic of Hong Kong.

Tribble, C., and Jones, G. (1990). *Concordancing in the classroom.* Harlow, UK: Longman.

Tulving, E., and Gold, C. (1963). Stimulus information and contextual information as determinants of tachistoscopic recognition of words. *Journal of Experimental Psychology, 66*(4), 319-327.

Tuman, M. C. (1992). *Word perfect: Literacy in the computer age.* London: Falmer Press; Pittsburgh: University of Pittsburgh Press.

Underwood, J. (1984). *Linguistics, computers, and the language teacher.* Rowley, MA: Newbury House.

Upitis, R. (1990). Real and contrived uses of electronic mail in elementary schools. *Computers and Education, 15* (1-3), 233-243.

Utsumi, T. (1993). Successful reception of CU-SeeMe winwindow in Moscow. Internet memorandum to participants in Glosas USA: U.S.-Russia EDES Project, GLH/TeleTeaching '93. August 26, 1993.

Van Campen, J. (1981). A computer-assisted course in Russian. In P. Suppes (ed.), *University-level computer-assisted instruction at Stanford: 1968-80* (pp. 603-646). Stanford, CA: Institute for Mathematics Studies in the Social Sciences.

Van Lier, L. (1988). *The classroom and the language learner: Ethnography and second-language classroom research.* London: Longman.

Van Waes, L. (1992). Writing profiles of computer writers. Paper presented at 9th annual Computers and Writing Conference. Indianapolis, May 1992.

Video Voice. MicroVideo, Ann Arbor, MI.

Visi-Pitch. Kay Elemetrics, Pine Brooks, NJ.

Viteli, J. (1989). Learning styles and individual differences in learning English idioms via computer assisted language learning in English as a second language. ERIC ED 320 559.

Voyager Expanded Book. Macintosh hypermedia software. Voyager Company.

Voyager Expanded Book Toolkit. Macintosh hypermedia program. Voyager Company.

Warschauer, M. (1995). *Email for English teaching.* Washington, DC: TESOL.

Watson-Gegeo, K. A. (1988). Ethnography in ESL: Defining the essentials. *TESOL Quarterly, 22*(4), 575-592.

Weizenbaum, J. (1976). *Computer power and human reason: From judgment to calculation.* San Francisco: W. H. Freeman.

Wells, R. (1993) The use of computer-mediated communication in distance education: progress, problems, and trends. In G. Davies and B. Samways (eds.), *Teleteaching* (pp. 79-88). Proceedings of a conference held at the University of Trondheim, August 1993. International Federation for Information Processing (IFIP), the University of Trondheim, and the Norwegian Computer Society.

Weltens, B., and de Bot, K. (1984). Visual feedback of intonation II: Feedback delay and quality of feedback. *Language and Speech, 27*(1), 79-88.

Wenden, A. (1985). Learner strategies. *TESOL Newsletter, 19*, 1-7.

Where in the World is Carmen Santiago. CD-ROM software. Broderbund Software Inc., Novato, CA.

Willis, J. D. (1990). *The lexical syllabus.* London and Glasgow: Collins.

Willis, J. D., and Willis, J. R. (1988). *Collins COBUILD English course.* London and Glasgow: Collins.

Windeatt, S. (1986). Observing CALL in action. In G. Leech and C. N. Candlin (eds.), *Computers in English language teaching and research* (pp. 79-97). New York: Longman.

Wise, B., Olson, R. K., Anstett, M., Andrews, L. Terjak, M. Schneider, V. Kostuch, J., and Kriho, L. (1989). Implementing a long-term computerized remedial reading program with synthetic speech feedback. *Behavior Research Methods, Instruments, and Computers, 21*, 173-180.

Wise, B., Olson, R. K., and Treiman, R. (1990). Subsyllabic units in computerized reading instruction: Onset-rime vs. Post-vowel segmentation. *Journal of Experimental Child Psychology, 24*, 234-267.

Womble, G. G. (1984). Process and processor: Is there room for a machine in the English classroom? *English Journal, 73*, 34-37.

Writer's Helper. Designed by William Wresch. Conduit, University of Iowa, Iowa City, IA.

Wusnack, T., and Strongman, R. (1993). Computer-mediated language learning: An overview and a case study. Unpublished paper, University of Texas at El Paso.

Wyatt, D. (1989). Computers and reading skills: The medium and the message. In M. C. Pennington (ed.), *Teaching languages with computers: The state of the art* (pp. 63-78). La Jolla, CA: Athelstan.

Yang, H. Z. (1991). Corpus-based learning: The JDEST corpus. Talk given to Department of English. City Polytechnic of Hong Kong, May 1991.

Young, R. (1988). Computer-assisted language learning conversations: Negotiating an outcome. *CALICO Journal, 5*(3), 65-83.

Youra, S. (1990). Computers and student writing: Maiming the Macintosh (A response). *Computers and Composition, 7*(3), 81-88.

Zampogna, J., Gentile, R., Papalia, A., and Silber, G. (1976). Relationships between learning styles and learning environments in selected secondary modern language classes. *Modern Language Journal, 60*, 443-447.

NAME INDEX

Abberton 160, 170
Abe 164
Abelson 124
Abraham 9, 36, 44, 178, 179
Adams 35, 36, 126
Adler 189
Alderman 35
Alderson 119, 130
Allen 118
Allwright 38
Anandam 34
Anderson 121
Anderson-Inman 173, 189
Anthony 17
Appel 34
Arden-Close 128
Armington 41
Armstrong 133
Ashworth 8, 13, 58, 79–94, 143, 159, 175, 183, 184, 186, 187
Atkin 23
Atkinson 37
Avner 40

Bachman 41, 42, 119
Bacon 118
Bailey 48
Balota 126
Baltra 178
Bangert-Drowns 53
Bar 37
Barnes 142
Barron 174
Batson 138, 149
Bean 138
Beard 37
Beazley 71
Benesch 137, 140
Berbisada 36
Berkemeyer 118
Bernhardt 118, 142
Berry 118
Bialystok 42
Biber 100

Bladon 189
Blake 36
Bland 41, 133
Boston 138
Bradley 137, 138
Bransford 124
Brebner 34, 35
Breen 47
Brock 10
Broderick 13
Brown 22, 154, 164, 176
Bruce 61, 75, 76
Bryson 138
Buckley 34
Buder 164, 189
Bueno 50
Busch 37
Butler 110

Campbell 89
Carton 2
Castine 53
Cazden 47, 50
Chamot 40
Chapelle 9, 11, 33–53, 115, 129, 135, 139, 140, 187
Chaudron 33, 47, 48
Christie 35
Chun 161, 184, 189
Ciarcia 157
Clark 35, 36, 51, 126
Clarke 125
Clifford 61
Coady 29, 125, 127
Cobb 7, 8, 11, 13, 92, 115–135, 175
Cobuild 113
Cohen 41, 48, 130, 138
Coleman 45
Collier 137, 138
Cranen 172
Craven 34, 183
Cron 189
Crookall 10, 73
Cross 137, 138, 139

Cullen 49
Cummins 154, 155
Cunningham 124
Curtin 36, 40

Daiute 13, 34, 61, 138, 159, 183
de Bot 160, 170, 171, 172, 184
De Cheveigne 164
Demel 118
Dever 178
Di Benedetto 161
Dick 121
Dickson 7, 9, 168, 170, 177, 178, 183
DiPardo 142
Divine 36
Dixon 53
Doshita 164
Doughty 8, 37, 38, 41, 42
Douglas 130
Drave 73
Dunkel 33, 51, 115

Eckhouse 58
Edmondson 133
Eichel 34, 35
Eisel 34
Eldred 142
Ellis 185
Endreweit 51
Erickson 47, 51
Ericsson 41
Esling 2, 7, 8, 44, 45, 72, 88, 153–188
Evans 34, 35
Faerch 41, 42
Farstrup 121
Favreau 127
Feldmann 119, 130, 131
Finnemann 118
Fletcher 37
Flowerdew 8, 97–112, 161
Foltz 174
Fortescue 178
Fought 41, 42
Fourcin 160, 170
Frederiksen 122
Freed 34
Freeman 49

Fröhlich 41

Garrett 107
Gay 41
Gentile 36
Goh 157, 158, 169, 170, 174
Gold 124
Goldman 126
Goodman 124, 125, 126
Grabe 125, 127
Graesser 126
Graney 29, 127
Gray 133
Greene 126

Haas 139
Halio 138
Hall 2
Halliday 43
Hanlon 89
Hasan 43
Hawisher 34, 138, 149
Haynes 127
Heath 47
Heppner 121
Herrmann 37, 48
Higgins 24, 40, 98, 102, 118, 120, 121, 133
Hill 139
Hiller 157, 161, 165, 166, 173, 186
Hillinger 189
Hoffman 2, 8, 9, 13, 43, 45, 55–77, 93, 94, 126, 141, 142, 143, 145, 147, 149, 152, 183
Hogaboam 126
Honeyfield 106, 108
Hosenfeld 41
Howard 57, 58
Hsu 39, 40
Hubbard 8, 9, 15–32, 37, 115, 127, 132
Huckin 127
Hulstijn 91, 92
Hunter 138
Hymes 47

Imagawa 172, 173
Imbier 8, 157, 159, 175

Name Index

Jack 157, 161, 165, 166, 173, 186
James 107, 170
Jamieson 9, 11, 33–53, 115, 129, 139, 140, 187
Jobs 137
Johns 40, 100, 107, 108
Johnson 34, 35, 44, 49, 124, 178
Jonassen 35
Jones 157, 159, 174, 175, 178, 185
Jonz 119
Joram 138
Jorden 91

Kalaja 61
Kalikow 170
Kane 51
Kaplan 138
Karrer 36
Kasper 41, 42
Keith 29
Kemmis 23
Kemp 142
Kent 164, 189
Khouri 138, 139, 140, 146
Kienbaum 118
King 36, 53
Kiritani 172, 173
Klatt 189
Kleinmann 118, 119
Kotler 34
Kozma 151
Krashen 8, 42, 46, 119
Kreeft Peyton 65, 183
Kremers 149
Kruglanski 2
Kulik 53
Kupper 40

Lafford 29
Larsen-Freeman 46, 47, 48, 51
Larson 53
Laurel 82
Laver 157, 161
Lawrenson 35
Lea 2, 3
Leather 170, 171, 184
Lee 130
Lefèvre 161
Leppänen 61

Lesgold 122, 126
Levin 48
Levine 51
Levy 15, 16, 32, 109
Lindsay 138
Lindstrom 53
Liou 9, 34, 35, 44, 178, 179
Long 38, 43, 46, 47, 48, 51, 129
Louth 138
Lozano 37
Lysiak 34, 35

Ma 101, 109, 112
MacLuhan 92
Madigan 138
Magoto 29, 127
Mailfert 170
Marcoulides 35
Martin 79
Marx 142, 149
Mathis 138
McAllister 138
McCaffrey 53
McLaughlin 128
McLeod 128
Mehan 47
Meredith 36
Michaels 50
Mikulecky 35, 36
Miller 124
Milton 110
Minsky 124
Mitchell 126
Mizuno 39, 40, 135
Mohan 3, 39, 44, 178, 179, 180, 181
Mokhtari 29, 127
Molholt 167, 170, 172
Monohan 138
Moran 149
Moulthrop 138
Mueller 37
Murison-Bowie 105, 106
Murphy 34, 138
Mydlarski 34, 35

Naiman 41
Nelson 50
Nichols 138

Noblitt 41, 133
Noda 91
Norfleet 36
Nunan 47, 50, 119, 130

O'Malley 40, 42
Oakhill 128
Oates 34, 35
Oller 110
Olofsson 174
Olson 174, 189
Owston 138
Oxford 10, 40, 42

Papalia 36
Park 9, 11, 33–53, 115, 129, 139, 140, 187
Papert 51
Pederson 24, 132, 133
Pennington 1–14, 34, 38, 44, 49, 88, 120, 138, 151, 153–188
Perfetti 122, 124, 125, 126, 127
Perkins 11
Peterson 34
Phillips 18, 20, 22, 23, 24
Phinney 2, 7, 8, 9, 13, 34, 45, 56, 61, 62, 137–152
Pickard 109
Piper 44, 137, 138, 140, 178, 179, 183
Pollatsek 126
Polson 124
Price 8, 157, 159, 175, 176, 185, 186
Prohaska 189
Provenzano 40
Pufahl 138

Rauch 34
Rayner 126
Read 164, 189
Reck 133
Reid 34, 35, 53
Renouf 110
Reynolds 149
Richards 17, 18, 20, 22, 23
Rieber 2
Robinson 37, 38
Roblyer 53, 115

Roche 34
Rochet 157, 165, 166, 167, 170, 173
Rodgers 17, 18, 20, 22
Rodrigues 141, 142, 151
Rooney 157, 161, 165, 166, 173, 186
Rubin 61, 75, 76, 119
Russel 118
Russo 40

Sabers 35
Salomon 9, 170
Sarracho 34, 35
Schaeffer 37
Schank 124
Schenk 144
Schiffrin 155
Schroder 133
Schrupp 37
Schumann 48
Schwartz 137, 138
Schwerin 80
Segal 130
Segalowitz 124, 127
Selinker 127
Sheingold 51
Shinall 36
Shwalb 53
Silber 36
Silberstein 125
Simon 41
Sinclair 100, 110
Singer 3
Sirc 149
Skehan 36
Skinner 122
Slatin 138
Smith 124, 125
Souviney 48
Spears 3
Spindler 48
Stanne 178
Stanovich 124, 126, 127, 128
Steinberg 135
Stemmer 119, 130, 131
Stern 41, 119
Stevens 7, 8, 11, 13, 21, 24, 37, 92, 115–135, 153, 172, 175

Name Index

Stewner-Manzanares 40
Strongman 149, 151
Stubbs 103
Susser 146
Suzuki 172, 173
Svartik 104
Swain 2, 46
Swales 154
Swets 170

Tammelin 73
Terrell 119
Thompson 39, 40
Tillyer 152
Todesco 41
Todman 35
Treiman 174
Tribble 100
Tulving 124
Tuman 11, 117, 159

Underwood 46
Upitis 69, 70, 71
Utsumi 95

Van Campen 34
Van Lier 47, 48, 51
Van Rossum 172
Van Waes 140
Viteli 36
Vygotsky 2

Wallace 34, 35, 139
Warren 61
Warschauer 78
Watson-Gegeo 47, 50
Weiderman 121
Weiss 130
Weizenbaum 178
Wells 76, 77
Weltens 160, 172
Welty 118
Wenden 42
West 126, 127, 128
Whanger 36
Wideman 138
Willis 110
Windeatt 39, 119, 132, 133
Wise 174

Womble 138
Woodruff 138
Wright 23
Wusnack 149, 151
Wyatt 115, 116, 117, 119

Yang 104
Young 178, 179
Youra 138
Yule 154, 176

Zampogna 36

SUBJECT INDEX

accessibility 1
activity type 24
advance preparation 42
affective factors 6, 35
annotation 81
approach-based design 21
approaches 17, 20, 27, 30
    evaluation of 38
authentic text 118, 120

bilingual dictionary 41
bulletin board 64

CALICO 80
CALL, evaluation 27, 39
CD-ROM 79, 83, 116, 118, 159, 161
chat 63, 149, 154
Chinese 171
Chinews 86
classroom management 23, 31
cloze 129, 130
COBUILD 97
cognitive outcome 34
collaborative writing 62, 64, 141
commenting 144
communications 56, 92
composing 138
computer mediated
    communication 3
computer, in education 3
concordance 97–112, 175
conferencing 63
consciousness-raising 102
context 38
corpus 98, 99, 100, 103, 120
    size 100, 101, 111
courseware 15, 20, 115, 159
creative construction 6
cyberspace 13, 93

delivery system 21
diary study 48
dictionary 83
discourse analysis 43, 45

discourse, see also output
distance learning 76

e-mail 9, 56, 59, 65, 66, 67, 69–74, 118, 147
ELIZA 44, 183
error analysis 106
ESP 100
ethnography 47–51

feedback 8, 10, 25, 67, 132
field dependence 36
field independence 36
fingertip effect 11

gap-filling 106

hyperdocument 92
hypermedia 8, 79–94, 173
hypertext 81, 116
hypothesis testing 42

i+1 8
ICONS 68, 72
IDEALS 68, 72
information superhighway 56
input 2, 7, 46, 105, 118, 155
interaction 39, 40, 56, 62, 64, 176, 179
interaction analysis 38
interactive reading 124, 128
interactive writing 61
interactivity 82, 122
Internet 56
intonation 163
introspective data 103

Kanji City 86
key word 98

LAN 56, 57, 60, 65
learner control 24, 132
learner profiles 22, 30
learning style 18, 23
learning zone 5

learning, inductive 107
learning, serendipity
linear predictive coding 158

materials development 105
meaning, negotiation 55
memory 38
messaging 63
method 16
methodology 15–32
MicroConcord 105
motivation 8
multimedia 81

netware 57
network 55, 67, 74, 76
    see also LAN, WAN
newsgroup 68
non-linear text 80
NREN 56

output 2, 7, 44, 45, 46, 154, 173, 176, 180
    comprehensible 46

pedagogy 39
pen pal 68, 71
phonology 160, 161
Prep Editor 142
pronunciation 88, 153, 170, 172
proximal development 2, 10
psycholinguistics 41, 124
psychometrics 33

QuickTime 91
QUILL 61, 74–76

reading 86, 115–135
    as writing 125
    second language 127
reconstruction 125
research 33–53, 90, 115
resourcing 40
revision 137

scaffolding 2
screen layout 24
Sequitur 121
simulation 55

smilies 64
sorting 98
speak-writing 8
speaking 153–188
speech analysis 161, 184
speech samples 161, 167
speed reading 120
SPELL 165
strategies, metacognitive 42
student queries 41
suprasegmental phonology 161
syllabus 22, 30
Système-D 133

teacher control 30
telnet 60, 73
text manipulation 119
transcript 150

variation 35
Victoria Project 68, 72
video 173, 175, 186
videodisc 161
virtual reality 13, 93
Visi-Pitch 161

WAN 56, 57, 65, 68
World Wide Web 56, 58
writing 61, 62, 88, 137–152

www.ingramcontent.com/pod-product-compliance
Lightning Source LLC
Chambersburg PA
CBHW071712160426
43195CB00012B/1655